Education
and the
Urban Crisis

Education and the Urban Crisis

Edited by

ROGER R. WOOCK
Associate Professor
The University of Calgary

INTERNATIONAL TEXTBOOK COMPANY
An **Intext** Publisher
Scranton, Pennsylvania

Standard Book Number 7002 2213 8

Preface

> If the problems of urban areas and urban schools are frightening to us, they are also mandating us to reevaluate objectives, methodology, content, and virtually everything we know (or thought we knew) about education in general. Moreover, we are beginning to see that what is happening in large urban areas is really a preview of coming attractions for a major portion of our country. The concentration of problems we now view in stark bas relief in the urban schools is beginning to emerge, we believe, even in the non-urban areas.[1]

This statement suggests two crucially important points in relating the process of education to the urban crisis. First, the urban crisis is clearly not confined to schools, and it is extremely difficult to separate schooling from other problems of the city. American society is rapidly becoming an urban society and this process has created a tremendous range of crises. Transportation, housing, air and water pollution, crime and delinquency, education, and indeed the quality of American life itself are all affected. Second, as Fantini and Weinstein suggest, the trend over the past decades makes it quite clear that suburban and even rural communities will not escape for long the developments and the problems which are now more evident in the city. The urban crisis is becoming the national crisis. Urban education, then, must be concerned with a variety of difficulties which characterize the schools now attended by the majority of American youth.

This collection concentrates on four areas which are particularly important in considering the relationship between education and the urban crisis — Communities, Youth, Teachers, and School Systems. Obviously any selection of articles on these topics is arbitrary and affected by the attitudes, opinions, and prejudices of the editor. Some of these attitudes and prejudices are clarified in the introductory essay, but it may be helpful to the potential user of this volume to make them more explicit here. The following convictions have shaped this book and the choice of contributors.

1. It is not justifiable to concentrate exclusively on "cultural deprivation" as the theoretical explanation for the failure of public schools to educate disadvantaged and/or minority group youngsters. There is, of

---

[1] Mario Fantini and Gerald Weinstein, *Making Urban Schools Work.* New York: Holt, Rinehart and Winston, 1968, p. 2.

v

course, no question that family and community make an impact on
school performance. However, too frequently the emphasis on "no
books in the home" or "the female headed family" have been used by
teachers, administrators, and professors of education as a sufficient
cause for school failure.

2. Insight into the problems of relating education to the urban crisis is
found not only within professional educationist circles but by academics in other fields, journalists, and classroom teachers. The hostility
which greets comments, criticisms, and suggestions made by non-
educationists is entirely inappropriate. This collection includes a number of selections from individuals outside of the educational power
structure.

3. One of the frequently overlooked but extremely important problems
relating to urban education is the organization of schools and school
systems. Beginning teachers must be given an introduction to the nature
of educational bureaucracy and to a variety of proposals for changing
it.

4. To look critically at present practices in all aspects of urban education
is both healthy and productive. The argument that students should only
be exposed to basic criticism after they have had experience in the
schools is not accepted. This argument, most often advanced by those
already in the educational power structure, seems in part designed to
defend the status quo. An important intent of this book is to be honestly and thoroughly critical of present practices in urban education.

Although this collection is primarily designed for undergraduate social
foundations courses, it has been the editor's experience that many master's level
students in teacher education have unfortunately not been exposed in their
undergraduate preparation to the problems raised in this book. The collection
should be useful on this level as well.

The editor's first debt of gratitude is, of course, to the men and women who
have written the books and articles from which selections were made. Without
their concern, talent, and ability the situation would indeed by hopeless. The
editor's colleagues at Hunter College, Lehman College, and Richmond College
have also been helpful. John Dugan of the International Textbook Company deserves a particular note of appreciation. Without his generous support the book
would not have been possible.

ROGER R. WOOCK

Calgary, Alberta
January, 1970

Contents

Introduction

Education and the Urban Crisis begins with an analysis of the "decentralization" issue in New York City. This case study cuts across the categories of Community, Youth, Teachers, and School Systems used throughout the book. The kinds of conflicts focused on here are those which will in a variety of forms plague most city school systems. At this writing, and for some time to come, it is unlikely that there will be a real settlement of the issues. This case study, then, is unfinished and the crisis continues.

Decentralization
in New York City: A Case Study
in Urban Crisis*

Phillip Allsworth and Roger R. Woock

In this essay the authors have tried to offer as reasonable and complete an analysis of New York's Ocean Hill-Brownsville controversy as the continuing nature of the crisis will allow. At this writing no fundamental settlement has been accomplished. Decentralization has not come to the public schools of New York City nor has the system returned to the monolithic structure which existed prior to the Spring of 1968. It is our position that the implications of the crisis, both for the futures of decentralization and teacher unionization, are considerably more important than placing blame. (However, when occasion demands, the stated positions of organizations and groups will be compared with their actions.) Since the Ocean Hill-Brownsville crisis did not erupt suddenly in the Fall of 1968, we have included a brief chronology. Our analysis is divided into two main sections dealing with first, educational questions; and, second, political and social implications. These two categories are not really separate but for purposes of analysis it seems reasonable to make such a division. It is unlikely that schools and educational policy can be kept out of the political arena. Indeed, the authors are convinced of just the opposite – politics, social change and education are by necessity intermingled and closely related.

CHRONOLOGY

1958

Board of Education decision to construct IS 201 in Harlem as an essentially segregated school.

1967

July – Ford Foundation provides funds for three demonstration projects: (Local districts) IS 201; Two Bridges; and Ocean Hill-Brownsville.

August 3 – Ocean Hill-Brownsville parents elect their local governing board. The Board of Education accepts the election and grants it power to elect the unit administrator and principals to the eight schools in the district.

*Phillip Allsworth and Roger R. Woock, "Decentralization in New York City: A Case Study in Urban Crisis," *Urban Education*, Vol. IV. No. 1, 1969.

September 2 – Teacher representatives on Ocean Hill-Brownsville local governing board refuse to vote for local principals. They never return to the board.

1968

May 10 – Local Ocean Hill-Brownsville governing board orders transfer of nineteen teachers charging them with attempts to sabotage the demonstration project.

May 14 – May 22 – United Federation of Teachers lobbies in Albany and defeats strong decentralization bill for New York City (predicted by Governor Rockefeller).

September 9 – First strike by UFT to protest refusal of the Ocean Hill-Brownsville district to reinstate teachers transferred in May.

September 10 – Agreement reached providing for the return of the teachers to Ocean Hill-Brownsville.

September 13 – Teachers strike again charging Ocean Hill-Brownsville governing board with failure to honor the agreement.

September 14 – State Commissioner of Education James Allen enters the picture and becomes party to the negotiations.

September 30 – Schools reopen again under a plan providing for the return of the disputed teachers under the surveillance of observers from the Union and the Board of Education.

October 14 – Teachers union goes out on strike again charging that members have been terrorized and threatened with death at JHS 271.

November 19 – Strike settled. Ocean Hill-Brownsville District to be operated as a trustee of the state.

December 3 – JHS 271 (Ocean Hill-Brownsville) closed by the State after disorders break out in and around the school.

December 4 – Trouble erupts in PS 39 (IS 201 District) as nine union teachers charged with insubordination are barred from entering school by community residents.

December 6 – Teachers escorted to PS 39 by police but school boycotted by students and other instructors.

December 12 – Unit administrator, Rhody McCoy, transferred out of Ocean Hill-Brownsville District by order of State Trustee William Firman.

EDUCATIONAL QUESTIONS

In many nonwhite urban neighborhoods the public school is viewed as an enemy fortress both by the local community and by the mostly white administrators and teachers. The educational failure and human waste contained in these schools, so poignantly described in DEATH AT AN EARLY AGE, and 36 CHILDREN, are clearly important motivating forces for the decentralization and community control of urban schools.[1] A twofold problem confronts American society with regard to the education of minorities and the urban poor. First, these youngsters are being educated separately: and second, their educational performance consistently falls far below that of the white majority. Since the 1954 Supreme Court decision which declared segregation in public schools to be unconstitutional, a hard look at northern urban centers shows that racial segregation has increased. For example, in Cincinnati in 1950 seven of every ten black elementary children attended 90 to 100% black schools. In 1965 the figures were nine out of ten. In Oakland, California, less than 10% of black elementary school children were in 90 to 100% black schools. In 1965 the percentage had increased to 50%. In Philadelphia the percentage of black youngsters attending 90 to 100% black schools went from 63.2% in 1950 to 72% in 1965. In the South, although the pattern is somewhat different, the direction is the same. In Houston, Texas with a history of completely segregated public schools until 1960 the number of black children in all black elementary schools increased by 20% from 1960 to 1965. As the United States Commission on Civil Rights Report states, "The rising Negro school enrollment combined with only slight desegregation has produced substantial increase in the number of Negroes attending all Negro or nearly all Negro schools in southern and border cities."[2] North or South, then, the pattern is clear. School desegregation in America is increasing rather than decreasing.

The pattern in New York City is unfortunately no exception. The number of elementary schools with 85% or more black and Puerto Rican pupils increased from 64 in the 1957-58 school year to 148 in the 1964-65 school year. On the junior high school level the number increased from 16 to 34.[3] Part of this increase may be accounted for by the decrease in the number of white pupils in the public schools of New York. But certainly not all of it. This trend in enrollment developed at a time when the New York City Board of Education was committed to a policy of desegregation. Some experimentation took place

[1] Herbert Kohl, *36 Children,* New York: New American Library, 1967. Jonathan Kozol, *Death at an Early Age,* Boston: Houghton Mifflin, 1967.

[2] *Racial Isolation in the Public Schools,* A Report of the United States Commission on Civil Rights, Washington, D.C.: U.S. Government Printing Office, 1967, p. 10.

[3] Eleanor B. Sheldon and Raymond A. Glazier, *Pupils and Schools in New York City, A Fact Book,* New York: Russell Sage Foundation, 1965, p. 120.

with programs like Open Enrollment, (a voluntary program allowing youngsters from predominantly nonwhite overcrowded schools to transfer and transport themselves to less crowded predominantly white schools): pairing, in which schools in adjacent areas, one predominantly white and one predominantly black, were attended by students from both districts; and, bussing, in which students on a non-voluntary basis were transferred out of their own segregated and crowded schools. Opposition by middleclass white parent groups was strong and the school board backed down. The history of this failure of the New York City school system to implement its own policies with regard to desegregation is brilliantly analyzed in David Roger's recent study, *110 Livingston Street.*[4] This pattern of segregation in New York and other urban areas would not assume the dimensions of a tragedy were it not for the fact that black youngsters consistently perform at lower levels on all standardized educational achievement tests. This is in spite of the ten year period of concern on the part of educators and several billions of dollars spent in the last five years on a wide variety of special educational programs.

The New York Times in December of 1966, 1967 and 1968 published a number of startling educational statistics — the reading scores by school of New York pupils in grades two, five, seven and nine. In addition to being reported by school, these scores were also reported by district. Thus, one could compare school scores in Bedford-Stuyvesant or Harlem, the two largest black communities, with those in Forest Hills or Rego Park, white middleclass communities in Queens. These figures showed a consistent and extensive discrepancy on every grade level between the scores of schools serving white youngsters and those serving black youngsters. In the introductory article to these statistics, Dr. Samuel D. McClelland, acting director of the Bureau of Educational Research, wrote the following.

> In the favored socio-economic areas of a large city, children have every access to many books, magazines, adult conversations, trips, and similar cultural experiences which enrich verbal knowledge. The enhanced verbal facility is reflected in reading proficiency and reading test scores. On the other hand many children in disadvantaged neighborhoods not only lack such cultural opportunities but often they must cope with negative influences which make it difficult to study. To judge the educational success obtained merely by comparing the reading test scores with the national norm without regard to the difficulties would be inappropriate.[5]

It is this sort of explanation about the failure of nonwhite youngsters to learn that has aroused the passion and hostility of black and Puerto Rican parents who are increasingly unwilling to accept the "bad environment — unteachable" formula so popular with many educators besides Dr. McClelland.

[4] David Rogers, *110 Livingston Street,* New York: Random House, 1968.
[5] *The New York Times.* September 23, 1966, p. 30.

The beginnings in New York City of specific and organized demands for community control of public schools may well be traced to the decision of the Board of Education to construct Intermediate School 201 in the center of East Harlem. Prior to that decision community residents had attempted to persuade the board to construct the school on the edge of the nonwhite community so that it might become an integrated school. After the site selection, parents and community groups, convinced that the Board was not serious about desegregation, began to change their emphasis to the now familiar demand for community control and black administrators and faculty.

Given the failure of the New York City Board of Education to implement any significant programs designed to desegregate New York's schools and given the growing awareness and the clear cut nature of the failures and educational deficiencies of the public schools, it is certainly understandable that schoolmen have been searching frantically for other remedies. The other remedies are probably best identified as "compensatory education." In an earlier article one of the authors described two of these efforts in New York City.

> In spite of wide support in the educational community and several billion dollars spent on a great variety of compensatory programs the results in educational terms are practically negligible.

> Higher Horizons in New York City was one of the most publicized and highly praised of the compensatory programs. It featured four different approaches designed to increase learning. First of all, teachers were trained and encouraged to improve the student's level of aspiration. Second, counseling and guidance services were extended and increased. Third, an effort was made to broaden the cultural background of the youngsters by visits to museums, libraries, concert halls, etc. Fourth, special remedial teachers were provided to upgrade reading, writing, and arithmetic skills. In 1964 five years after its inception, the Higher Horizons program was evaluated by the New York City Board of Education. No significant difference in performance was found between students who participated in Higher Horizons and similar students in schools without the program. There was no difference in academic achievement.

> The More Effective Schools program in New York City is more difficult to judge at this time since it has been in operation only since 1964. MES was initiated in ten elementary schools and expanded to 11 more schools in 1965-66. The program includes small class size, extra teachers, guidance personnel, psychological services, and administrative personnel. An evaluation completed by the New York Center for Urban Education in September of 1967 indicated that MES had improved the climate and morale in the schools, but there was little comparable improvement in reading scores. From the fourth grade on not one nonwhite school in the MES program is reading at grade level.

> There seems no doubt that the report of the United States Commission on Civil Rights, RACIAL ISOLATION IN THE PUBLIC SCHOOLS, was correct in this thesis that compensatory programs in predominantly

nonwhite schools have just not provided sustained success in raising achievement levels of nonwhite youngsters. The future of compensatory education at this point seems rather bleak. Although there are no new radical proposals on the horizon, the federal government and school systems themselves are providing more funds for programs which simply are not working. Indeed, it seems that as more evidence of failure accumulates, more money becomes available.[6]

Given the failure of desegregation and compensatory programs, what do the proponents of community control expect to accomplish through decentralization? Writers such as Professor Kenneth Clark, Jonathan Kozol, and Herbert Kohl, begin by focusing on the general attitude of hopelessness which pervades the traditional ghetto school. They describe a meaningless curriculum, a lack of adequate materials, few well qualified teachers, and a general atmosphere of disorganization. A recent study by Robert Rosenthal and Leonore Jacobson, entitled *Pygmalion in the Classroom,* suggests that teacher attitude and expectation significantly affect whether or not a "disadvantaged" child will learn in school.[7] The Rosenthal study does not demonstrate just how important teacher attitude is for learning and has nothing to say about how these attitudes and expectations are communicated from teacher to student. It does, nevertheless, point to an important factor in ghetto schools, the prejudgment on the part of middleclass teachers that the lower class or minority group youngster will be less successful academically than would a white middleclass child.

If one were to ask a supporter of community control what specifically it would accomplish educationally the answers would fall roughly into the following four categories.

1. A significantly increased parental and community involvement in the school. This involvement would be important educationally since recent research studies suggest that parental attitude has an important effect on the child's motivation and desire to succeed in school. Increased parent involvement leads to increased student motivation, and thus to increased performance.

2. Curriculum and school services better designed to meet the needs of the local community. Those familiar with the local community, both professional and non-professional, would be better able to judge the particular programs, curricular and extra-curricular, that would benefit the youngsters in the local community.

3. A hiring policy to attract and select teachers with a dedication and desire to teach minority group urban children. Giving local school boards the power to hire teachers from approved city or state lists would reduce the

---

[6] Roger B. Woock, "Community Operated Schools – A Way Out?" Arthur I. Blaustein and Roger R. Woock (eds). *Man Against Poverty: World War III,* New York: Random House, 1968, pp. 248-250.

[7] Robert Rosenthal and Lenore Jacobson, *Pygmalion in the Classroom,* New York: Holt, Rinehart and Winston, 1968.

chance of forced assignment of those who do *not* want to teach in a ghetto school. Most community control advocates would argue for only the limitation of state law or the right to go outside of the city approved lists to hire both administrators and teachers.

4. Most important of all, a significant increase in achievement level. Community control would bring a change in attitude of the professional staff and the parents in the community and to an improved self image on the part of youngsters themselves. The school would not longer be viewed as a hostile fortress but as an integrated community institution.

Can these very ambitious goals be achieved? Many concerned educators argue that there is no evidence to support the contention that decentralization would significantly improve educational performance. While it is true that we do not yet have evidence which allows us to compare the performance of youngsters under decentralization with those in a centrally controlled school, one must keep in mind the past inadequacies of the centrally controlled system in New York. Certainly if nonwhite youngsters had been learning at or even near grade level, it seems unlikely that very much enthusiasm could have been aroused for community control. But in point of fact urban desegregation has never been tried and compensatory programs have thus far failed to provide the education so desperately needed by nonwhite youngsters. Given this background it seems a reasonable educational gamble to support and encourage a genuine program of community control.

THE POLITICAL AND SOCIAL IMPLICATIONS

Although the New York City school system has been divided for some time into thirty local districts, each with an advisory board, the first real proposals for decentralization of the school system grew out of Mayor John Lindsay's bid for more state aid for education in 1967.

Under the present plan state aid is computed for New York City on a single district basis since the central Board of Education has legal responsibility for education in the city. Because of the high assessed valuation of real estate in the boroughs of Manhattan and Queens, New York City receives less state aid than if the school system were divided into five separate districts, one for each borough.

The Mayor first advocated that state aid be computed on a county basis since the boundaries of the five boroughs are contiguous with county lines. This would have brought the city $108,000,000 more aid during fiscal 1969. When the state Legislature indicated that the school system would have to be divided into five separate districts to qualify for the additional funds, considerable objection was raised. As a result, the New York State Legislature empowered the Mayor to develop plans for decentralization to provide "greater community initiative and participation in the development of education policy for the public schools. . .and to achieve greater flexibility in the administration of such schools."

The outcome was the controversial "Bundy Report," *Reconnection for Learning,* developed by the Mayor's Advisory Panel on Decentralization and headed by McGeorge Bundy, president of the Ford Foundation.[8] The plan called for radical restructuring of the school system by breaking up the monolithic structure into a federation of thirty to sixty largely autonomous districts which, unlike the existing thirty districts, would have real power. In local hearings as well as in the Legislature the report met considerable opposition. The New York City Board of Education, the United Federation of Teachers, and the Board of Regents presented alternate plans; but, under pressure from the UFT and supporting unions the Legislature backed off. In effect the entire issue was postponed for a year with the passage of the Marchi Bill which directed the Board of Education to develop a plan to be submitted to the 1969 session of the Legislature. In the intermin, the central Board of Education has delegated some powers, such as selection of local superintendents from eligible lists, to the local boards. But for the most part, the central agency is in control of the schools.

The people of Ocean Hill-Brownsville like most ghetto residents, long denied the opportunity to take part in decision-making in the schools, recently have become less inclined to accept decisions imposed upon them by the educational establishment. They are no longer willing to wait indefinitely for those who hold power to delegate it. Especially among the militants there exists the feeling that the establishment must be confronted and demands for local control of the schools not only be made but acted upon.

In Ocean Hill-Brownsville following the central Board of Education's failure to implement integration plans in the face of white opposition, a group representing diverse interests in the community began meeting early in 1967 to plan for more active involvement in educational affairs. The chronology of events leading up to the 1968 teacher strikes lists several occasions when the Ocean Hill-Brownsville planning group, faced with delaying or obstructionist tactics by the Board of Education, simply went ahead and took action. At the outset, they were apparently willing to settle for something less than complete community control, for in its July, 1967 proposal outlining powers, responsibilities, and functions of a local governing board for the district, the group indicated that the board would be responsible to the central Board of Education.

As time went by it became apparent that the Ocean Hill-Brownsville planning group was getting little encouragement from the Board of Education. When the plans for election of a governing board were being set up, the Board of Education refused to cooperate by providing names of parents in the district. As the opening of the 1967-68 school year approached, the Board had not responded to the planning group's proposals. In fact, at this writing, the Board still has taken no action. According to the New York Civil Liberties Union:

[8]*The New York Times,* November 9, 1967.

Apparently, once the Board of Education understood that what Ocean Hill-Brownsville really wanted was an experiment in genuine community control, it backed off even before it had begun.[9]

In January, 1968, the Board drew up a set of guidelines which removed practically all power from the Ocean Hill-Brownsville governing board, but left undefined the lines of authority between the two boards. During this period it became more and more evident that the Board of Education was not really interested in community control. Then, in March, 1968, the Board said:

> We believe that the advantages of flexibility and increased local responsibility which we favor can be achieved without the dangers and risks involved in a drastic change of administrative structure which seeks to give basic control of many school districts to different groups.[10]

While the Ocean Hill-Brownsville group was talking about community control, the central Board of Education was talking about community involvement. The confrontation that eventually set off the city-wide teacher strikes in the Fall of 1968 came when the Ocean Hill-Brownsville unit administrator Rhody McCoy and the governing board decided to transfer nineteen teachers and administrators out of the district. School Superintendent Bernard Donovan blocked the transfer, even though teachers had always been routinely transferred from district to district. The United Federation of Teachers claimed that the nineteen were being discharged without due process. The Union gave the impression that the teachers were being fired rather than transferred. Ironically, according to the UFT-Board of Education contract, union teachers had been given the right to transfer out of the experimental district if they so desired.

In the process of development Ocean-Hill Brownsville people who previously had little or no power or experience in community affairs, suddenly were learning how to cope with the intricate bureaucracy of the public schools. It may well be that one result of this crisis will be the emergence of experienced community leaders. As these leaders refine their skills in dealing with the educational establishment they will certainly later move to correct injustices existing in other aspects of ghetto life.

If under decentralization local groups are given control over personnel and budget matters, policies certainly will change so that more blacks and Puerto Ricans will be employed. Contracts for construction, maintenance, and supplying the schools will go to black and Puerto Rican businessmen. More pressure will be brought on white trade unions to admit members from the

[9]"The Burden of Blame: A Report on the Ocean Hill-Brownsville School Controversy," New York: New York Civil Liberties Union, October 9, 1968.

[10]Board of Education, City of New York, "A Plan for Educational Policy and Administrative Units," New York: *The Board,* March 7, 1968, p. 1.

urban ghetto. The long range effects would mean a considerable shifting of power now concentrated in the hands of the white middle-class to the black and Puerto Rican population. It would also increase the 9% black and Puerto Rican teachers and administrators in the public schools. (The student population is now 52% nonwhite.)[11]

Local control of ghetto schools may well be the starting point for the powerless minority to begin to exert greater organized pressure in the political life of the city. Strong leadership may be able to mobilize the urban poor to gain better education, housing, police and fire protection, and in general a better life for the inner-city dweller. City-wide political leaders may be developed in this process.

The United Federation of Teachers, bargaining agent for the city's 57,000 teachers, has in less than a decade become a dominant educational force. Although in the past generally regarded as a progressive force, the union in the current struggle finds itself allied with those in the education establishment who are opposed to community control or those who favor a very limited type of community involvement with the real control still residing with the central Board of Education and the existing bureaucracy. Despite the Union's statements that it is not opposed to decentralization, it appears to be interested only in insuring continuance of the existing structure with modification to encourage more community participation. Elements in the population who are disenchanted with the present system and accuse the establishment, both board and union, of failing to educate black and Puerto Rican children are seen as threatening and irresponsible extremists by the union.

In the early development of the Ocean Hill-Brownsville struggle the union allied itself with black groups who had cut off relations with the larger district of which Ocean Hill was a part. When the governing board was selected union teachers were among its membership. But when the governing board wanted to appoint its own principals, based on a special ruling by Commissioner Allen permitting them to do so, the UFT teachers refused to cooperate and withdrew from the local board. The UFT as well as the Council of Supervisory Associations, an organization of administrators, viewed the governing board's action as a threat to job security for all teachers and administrators. If this local board could ignore the city's civil service examination list for personnel, would not other boards do the same?

The UFT strike in September, 1967 came at a critical juncture, for it occurred simultaneously with the opening of Ocean Hill-Brownsville as an experimental district. Relations between the Ocean Hill governing board and the union deteriorated since the governing board not only refused to back the strike but took the position that it was a strike against black and Puerto Rican

___

[11] *The Public Schools of New York City Staff Bulletin,* Vol VI, No. 10 (April 8, 1968), p. 6.

community control. When the governing board tried to keep its schools in operation, the UFT charged them with strike-breaking.

During March and April of 1968 the governing board's unit administrator, Rhody McCoy, accused the UFT teachers of trying to sabotage the experimental district by refusing to respond to the authority of McCoy and the principals in the district.

While this crisis between the union teachers and the governing board was developing, UFT leaders as mentioned earlier successfully lobbied against passage of decentralization in the state Legislature. Instead the Legislature enacted a bill directing the New York City Board of Education to develop a new plan for decentralization using criteria which would provide for community involvement, rather than community control, and would insure considerable central control over the local districts.

The UFT, concerned about protecting teacher rights, raised the spectre of extremist groups taking over the schools, operating them on the basis of racial and religious preference, firing teachers and replacing them with unqualified personnel. The existing city licensing procedure provides teachers and adminis-trators alike mobility up the bureaucratic ladder if they "play the game" properly. If local boards had the power to hire on the basis of state certification requirements rather than city licensing standards, open competition for jobs might result.

Success or failure of the UFT in its objectives in New York City may have considerable effect on whether the American Federation of Teachers, the UFT parent organization, can successfully unionize teachers in other large cities.

The UFT city-wide contract is much more easily negotiated and provides a greater power base from which to control its membership than thirty or more independent districts.

In defending the rights of teachers, including the nineteen suspended by the Ocean Hill-Brownsville governing board, the union raised the issue of due process. Ironically, the union raised few objections to earlier transfers of teachers in the New York City system, but in Ocean Hill-Brownsville dangers were apparently seen in letting a black and Puerto Rican dominated governing board have this power. A dangerous precedent might be set encouraging other dissatisfied ghetto communities to pressure school officials for change. Although the UFT position has been one of voicing support for decentralization, union actions make it appear that this is the last thing the UFT leaders want to see happen in New York City.

In New York as in other urban centers the days of the ghetto resident's quiet acquiescence to whatever the white establishment decides to impose on him are gone forever. Led by black and Puerto Rican men and women who are willing to risk their jobs and their careers in the educational establishment, by neighborhood people who are angry at promises unkept, at educational colonialism, and at their own powerlessness, the urban poor are making demands which shake the educational bureaucracy of the New York City schools to its foundation. At this stage activists are few in number, but their claim of wide support by ghetto residents is probably correct. When unit administrator McCoy was ordered transferred out of Ocean Hill, an unofficial school boycott resulted in 80% of the students and teachers remaining away from schools in the district.

The leaders want control of their schools – not next month or next year – but now. The militants are often in the vanguard, testing the establishment for weaknesses, taking power whether it be delegated or not, exerting pressures to retain whatever powers they have gained. Such actions do little to insure peace of mind for those with a vested interest in the status quo. The major fear in the minds of many school people is that community control will result in the destruction of the teaching profession's hard won rights; that race, religion, and politics will become criteria for the selection and retention of personnel.

Under any plan for community control the guidelines must be carefully spelled out – something that was not done when the Ocean Hill-Brownsville demonstration district was set up. There must be a commitment on the part of those now in control of education to see that decentralization will work and to mobilize their resources to that end. Had the central Board recognized the aspirations of Ocean Hill-Brownsville and provided greater cooperation, much of the chaos might have been avoided.

The attention focussed on Ocean Hill-Brownsville may have delayed but not stopped the movement toward community control of local schools. Educational power groups such as the UFT and the Council of Supervisory Associations, which supported the UFT during the 1968 strikes, will at best accept a limited form of decentralization with strong central controls. The attitude of the Union, judged by black and Puerto Rican leaders as not only anti-decentralization but anti-black and Puerto Rican, has, if anything, intensified their desire for complete community control.

Other big city school systems are likely to decentralize. Designs will vary from increased community participation to complete control. Whatever the plans, the need to make city schools accountable to the public is apparent.

chapter 1

Communities

To be effective any school must have a close and indeed intimate relationship with the community in which it is located. It should also receive its greatest support from the local community. One of the tragedies of our rapid and unplanned urban development has been that for many urban neighborhoods this supportive relationship has broken down. Indeed some city schools have become a kind of fortress in hostile territory. It is important that educators understand the communities in which their schools are located since students to some extent cannot help but reflect the social environment in which they live. This section while focusing on specific community problems also indicates the great variety of urban communities which do exist, each with its distinctive strengths and weaknesses.

Kenneth Clark begins by outlining ghetto dynamics in Harlem, frequently referred to as the black capital of America. Patricia Cayo Sexton views the neighboring ghetto of Spanish Harlem in her selection. "New York's Lower Depths." She indicates that this Puerto Rican slum has particular problems, some of which are not shared by black communities. Robert Conot's study, *Rivers of Blood, Years of Darkness,* is generally acknowledged to be the best study of the 1965 Watts riot. In "The City's Not for Burning" from that book, he suggests some remedies applicable to Watts and also to other poor urban communities. Walter Williams' analysis of the ghetto in Cleveland (the only major American city which had a special census in 1966) attacks the all too widely held but erroneous idea that things are getting better in slum neighborhoods. While Williams suggests that this is true for those residents who have been able to move out, it is not true for a large group of ghetto residents for whom conditions are deteriorating rather than improving. The urban crisis, of course, includes more than poor nonwhite areas in the center of large cities. In "The New School System," Herbert Gans views some of the problems in educational planning which face new suburban towns.

The Social Dynamics of the Ghetto*

Kenneth B. Clark

White America is basically a middle-class society; the middle class sets the mores and the manners to which the upper class must, when it wishes influence, seek to conform, at least in appearances, and which the lower class struggles to attain or defensively rejects. But dark America, of the rural and of the urban Negro, has been automatically assigned to be a lower-class society; the lower class sets the mores and manners to which, if the Negro upper class wishes influence, it must appeal; and from which the Negro middle class struggles to escape. As long as this chasm between white and dark America is allowed to exist, racial tensions and conflict, hatred and fear will spread. The poor are always alienated from normal society, and when the poor are Negro, as they increasingly are in American cities, a double trauma exists — rejection on the basis of class and race is a danger to the stability of society as a whole. Even though Negroes are a minority in America — approximately one-tenth of the population — a minority that is sick with despair can poison the wellsprings from which the majority, too, must drink. The social dynamics of the dark ghettos can be seen as the restless thrust of a lower-class group to rise into the middle class.

The problem of the American Negro, once predominantly Southern, has gradually over the past few decades become predominantly a Northern problem. Millions of Negroes have come North seeking escape from the miasma of the South, where poverty and oppression kept the Negro in an inferior caste. Three out of every four Negroes live in cities; approximately one of two lives in Northern cities. A million and a half left the South in the years 1950-1960, the largest number heading for California, New York, Illinois, and Michigan. Of the Negroes who live in the North, 95 percent now live in cities (in 1890 it was 65 percent).

There are Negro residential areas in such Southern cities as Atlanta, Birmingham, and New Orleans, but the Negro ghetto in America is essentially a Northern urban invention. There are racially mixed residential areas in a number of Southern cities, few in Northern cities. Although the South often criticizes the North for its urban segregation and explains its own comparatively mixed

*Kenneth B. Clark, *Dark Ghetto,* New York: Harper & Row, 1965. Selection from Chapter III, "The Social Dynamics of the Ghetto," pp. 21-41.

residential patterns as illustrative of a more intimate and more tolerant relationship to the Negro, the fact is that in the South mixed neighborhoods are permitted only so long as Negroes are not seen as a threat. In Charleston, South Carolina, for example, racial residential patterns reflect slavery days, and whites and Negroes tend to live in the same area as they did before Emancipation. Negro servants can come into any area and live in white homes without a lifted eyebrow. Racial problems have not been problems of racial contact – despite the implications of those who refuse to join Negroes at a college dormitory table or to use the common washroom in a factory. It is not the sitting next to a Negro at a table or washing at the next basin that is repulsive to a white, *but the fact that this implies equal status.* Historically, the most intimate relationships have been approved between Negro and white so long as status of white superiority versus Negro inferiority has been clear. Trouble comes only when Negroes decide not to be servants or mistresses and seek a status equal to that of whites. When Negroes start to assume symbols of upward mobility, then a pattern of residential segregation develops in the South, too. In Little Rock and Pine Bluff, Arkansas, and Atlanta, Georgia, to illustrate, as the status of Negroes improved, housing segregation increased. The South is today becoming more "Northern" in its discriminatory pattern. As its economic level rises, it will steadily become more and more like the North. Then urban ghettos will be created, and the Negro will be forced to deal with a different kind of rejection. Part of the social dynamics of the ghetto is the tension between those Negroes who wish to resist and eventually to destroy the ghetto and those whites who seek to maintain and strengthen it.

Eleven metropolitan areas have Negro communities of between 200,000 and one million: New York, Chicago, Los Angeles, Detroit, Philadelphia, Washington, D.C., St. Louis, Baltimore, Cleveland, Houston and New Orleans. (See Tables 1,2,2A,3.) In Washington, D.C., Negroes are in the majority; in Philadelphia, one in four persons is Negro. In the half century between 1910 and 1960 when the nation's Negro population doubled, New York City's Negro population multiplied ten times over.[1] Now the largest concentration of Negroes in an urban ghetto area is in Chicago; the largest number of Negroes lives in New York; and the largest percentage of Negroes (of total population) is in Washington, D.C.

In every one of these cities, Negroes are compelled to live in concentrated ghettos where there must be a continuous struggle to prevent decadence from winning over the remaining islands of middle-class society. A possible exception to this picture of creeping blight seems to be the Bay Area of San Francisco, Berkeley, and Oakland, where the Negro residential areas do not stand out from the other middle-class areas; the usual signs of congestion, deterioration, dirt,

---

[1] E. Franklin Frazer noted in *Condition of Negroes in American Cities,* when the first federal census was taken, Negroes constituted 13.1 percent of the New York City population and 5.7 percent of Philadelphia's.

TABLE 1
Residential Concentration of Negroes

Tracts with 90 Percent + Negro Population	City	In City	In Tracts 90 Percent + Negro	Percentage in Tracts 90 Percent + Negro
122	Chicago, Ill.	812,637	533,214	65.6
31	Baltimore, Md.	325,589	184,992	56.8
27	Cleveland, Ohio	250,818	134,142	53.5
29	Washington, D.C.	411,737	200,380	48.7
10	St. Louis, Mo.	214,377	94,041	43.9
8	Houston, Texas	215,037	87,222	40.6
27	Philadelphia, Penn.	529,240	207,627	39.2
17	New Orleans, La.	233,514	85,968	36.8
71	New York, N.Y.	1,087,931	362,370	33.3
45	Detroit, Mich.	482,223	140,546	29.1
19	Los Angeles, Calif.	334,916	68,715	20.5

Source: U.S. Census of Population: 1960. The data presented in Tables 1 and 3 were prepared by James A. Jones, research director of Haryou, for this book.

ugliness are not yet present there. In all of these ghettos whites had lived before and, as Negroes came, gradually moved away. The origin of Harlem — symbol of Negro ghettos everywhere — is, in many ways, typical of the blight that has already affected almost all.

In the early years of the century an upper-class community of luxury, Harlem by World War 1 became a moderately populated area of middle-class

TABLE 2
Cities with 200,000 or More Negroes

City	Total Population	Total	Negroes Males	Females	Percent Negro
New York, N.Y.	7,781,984	1,087,931	498,167	589,764	14.0
Chicago, Ill.	3,550,404	812,637	387,718	424,919	22.9
Philadelphia, Penn.	2,002,512	529,240	250,256	278,984	26.4
Detroit, Mich.	1,670,144	482,223	232,829	249,394	28.9
Washington, D.C.	763,956	411,737	196,257	215,480	53.9
Los Angeles, Calif.	2,479,015	334,916	160,118	174,798	13.5
Baltimore, Md.	939,024	325,589	157,130	168,459	34.7
Cleveland, Ohio	876,050	250,818	120,873	129,945	28.6
New Orleans, La.	627,525	233,514	110,096	123,418	37.2
Houston, Texas	938,219	215,037	103,471	111,566	22.9
St. Louis, Mo.	750,026	214,377	100,159	114,218	28.6

A Sampling of Other Cities

City	Total Population	Total	Negroes Males	Females	Percent Negro
Pittsburgh, Penn.	604,332	100,692	48,670	52,022	16.7
Kansas City, Mo.	475,539	83,146	39,723	43,423	17.5
Boston, Mass.	697,197	63,165	30,081	33,084	9.1
Rochester, N.Y.	318,611	23,586	11,491	12,095	7.4
Minneapolis, Minn.	482,872	11,785	5,792	5,993	2.4

TABLE 2A
**Cities with 200,000 or More Negroes in Terms
of Percentages of Negroes**

City	Percent Negro
Washington, D. C.	53.9
New Orleans, La.	37.2
Baltimore, Md.	34.7
Detroit, Mich.	28.9
Cleveland, Ohio	28.6
St. Louis, Mo.	28.6
Philadelphia, Penn.	26.4
Chicago, Ill.	22.9
Houston, Texas	22.9
New York, N.Y.	14.0
Los Angeles, Calif.	13.5

Sample Cities in Terms of Percentage of Negroes

City	Percent Negro
Kansas City, Mo.	17.5
Pittsburgh, Penn.	16.7
Boston, Mass.	9.1
Rochester, N. Y.	7.4
Minneapolis, Minn.	2.4

Source: U.S. Census of Population: 1960.

Jews, Italians, Irish, Germans, and Finns and then, during the twenties and thirties, was transformed into one of the largest and most densely populated Negro communities in the country.

The Negro came to Harlem, as all migrants do, seeking better living conditions and expanded economic opportunities. Harlem became the center of Negro culture and talent. It is here that most Negro artists and intellectuals lived, drawing their ideas and inspiration from the life of the community. But the Negro in Harlem found himself increasingly isolated culturally, socially, and economically by a wall of racial prejudice and discrimination. He was blocked from the training necessary to prepare himself for the highly skilled jobs in private industry or government, and he was pushed into the most menial occupations. His housing and schools deteriorated, and he was forced to pay more for less. He discovered that his new neighbors resented his presence, his aspirations, and his talents. They left in droves, and Harlem became a prison of its new residents. During the thirties Harlem seethed with discontent and racial strife, gaining an exaggerated reputation as a center of vice and crime. White persons ventured into the community only in search of exotic primitive glamour. Today, Harlem, no longer the mecca for white bohemia, is a center both of trouble and potential talent, the fountainhead of Negro protest movements.

TABLE 3
Negro Residential Concentration by Areas of Cities

City and Area	Population	Negroes	Percent
New York, N. Y.			
Brooklyn ghetto	91,391	87,654	95.9
Queens ghetto	20,324	19,091	93.9
Manhattan ghetto	241,125	236,051	97.9
Los Angeles, Calif.			
Area I	48,806	46,865	96.0
Area II	15,489	14,990	96.8
Baltimore, Md.			
Area I	149,197	143,849	96.4
Washington, D. C.			
Area I	120,060	115,552	96.2
Area II	66,043	64,196	97.2
Cleveland, Ohio			
Area I	70,060	68,700	98.1
Area II	49,815	46,863	94.1
St. Louis, Missouri			
Area I	97,144	93,807	96.6
New Orleans, Louisiana			
Area I	45,111	44,044	97.6
Chicago, Illinois			
Area I	347,806	340,599	97.9
Area II	105,307	102,096	97.0
Area III	21,133	20,401	96.5
Area IV	22,168	21,347	96.3

Source: U.S. Census of Population: 1960.

Despite the apathy and despair of many of its residents, it is a vibrant, exciting and, all too frequently, a turbulent community.[2]

In most important ways — social and economic structure, community culture, quality of education, and the like — all urban ghettos in America are similar. As one Negro told a Haryou interviewer: "I don't limit the black man to Harlem alone. Harlem is only one of the accidents in time that have beset the children along the way. Problem of the black man is universal, the world over."

ECONOMIC AND SOCIAL DECAY

The symptoms of lower-class society afflict the dark ghettos of America — low aspiration, poor education, family instability, illegitimacy, unemployment, crime, drug addiction and alcoholism, frequent illness and early death. But because Negroes begin with the primary affliction of inferior racial status, the burdens of despair and hatred are more pervasive. Even initiative

[2]The name "Harlem," as used in this book, refers to that section of Manhattan sometimes referred to as Central Harlem, and excluding Spanish Harlem. Its boundaries are: 110th Street on the south; Third Avenue on the east; Harlem River, northeast; the parks bordering St. Nicholas, Morningside, and Manhattan avenues on the west.

usually goes unrewarded as relatively few Negroes succeed in moving beyond menial jobs, and those who do find racial discrimination everywhere they go.

The most concrete fact of the ghetto is its physical ugliness — the dirt, the filth, the neglect. In many stores walls are unpainted, windows are unwashed, service is poor, supplies are meager. The parks are seedy with lack of care. The streets are crowded with the people and refuse. In all of Harlem there is no museum, no art gallery, no art school, no sustained "little theater" group; despite the stereotype of the Negro as artist, there are only five libraries — but hundreds of bars, hundreds of churches, and scores of fortune tellers. Everywhere there are signs of fantasy, decay, abandonment, and defeat. The only constant characteristic is a sense of inadequacy. People seem to have given up in the little things that are so often the symbol of the larger things.

The dark ghetto is not a viable community. It cannot support its people; most have to leave it for their daily jobs. Its businesses are geared toward the satisfaction of personal needs and are marginal to the economy of the city as a whole. The ghetto feeds upon itself; it does not produce goods or contribute to the prosperity of the city. It has few large businesses. Most of the businesses are small, with what that implies in terms of degree of stability. Even the more substantial-appearing businesses (e.g., real estate and insurance companies) are, by and large, marginal. Of 1,617 Harlem businesses listed in the yellow pages of Manhattan's telephone directory, 27 percent are barber shops, beauty shops, or cleaning establishments — all devoted to tidying up, a constantly renewable service. Thirty-five percent are involved in the consumption of food and drink (bakeries, caterers, grocery stores, liquor stores, luncheonettes, restaurants, bars, and taverns). In general, a ghetto does not produce goods of lasting worth. Its products are used up and replaced like the unproductive lives of so many of its people. There are 93 funeral homes in Harlem.

Even though the white community has tried to keep the Negro confined in ghetto pockets, the white businessman has not stayed out of the ghetto. A ghetto, too, offers opportunities for profit, and in a competitive society profit is to be made where it can.

In Harlem there is only one large department store and that is owned by whites. Negroes own a savings and loan association; and one Negro-owned bank has recently been organized. The other banks are branches of white-owned downtown banks. Property — apartment houses, stores, business, bars, concessions, and theaters — are for the most part owned by persons who live outside the community and take their profits home. Even the numbers racket, a vital and indestructible part of Harlem's economy, is controlled by whites. Here is unproductive profit-making at its most virulent, using the Negro's flight from despair into the persistent dream of quick and easy money as the means to take from him what little money he has.

When tumult arose in ghetto streets in the summer of 1964, most of the stores broken into and looted belonged to white men. Many of these owners responded to the destruction with bewilderment and anger, for they felt that they had been serving a community that needed them. They did not realize that the residents were not grateful for this service but bitter, as natives often feel toward the functionaries of a colonial power who, in the very act of service, keep the hated structure of oppression intact. Typical of this feeling are the following views expressed to Haryou investigators in 1962 and 1963. None who heard their contempt, their anti-Semitic overtones, would have been surprised at the looting of 1964 — rarely does a social revolt occur without decades of advance warning.

> That Jew, he's got a wagon out here, and he will send his son through college, you understand? Nothing but a wagon, selling to these people in this junky neighborhood right here, and he's got a house in the Bronx, and he's paying for it, and the child is going to college, and he's selling you stringbeans at fifteen cents a pound.
>
> — Man, age 27

> Another thing I am sick and tired of, I am sick and tired of all these Jew business places in Harlem. Why don't more colored business places open? This is our part of town. They don't live here but they got all the businesses and everything.
>
> — Woman, age 38

Negroes have left business in the ghettos to whites not from a dislike of business but for a complex of other reasons. In those Southern cities like Birmingham, Atlanta, and Memphis, where the pattern of segregation is so complete that the dark ghettos must be almost self-sufficient, there are a number of Negro-owned stores, restaurants, and banks. But, in the North, the Negro is allowed to involve himself partially in the total city, and whites are willing to open businesses within the ghetto, sensing a profit among the tenements. The white power structure has collaborated in the economic serfdom of Negroes by its reluctance to give loans and insurance to Negro business. Eugene P. Foley, administrator of the Small Business Administration, told a meeting called in August 1964 to encourage economic investment among minorities that, before its field office opened in Philadelphia in that year, "I am ashamed to admit that my agency had made seven loans to Negroes in ten years." The situation has somewhat improved since then; in the six months after the field office opened fifty-five loans were granted and sixteen new businesses opened; new field offices were organized, also, in Harlem and in Washington, D.C.

There are insufficient economic resources within the ghetto to support its future development. Therefore any economic growth — as in fact is true of suburbs — must be supported and developed from without. But unlike the suburbs, where residents have high income and good credit, the ghetto has inadequate resources to command the attraction of economic power outside and cannot lure capital into its limits. Most ghetto residents are permitted only menial jobs and marginal income. The suburbs drain the economy of the city — through subsidized transportation, housing development, and the like. The economy of the ghetto is itself drained and is not replenished.

HOUSING DECAY

Another important aspect of the social dynamics of the Northern urban ghettos is the fact that all are crowded and poor; Harlem houses 232,792 people within its three and one half square miles, a valley between Morningside and Washington Heights and the Harlem River. There are more than 100 people per acre. Ninety percent of the 87,369 residential buildings are more than thirty-three years old, and nearly half were built before 1900. Private developers have not thought Harlem a good investment: Few of the newer buildings were sponsored by private money, and almost all of those buildings erected since 1929 are post-World War II public housing developments, where a fifth of the population lives.

The condition of all but the newest buildings is poor. Eleven percent are classified as dilapidated by the 1960 census; that is, they do "not provide safe and adequate shelter," and thirty-three percent are deteriorating (i.e., "need more repair than would be provided in the course of regular maintenance"). There are more people in fewer rooms than elsewhere in the city. Yet the rents and profits from Harlem are often high, as many landlords deliberately crowd more people into buildings in slum areas, knowing that the poor have few alternatives. The rent per room is. often higher in Harlem than for better-equipped buildings downtown. Slum landlords, ready enough when the rent is due, are hard to find when repairs are demanded. Even the city cannot seem to find some of them, and when they go to trial for neglect, they are usually given modest and lenient sentences — compared to the sentences of Harlem teen-agers who defy the law. Cruel in the extreme is the landlord who, like the store owner who charges Negroes more for shoddy merchandise, exploits the powerlessness of the poor. For the poor are not only poor but unprotected and do not know how to seek redress. One is reminded of the Biblical admonition: "For whosoever hath, to him shall be given, and he shall have more abundance: but whosoever hath not, from him shall be taken away even that he hath."

The effects of unsafe, deteriorating, and overcrowded housing upon physical health are well documented and understood.[3] The multiple use of toilet and water facilities, inadequate heating and ventilation, and crowded sleeping quarters increase the rate of acute respiratory infections and infectious childhood diseases. Poor facilities for the storage of food and inadequate washing facilities cause enteritis and skin and digestive disease. Crowded, poorly

---

[3] Among others, see D. M. Wilner, R. P. Price, and M. Tayback, "How Does the Quality of Housing Affect Health and Family Adjustment?" *American Journal of Public Health,* June 1956, pp. 736-744; "Report of the Subcommittee on Housing of the Committee on Public Health Relations," *Bulletin of the New York Academy of Medicine,* June 1954; M. Allen Pond, "The Influence of Housing on Health," *Marriage and Family Living,* May 1957, pp. 154-159; Alvin L. Schorr, *Slums and Social Insecurity,* Social Security Administration, Division of Research and Statistics, no date; D. M. Wilner, R. P. Walkley, T. Pinkerton, and M. Tayback, *The Housing Environment and Family Life: A Longitudinal Study of the Effects of Housing on Morbidity and Mental Health,* Baltimore, Johns Hopkins Press, 1962.

equipped kitchens, poor electrical connections, and badly lighted and unstable stairs increase the rate of home accidents and fires. Nor is the street any safer. Harlem's fourteen parks, playgrounds, and recreational areas are inadequate and ugly, and many of the children play in the streets where heavy truck traffic flows through the community all day. Far more children and young adults are killed by cars in Harlem than in the rest of the city (6.9 per 100,000 population compared to 4.2 per 100,000 for New York City as a whole).

The physical health of the residents of the ghetto is as impaired as one would expect based on knowledge of its housing conditions. The best single index of a community's general health is reputed to be its infant mortality rate. For Harlem this rate in 1961 was 45.2 per 1,000 live births compared to 25.7 for New York City. For Cleveland's Hough area the infant deaths are also about double that of the rest of the city. Poor housing conditions, malnutrition, and inadequate health care are undoubtedly responsible; where flies and maggots breed, where the plumbing is stopped up and not repaired, where rats bite helpless infants, the conditions of life are brutal and inhuman. All are symptoms of the underlying fact of poverty. Perhaps even more extraordinary than the high rate of disease and death is the fact that so many human beings do survive.

The effect of housing upon the social and psychological well being of its occupants is much discussed but less well documented. The most careful of the few relevant studies (those by Wilner, Walkley, Pinkerton and Tayback) on the psychological effects of poor housing have produced findings less dramatic than one would expect. The link between housing and mental health is not clearly established, but residents of public housing do have higher morale and greater pride in their neighborhoods than those who live in slums, and they are more likely to say that they have improved their lot in life and are "rising in the world." Nevertheless, their pride is generally not followed by genuine aspiration. They often express hope, but it usually is, alas, a pseudohope unaccompanied by an actual struggle to win better jobs, to get their children into college, to buy homes. Real hope is based on expectations of success; theirs seems rather a forlorn dream. Wilner and Walkley point out that "for all the housing improvement, many other circumstances that would be expected to affect the way of life [of these families] remained substantially the same. These were still families at the lowest end of the economic scale; practical family situations remained materially unimproved; in one-third of the families there was no husband present; and one-third were on public welfare."[4] Housing alone does not lead to sound psychological adjustment, for to build new housing or to spruce up the old is not to abolish the multiple pathology of the slums. Still, at the very least, good housing improves health, lifts morale, and thereby helps to generate a restless eagerness for change, if not in the adult generation then in their children; a fact, incidentally, that might give pause to some of those in

[4] Daniel M. Wilner and Rosabelle Price Walkley, "Effects of Housing on Health and Performance," in *The Urban Condition*, L. J. Duhl, editor, New York, Basic Books, 1963, p. 224.

society who support aid to public housing believing it will decrease the demands of Negroes. It will in fact, stimulate them to further demands, spurred by hope for a further identification with middle-class society. Housing is no abstract social and political problem, but an extension of a man's personality. If the Negro has to identify with a rat-infested tenement, his sense of personal inadequacy and inferiority, already aggravated by job discrimination and other forms of humiliation, is reinforced by the physical reality around him. If his home is clean and decent and even in some way beautiful, his sense of self is stronger. A house is a concrete symbol of what the person is worth.

In Harlem, a Haryou interviewer had a conversation with a little girl about her home that revealed both the apathy and the hope of the ghetto:

Interviewer: Tell me something about you – where you were born, you know, where you grew up, how everything went for you?

Gwen D: When I was born I lived on 118th Street. There was a man killed in the hallway, and a man died right in front of the door where I lived at. My mother moved after that man got killed.

I liked it in 97th Street because it was integration in that block. All kinds of people lived there.

Interviewer: Spanish people? White people?

Gwen D: Spanish people, Italian people, all kinds of people. I liked it because it wasn't one group of whites and one group of Negroes or Spanish or something like that; everybody who lived in that block were friends.

Interviewer: How come you moved?

Gwen D: Well, my mother she didn't like the building too well.

Interviewer: What didn't she like about it?

Gwen D: Well, it was falling down!

Interviewer: In your whole life, has anything happened to you that you really got excited about?

Gwen D: I can't remember.

Interviewer: Tell me about some real good times you've had in your life.

Gwen D: In Harlem?

Interviewer: In your life, that you've really enjoyed.

Gwen D: One year we was in summer school, and we went to this other school way downtown, out of Harlem, to give a show, and everybody was so happy. And we were on television and I saw myself, and I was the only one there with a clean skirt and blouse.

Interviewer: And you really got excited about that. Anything else ever happen to you that you had a really good time?

Gwen D: No.

Interviewer: What kind of changes would you want to make? Changes so that you can have a better chance, your sisters can have a better chance and your brother?

Gwen D: Well, I just want a chance to do what I can.

THE DYNAMICS OF UNDER-EMPLOYMENT

The roots of the pathology of ghetto communities lie in the menial, low-income jobs held by most ghetto residents. If the occupational level of the community could be raised, one would expect a corresponding decrease in social pathology, in dependency, disease, and crime.

With the growth of the civil rights movement, Negroes have won many footholds earlier forbidden to them, and it would seem logical to conclude, as many do, that Negroes are better off than ever before in this gradually desegregating and generally affluent society. But the fact is that in many ways the Negro's situation is deteriorating. The Negro has been left out of the swelling prosperity and social progress of the nation as a whole. He is in danger of becoming a permanent economic proletariat.

About one out of every seven or eight adults in Harlem is unemployed. In the city as a whole the rate of unemployment is half that. Harlem is a young community, compared to the rest of New York, and in 1960 twice as many young Negro men in the labor force, as compared to their white counterparts, were without jobs. For the girls, the gap was even greater — nearly two and one-half times the unemployment rate for white girls in the labor force. Across the country the picture is very much the same. Unemployment of Negroes is rising much faster than unemployment of whites. Among young men eighteen to twenty-four, the national rate is five times as high for Negroes as for whites.

An optimist could point to the fact that the average family income of Negroes has increased significantly within the two decades 1940 – 1960, but a more realistic observer would have to qualify this with the fact that the *discrepancy* between the average family income of whites and that of Negroes has increased even more significantly. The real income, the relative status income, of Negroes has gone down during a period when the race was supposed to have been making what candidates for elective office call, "the most dramatic progress of any oppressed group at any period of human history."

The menial and unrewarding jobs available to most Negroes can only mean a marginal subsistence for most ghetto families. The median income in Harlem is $3,480 compared to $5,103 for residents of New York City — a similar gap exists in the country as a whole. Half the families in Harlem have incomes under $4,000, while 75 percent of all New York City residents earn more than $4,000. Only one in twenty-five Negro families has an income above $10,000, while more than four in twenty-five of the white families do.

Nor do Negroes with an education receive the financial benefits available to whites. Herman P. Miller in his book, *Rich Man, Poor Man,*[5] states that Negroes who have completed four years of college *"can expect to earn only as much in a lifetime as whites who have not gone beyond the eighth grade."* This is true both in the North and in the South. The white high school graduate will earn just about as much as a Negro who has gone through college and beyond for graduate training. One young man in Harlem asked: "What is integration into poverty?" The question is not easy to answer.

Both the men and the women in the ghetto are relegated to the lowest status jobs. Sixty-four percent of the men in Harlem compared to only 38 percent of New York City's male population, and 74 percent of the women, compared to 37 percent for New York City, hold unskilled and service jobs. Only 7 percent of Harlem males are professionals, technicians, managers, proprietors, or officials. Twenty-four percent of the males in the city hold such prestige posts.

An eighteen-year-old Negro boy protested: "They keep telling us about job opportunities, this job opportunity, and that, but who wants a job working all week and bringing home a sweat man's pay?" Most of the men in the dark ghetto do work for a "sweat man's pay," and even *that* is now threatened by the rise of automation.

Many of the jobs now held by Negroes in the unskilled occupations are deadend jobs, due to disappear during the next decade. Decreases, or no expansions, are expected in industries in which more than 43 percent of the labor force in Harlem is now employed (i.e., transportation, manufacturing, communication and utilities, and wholesale and retail trades). Employment in those industries and occupations requiring considerable education and training is expected to increase. As the pressure of unemployed white workers in the few expanding areas of unskilled jobs grows, the ability of ghetto residents to hold on to such jobs becomes doubtful. And by 1970 there will be 40 percent more Negro teen-agers (16-21) in Harlem than there were in 1960. The restless brooding young men without jobs who cluster in the bars in the winter and on stoops and corners in the summer are the stuff out of which riots are made. The solution to riots is not better police protection (or even the claims of police brutality) or pleas from civil rights leaders for law and order. The solution lies in finding jobs for the unemployed and in raising the social and economic status of the entire community. Otherwise the "long hot summers" will come every year.

By far the greatest growth in employment in New York City is expected in professional, technical, and similar occupations — some 75,000 to 80,000 jobs by the end of the present decade.[6] Of the 3 percent of Harlem residents in this

[5] New York, Thomas Y. Crowell Co., 1964

[6] *Manpower Outlook 1960-1970,* New York City Department of Labor, 1962, pp. 1 and 12, provides the projections that pertain to job expectations.

group, the major portion are in the lower-paying professions: clergymen, teachers, musicians, and social welfare and recreation workers. A substantial increase of 40 percent in the number of managers, officials, and proprietors is expected in business and government, but the Negro has made few advances here. This will be offset by declines expected in retail business, where the trend toward bigness will result in fewer small store proprietors, another prophecy with grim implications for Negroes since the only business where Negro ownership exists in number is small stores. The number of clerical positions is due to grow in New York by 35,000 to 40,000 jobs. Approximately 14 percent of the residents of Harlem have such jobs, but most of them are in the lower-paying positions. Electronic data-processing systems will soon replace many clerks in routine and repetitive jobs, such as sorting, filing, and the operation of small machines — the kind of jobs Negroes have — while workers in jobs requiring contact with the public, such as claim clerks, complaints clerks, and bill collectors — usually white — will be least affected by office automation. The number of sales workers will decline as self-service increases, and here too, Negroes who have been successfully employed will lose out.

Jobs for skilled workers are due to grow in New York State by 28,000 yearly. Building trades craftsmen will be particularly in demand. But the restrictions to apprenticeship training programs in the building trades industry have kept Negroes from these jobs. Semiskilled and unskilled jobs (excluding service workers) will decrease by 70,000 to 80,000 jobs between 1960 and 1970. Thirty-eight percent of the Negro male workers living in Harlem have such jobs now. If present employment patterns persist, Negro and white workers who might ordinarily qualify for semiskilled jobs will undoubtedly be pushed into the unskilled labor force or become unemployed in the face of increasing competition with those who are better trained. Negro unemployment will rise as the unskilled labor supply exceeds the demand. The only jobs that will increase, and in which Negroes now dominate, are jobs as servants, waitresses, cooks — the traditional service jobs which have added to the Negro's sense of inferiority. But as the requirements of skilled jobs grow stiffer and as semiskilled jobs decline, Negroes will face strong competition from whites to hold even these marginal jobs.

It is illegal in New York to deny a job to anyone on the basis of skin color, but it is common practice anyway. First, Negro applicants are often said to lack the qualifications necessary for a particular job. Who can prove this to be disguised racial discrimination? Like any charge with some truth, the extent of the truth is hard to determine. Second, often working against the Negro applicant, though sometimes in his favor, are ethnic quotas applied to certain types of jobs, employed with the conscious intent of maintaining an "ethnic balance" in the work force. When the quota is filled, the Negro applicant, no matter how well qualified, is told that there are no openings. Third, and much more subtle, although no less discriminatory, is the practice employed by some unions of requiring that a member of the union vouch for an applicant. When the union has no Negro members, the possibility of finding someone to vouch for a Negro applicant is extremely remote.

Through historical processes certain ethnic or religious minority groups come to predominate in certain kinds of jobs: in New York, the waterfront for the Italians, the police force for the Irish, the school system for Jews, and the personal services for Negroes.[7]

A study by the Bureau of Social Science Research, Inc., showed a fourth technique of exclusion; that employers tend to label some jobs, usually the lowest, as "Negro jobs" – Negroes are hired by many firms, but at "Negro jobs," with menial status, minimum wages, and little if any security.

Furthermore, many Negroes are discouraged before they begin. Guidance counselors often in the past advised Negro students not to prepare for jobs where employment opportunities for Negroes were limited. Doubtless they believed they did so in the best interests of the youth – better not to encourage him to pursue a career which is likely to end in bitter frustration and unemployment. There is some evidence that this form of root discrimination is now being reduced under persistent pressure from groups like the Urban League and the National Scholarship Service and Fund for Negro Students. The plethora of ineffective antidiscrimination and equal opportunities legislation – contrasted with the clear evidence of acutal exclusion – leads one to suspect that this type of discrimination works in such a way as to be relatively immune to laws. It would appear that effective techniques for reducing discrimination in employment must, therefore, be as specific, subtle, and as pervasive as the evil they seek to overcome.

It has been charged over and over again that Negro youth lack motivation to succeed. To the extent that this is true, it is largely a consequence of ghetto psychology. Teen-age boys often help to support their families, and they have neither the time nor money nor encouragement to train for a white-collar job or skilled craft. Negroes often dread to try for jobs where Negroes have never worked before. Fear of the unknown is not peculiar to one racial group, and Negroes have had traumatic experiences in seeking employment. The Negro youth is caught in a vicious cycle: Poor preparation means poor jobs and low socio-economic status. Low status and poor jobs result in poor preparation for the next generation to come.

A comprehensive employment program for the youth of dark ghettos everywhere must be geared toward revamping the various systems which feed upon one another. It must upgrade the educational system which spawns functional illiterates and which helps perpetuate personnel practices which exclude Negro youth. Even if a personnel officer is free of racial prejudice, the

[7]A similar conception has been formulated by Eli Ginsberg in *A Policy for Skilled Manpower,* New York, Columbia University Press for the National Manpower Council, 1954, especially p. 249.

majority of Negro applicants can be rejected for jobs which require basic educational skills. Inferior schools, which discriminate against the masses of Negroes, have made Fair Employment Practices regulations virtually irrelevant. A crash program of rehabilitation with specific skill training is imperative. So, too, is a systematic procedure to inform ghetto youth about the occupations for which they might qualify. A realistic and comprehensive occupational training and employment program would include a counseling service not only to develop motivation and self-respect but also to help young people with concrete problems related to getting and keeping a job — many do not know how to apply for a job, how to speak to an employer, how to fill in an application blank. Many must learn the importance of promptness, appropriate dress and speech, and to modify habits that had been appropriate in the menial jobs to which Negroes had been relegated in the past. They must learn to appear and to behave like other middle-class applicants with whom they will be required to compete.

The Haryou proposal[8] to the City of New York included such a many-pronged attack. Over a three-year period, 7,000 Harlem youths, ages 16 through 21, were to receive job training. In on-the-job training the youth was to be paid the standard wage of the job for which he was being trained, with the employer and the project sharing the cost. As he improved, the employer would assume more of the salary costs. Also part of the Haryou plan was to establish a special counseling and guidance program for high school dropouts, for those who could be encouraged to re-enter high school. Those who chose not to return to school were to be referred to training programs appropriate to their specific needs and interests. High school graduates with marketable work skills were to be referred for employment through the program placement services. Graduates in need of further training would get it.

The young people associated with Haryou during its planning stage (the Haryou Associates) pointed out that Negro youth in Harlem did not have the opportunity to learn how to manage even a small business or store since, unlike other lower-middle-class groups in the city, their parents did not own stores. They believed that this was a major handicap and suggested the organization of a Harlem Youth Enterprises, Unlimited, which would sponsor a cluster of local business enterprises owned by youth so as to provide them with on-the-job training opportunities.

For those who have been so severely damaged that they are not at present able to profit from organized job training and not able to benefit from the small-business management program, Haryou proposed to recruit in the poolrooms and other hangouts for a Community Service Corps, designed to perform various needed community services at whatever level of competence

---

[8]See author's introduction and *Youth in the Ghetto, A Study of the Consequences of Powerlessness and a Blueprint for Change,* Harlem Youth Opportunities Unlimited, Inc., New York, 1964.

these young people had. The corps would try to raise their level of competence so that they would eventually be able to move into a more demanding job training program. Since each corps trainee would get enough money to meet his normal living needs, it might turn out that in a time of severe job scarcity, young people would "make a career" of job training. The alternative — larger welfare rolls, more jails, bigger police force to constrain hordes of desperate, jobless young people — is clearly more expensive. But the emphasis in all these programs would not be on "make-work" jobs designed to provide pocket money or to keep youths out of trouble during the stormy adolescent years. Rather, they would concentrate on providing young people with salable skills and insure a boost to the socio-economic status of ghetto residents of all America's urban ghettos, crucial if the pathology rooted in social and economic inferiority is to be remedied. One man expressed to a Haryou interviewer the view of many in the dark ghettos of America:

> Most of all, I am trying to impress on them that the people are not chaining themselves to posts, that demonstrations are not being held, that people are not exposing themselves to dogs and tear gas so they can go on being delivery boys forever.

And another said with wistfulness:

> If you go down and say well, man, I want a job, and showed that you really want to work and were given a job, then that's hope.

The main hope, however, may be that stated by Gunnar Myrdal in his book, *The Challenge of Affluence.*

> ... at this juncture of history there is a striking convergence between the American ideals of liberty and equality of opportunity on the one hand, and of economic progress on the other. Indeed, the chief policy means of spurring economic progress will have to be huge reforms that are in the interests of social justice.

New York's Lower Depths*

Patricia Cayo Sexton

I like Long Island, good houses, and the parents are better. Right here you see them take numbers, and they drink a lot. Sometimes I get angry, and I always say I'm going to run away from home. Then sometimes I say, "Well, where am I going to sleep? Where am I going to eat and all that?" Then I say, "How could I be a scientist if I don't go to school or nothing like that." I start to bother my sister. My mother comes. Sometimes she hits me. I get angry. I say I'm going to run away tonight. I wake up in the middle of the night. I'm ready to leave, and then I say, "Should I stay or shouldn't I?" And I go back to sleep.
— An Eleven-Year-Old Puerto Rican Boy

But is the whole of East Harlem a slum? In its low income housing projects, families on welfare range from 13 per cent in one to 21 per cent in another. Still, the majority of families are self-supporting.

The Triangle is an American Casbah, loaded with troubles and despair, but even there can be found much hope. In the Triangle's thirty-six acres, more than half the families are stable enough to have lived there for from eleven to twenty-one years. In a study done by a local group, 15 per cent of the residents were found to have criminal records and 10 per cent to be narcotics addicts. The reverse is that even in this trouble spot only a small minority were addicted and relatively few had criminal records.

On a warm summer day the broken and derelict men are visible on the Triangle streets, sodden with despair and whatever they take to make their internal escape from the slum. But far more numerous at some hours of the day are the spirited and attractive young men and women. While some of the Triangle's citizens look sullen and resentful, many do not. No stereotype fits; and, what outsiders would call a slum, many insiders would not.

One young Puerto Rican described East Harlem this way: "I'm 23 years old, and I've been living here all my life. I never been out of this neighborhood. To me this neighborhood is all right. People who have money — maybe it's a dump, as they call it, but this is my home." It is not a slum to everyone.

The relevant facts about East Harlem's poverty were turned up by a mayor's study. They showed that one in five New Yorkers lives in conditions of poverty. Though more than half of the poor are white, nonwhites are 29 per cent of the

*Patricia Cayo Sexton, *Spanish Harlem*, New York: Harper Colophon Books, 1965, Chapter III, "New York's Lower Depths," pp. 22-34.

poor and Puerto Ricans 19 per cent. The poor are largely confined to sixteen of the seventy-four recognized communities of the city — one of them East Harlem, the poorest of the poor.

Nothing more meaningful about East Harlem can be found than the fact that its median family income of $3,700 is $2,300 a year lower than the median for the city, or that jobless rates for Negroes run about 50 per cent above the norm of whites and for Puerto Ricans about 100 per cent.

About half of all private dwellings in East Harlem are dilapidated. Almost one in three is overcrowded. It is possible that crowding alone may produce much of the slum's stress. Experimental biologist Dr. Hudson Hoagland has found that over-crowding in animal society can produce stress-induced maladies — liver disease, heart trouble, sexual deviation — that serve as natural population controls. When crowded, animals die off despite adequate food; rats show abnormal sexual and social behavior. It is part of the "acute stress syndrome," he suggests, that results from the overactivity of the pituitary adrenal system, which regulates the release of hormones during stress.

Slum dwellers may be reacting in the same physiological way as the biologist's animals. Most people need and want privacy, at least on occasion — a room of one's own, an escape from family demands, noise, conflict. Because of the continuing bombardment of the senses, day and night, many slum children wake up nervous and tired. But the children are not lonely, and they are less likely than the more isolated "only child" of the middle class family to commit suicide.

A Negro woman in East Harlem expressed a common opinion: "We're in such crowded tenements down here, that it's hard to live privately. Your neighbors can't move — because of the salaries that are being made — into a decent neighborhood. The mix is good. You have to mix in order to get along with people. But the living *so close together,* that's a bit too much."

In East Harlem tuberculosis rates are high and venereal disease (VD) rates are more than twice the city average. Crowding helps spread disease. So does the inability of the poor to pay for decent medical care.[1]

Crowded rooms and lack of privacy no doubt help persuade East Harlem's youths (indeed the poor everywhere) to marry younger than do their middle class peers. Since the young are even less able to buy medical care, *one out of three pregnant mothers gets no prenatal attention.* Not surprisingly then, infant mortality is 37 per 1,000 live births (compared with the city average of 26), and 50 per cent of the infant deaths occur on the first day of life.

The typical East Harlem resident has never been to high school. Median

[1] More than 90 per cent of East Harlem school children depend on institutional medical care. New York's Health Commissioner, Dr. George James, said that "poverty is the third leading cause of death" in the city. He attributes 13,000 deaths a year to it, including cancer, diabetes, pneumonia, influenza, cardiovascular diseases, and accidents, along with tuberculosis and VD.

school years finished are 8.2. Only one out of five has graduated from high school. Only one out of twenty has had any college. Of all residents in upper Manhattan who have had no formal education, 50 per cent live in East Harlem, and most are Puerto Ricans.

In East Harlem few residents (and those mainly Italians) own their own homes. By contrast, nationally 38 per cent of Negroes and 64 per cent of whites in 1960 owned their own homes.[2]

The typical New Yorker is a tenant. As such he is denied the status, power, and stability that the American's chief property assets can offer: a home and the car that usually goes in its garage. The New Yorker, the poorer one in particular, typically has neither. Many like it this way and prefer apartment living when there are no young children in their families. But it is not clear what the effect the total denial of these assets has on the poor and others. The lack of these major creative and recreational outlets may result in significant psychological deprivation. Though caring for a house and car is simply a chore for many middle class people, manual workers often find in it a major source of satisfaction. If a worker is handy with his hands he will spend much of his time with his house and car, finishing the basement or attic, building a fence or porch, repairing his car. Do-it-yourself attitudes and skills are by-products of car and home ownership. So is the sense of control over the environment and the machine. It is a vital part of the American style of life that is missing in East Harlem and other rental areas. If the residents of East Harlem owned these buildings they would not permit them to remain in their present state of decay. They would be moved to clean, paint, and fix. As it is they think it is the landlord's responsibility — and almost always it is. In the rental slums of New York, apartment ownership may offer a substitute for home ownership.

In other cities, even the poor, unless they are desperate, often buy their homes if only on land contract. In New York the poor rent. As renters they usually contend with absentee landlords, who neglect their property. The tenants complain. The landlords ignore them. The city investigates; nothing happens. Tenants are helpless, unable to move either landlords or the city to action. Since a serious housing shortage still exists in the city, they are unable to move out to better housing.

RENT STRIKE

My days are swifter than a weaver's shuttle, and are spent without hope.
— Job

[2] The typical owner-occupied Negro home was valued at $6,700 in 1960, compared to $12,230 for the white home. In 1950, 35 per cent of Negroes and 57 per cent of whites owned their homes; thus the rate of increase has been greater for whites.

It was natural that the rent strike, one of the most potent (if controversial and short-lived) direct action devices New York's poor have found, should have begun inside East Harlem.

The Community Council on Housing, led by Jesse Gray, had its offices in East Harlem. One of the first buildings struck was 16 East 117 Street, in East Harlem, owned by a matron living in Teaneck, New Jersey. After the strike began in this building, the landlord tried to disposses the tenants. The court, inspecting building violations, ordered the rent paid to the court rather than the landlord. Later the city started receivership proceedings, and the rent money was returned to the tenants.

Mrs. Inocencia Flores, Apartment 3 W, was among the striking tenants. Born in Puerto Rico, where she attended high school and for a time the University of Puerto Rico, she came to New York in 1944 and began work in the garment district, trimming and making clothes. At the time of the strike, she had four children, was on relief, and separated from her husband.

Her diary, kept while her building was on strike, tells part of her story.[3]

Wednesday, Feb. 5: I got up at 6:45. The first thing to do was light the oven. The boiler was broke so not getting the heat. All the tenants together bought the oil. We give $7.50 for each tenant. But the boiler old and many things we don't know about the pipes, so one of the men next door who used to be superintendent is trying to fix. I make the breakfast for the three children who go to school. I give them orange juice, oatmeal, scrambled eggs, and Ovaltine. They have lunch in school and sometimes they don't like the food and won't eat, so I say you have a good breakfast. Miss Christine Washington stick her head in at 7:30 and say she go to work. I used to live on ground floor and she was all the time trying to get me move to third floor next door to her because this place vacant and the junkies use it and she scared the junkies break the wall to get into her place and steal everything because she live alone and go to work.

I'm glad I come up here to live because the rats so big downstairs. We all say the "rats is big as cats." I had a baseball bat for the rats. It's lucky me and the children never got bit. The children go to school and I clean the house and empty the pan in the bathroom that catches the water dripping from pipe in the big hole in the ceiling. You have to carry umbrella to the bathroom sometimes. I go to the laundry place this afternoon and I wash again on Saturday because I change my kids clothes every day because I don't want them dirty to attract the rats.

At 12:15 I am fixing lunch for myself and the little one, Tom. I make for him two soft boiled eggs and fried potatoes. He likes catsup and he has one slice of spam and a cup of milk. I have some spam for myself and salad because I only drink a cup of coffee at breakfast because I'm getting too fat. I used to work in the shipping department of bathing suits and the boss used to tell me to model for the buyers. I was a model, but now I'm too fat.

[3] Francis Sugrue, "Diary of a Rent Striker," *New York Herald Tribune,* February 16, 1964, p. 28.

After I go out to a rent strike meeting at night, I come home and the women tell me that five policemen came and broke down the door of the vacant apartment of the ground floor where we have meetings for the tenants in our building. They come looking for something — maybe junkies, but we got nothing in there only paper and some chairs and tables. They knocked them all over. The women heard the policemen laughing. When I come up to my place the children already in bed and I bathe myself and then I go to bed and read the newspaper until 11:30.

Thursday, Feb. 6: I wake up at six o'clock and I went to the kitchen to heat a bottle for my baby. When I put the light on the kitchen I yelled so loud that I don't know if I disturbed the neighbors. There was a big rat coming out from the garbage pail. He looks like a cat. I ran to my room, I called my daughter Carmen to go to the kitchen to see if the coast was clear. She's not scared of the rats. So I could go back to the kitchen to heat the bottle for my baby. Then I left the baby with a friend and went downtown.

Friday, Feb. 7: This morning I woke up a little early. The baby woke up at five o'clock. I went to the kitchen but this time I didn't see the rat.

After the girls left for school I started washing the dishes and cleaning the kitchen. I am thinking about their school. Today they ain't teaching enough. My oldest girl is 5.9 in reading. This is low level in reading. I go to school and English teacher tell me they ain't got enough books to read and that's why my daughter behind. I doesn't care about integration like that. It doesn't bother me. I agree with boycott for some reasons. To get better education and better teachers and better materials in school. I don't like putting them in buses and sending them away. I like to stay here and change the system. Some teachers has to be changed. My girl take Spanish in junior high school, and I said to her, "Tell your teacher I'm going to be in school one day to teach him Spanish because I don't know where he learns to teach Spanish but it ain't Spanish."

I'm pretty good woman. I don't bother anyone. But I got my rights. I fight for them. I don't care about jail. Jail don't scare me. If have to go to jail, I go. I didn't steal. I didn't kill nobody. There's no record for me. But if I have to go, I go.

Saturday, Feb. 8: A tenant called me and asked me what was new in the building because she works daytimes. She wanted to know about the junkies. Have they been on the top floor where the vacant apartment is? That's why I have leaking from the ceiling. The junkies on the top floor break the pipes and take the fixtures and the sink and sell them and that's where the water comes. . . . I'm not ascared of the junkies. I open the door and I see the junkies I tell them to go or I call the police. Many people scared of them, but they scared of my face. I got a baseball bat for the rats and for the junkies. I sometimes see a junkie in the hallway taking the junk and I give him a broom and say "Sweep the hall." And he does what I tell him and hand me back the broom after he sweep the hall. I'm not scared of no junkies. I know my rights and I know my self-respect. After supper I played cards (casino) for two hours with the girls and later I got dressed and I went to a party for the rent strike. This party was to get funds to the cause. I had a good time. Mr. Gray was there dancing. He was so happy.

Sunday, Feb. 9: I dressed up in a hurry to go to church. When I go to church I pray for to have better house and have a decent living. I hope He's hearing. But I don't get discouraged on Him. I have faith. I don't care how cold I am I never lose my faith. When I come out of church I was feeling so good.

Monday, Feb. 10: At 9:30 a man came to fix the rat holes. He charged me only $3. Then one of the tenants came to tell me that we only had oil for today and every tenant have to give $7.50 to send for more oil. I went to see some tenants to tell them there is no more oil. We all have to cooperate with money for the oil. It's very hard to collect because some are willing to give but others start fussing. I don't know why because is for the benefit of all, especially those with children. We have to be our own landlord and supers. We had to be looking for the building and I tell you we doing better than if there is an owner. Later I went down in the basement with another tenant to see about the boiler, but we found it missing water in the inside and she didn't light it up and anyway there was not too much oil in it. I hope nothing bad happens, because we too had given $5 each tenant to buy some material to repair the boiler. If something happens is going to be pretty hard to make another collection.

Tuesday, Feb. 11: This morning was too cold in the house that I had to light the oven and heat hot water. We had no steam, the boiler is not running good. I feel miserable. You know when the house is cold you can't do nothing. When the girls left for school I went back to bed. I just got up at 11:30 and this house is so cold. Living in a cold apartment is terrible. I wish I could have one of those kerosene stoves to heat myself.

My living room and my room is Alaska. I'm going to heat some pea soup and make coffee. I sat down in the kitchen by the stove to read some papers and keep warm. This is terrible situation. Living the way I live in this slum house is miserable. I don't wish no body to live the way I live. Inside a house in this condition, no steam, no hot water, ceiling falling on you, running water from the ceiling, to go to the bathroom you have to use an umbrella, rats everywhere. I suggest that landlords having human being living this way instead of sending them to jail they must make them live at least a month is this same conditions, so they know the way they pile up money in a bank.

Wednesday, Feb. 12: I wake up around 5 o'clock and the first thing I did was light the oven and the heater so when the girls wake up is a little warm. I didn't call them to 11 because they didn't have to go to school. It still so cold they trembling. You feel like crying looking your children in this way.

I think if I stay a little longer in this kind of living I'm going to be dead duck. I know that to get a project you have to have somebody prominent to back you up. Many people got to the projects and they don't even need them. I had been feeling [filling] applications I don't know since when. This year I feel another one. My only weapon is my vote. This year I *don't vote* for nobody. May be my vote don't count, but don't forget if you have fourteen cent you need another penny so you take the bus or the subway. At least I clean my house and you could eat on the floor. The rest of the day I didn't do nothing. I was so mad all day long. I cooked a big pot of soup. I leave it to God to help me. I have faith in Him.

Thursday, Feb. 13: I couldn't get up this morning. The house was so cold that I came out of bed at 7:15. I heated some water I leave the oven light up all night because the heater gave up. I fixed some oatmeal, eggs and some Ovaltine for the girls. I had some coffee. I clean the house. The baby was sleeping. Later on, the inspector came. They were suppose to come to every apartment and look all violations. They knock at the door and asked if anything had been fixed. I think even the inspectors are afraid of this slum conditions thats why they didn't dare to come inside. I don't blame them. They don't want to take a rat or any bug to their houses, or get dirty in this filthy houses. My little girl come from school with Valentine she made for me. Very pretty. At 8:30 I went downstairs to a meeting we had. We discuss about why there is no heat. We agreed to give $10 to fix the boiler for the oil. A man is coming to fix it. I hope everybody give the $10 so we have some heat soon.

Friday, Feb. 14: I didn't write this about Friday in my book until this Saturday morning, because Friday night I sick and so cold I go to bed and could not write in the book. But this about Friday. I got up at five and light the oven and put some water to heat. At seven I called the two oldest girls for school, I didn't send the little one, because she was coughing too much and with a running nose. I gave some baby aspirin and I put some Vick in her nose and chest and I gave some hot tea. I leaved her in bed.

It was so cold in here that I didn't want to do nothing in the house. I fixed some soup for lunch and read for a while in the kitchen and after a while I went out and clean the hallway. I didn't mop because there was no hot water, but at least the hallway looked a little clean.

Later on I fixed dinner I was not feeling good. I had a headache and my throat hurt. I hope I do not catch a cold. I hope some day God help me and all this experience I had be restore with a very living and happiness. It is really hard to believe that this happens here in New York and richest city in the world. But such is Harlem and hope. Is this the way to live. I rather go to the Moon in the next trip.

The building at 16 East 117 Street is one of 43,000 old-law tenements in New York City, which house about 900,000 people, a population the size of Baltimore, the nation's sixth largest city. Most old-law tenements, particularly those used by generations of poor and transient tenants, are not fit to live in and not economic to renovate. On the other hand, many old buildings, brownstones, and others, are often suitable for tenants or rehabilitation. Welfare Commissioner James Dumpson has said it will take fifty years to meet the housing needs of the city's welfare population alone at present construction rates, and another 100 years to house all the poor. By then the buildings that are habitable now will be in decay.[4]

In the building on 117 Street, decay set in after a fast shuffle of owners who didn't care and often could not be located: "The superintendent was replaced by a handy man. Then the handy man was made to be handy in so many places that he became handy in none. When the bell system failed, it was left unrepaired; when the lock was broken, the front door stood open. Tenants endured broken windows, falling plaster, peeling paint, leaking pipes, cracked sinks and toilets, clogged drains, rotten window frames, jammed doors, unlighted halls, unswept stairs, winter days and nights without heat. Then too, there were rats. Traps were set and poisons laid out, but, though some of the rats were caught and some wandered off to die in the walls, a population established itself and fattened and bred on the trash that wasn't collected and the garbage left out in the halls."[5]

None of the many owners of the house applied to raise rents under the law that guarantees landlords a fair return of at least 6 per cent on investment, plus 2 per cent for depreciation. Apparently the landlords made profits in excess of this legal guarantee.

A group of enterprising women from the Women's City Club of New York, instead of folding bandages or sponsoring talks on poverty, set out to learn for themselves what the slums are like. They chose a block of relatively "good" housing in East Harlem where the "decay of completely neglected slum areas was absent." In 59 apartments they found 1,319 violations of the housing code and unattended decay everywhere.

STRIKE GENESIS

The protector of the tenement is less the inspectors than the judges. Courts seldom convict landlords or impose real penalties. The judges are often landlords themselves, some say, and see only the landlord's side. Others say the landlords make big contributions to the political clubs that elect judges. Again, the relative political impotence of the poor is their housing handicap.

One judge came to the aid of tenants. When thirteen tenants, haled to court by their landlords, brought five dead rats to court, hidden under coats, the rent strike lid was lifted. Tenants were permitted to give rents to the court until repairs were made and the rats evicted. A second judge ruled that tenants could keep their own rents until repairs were made.

A flurry of tenant self-help activity followed. East Harlem's first tenement cooperative was soon set up. Tenants in one building voted to continue paying

---

[4] In New York City, according to the 1960 census, there are 2,758,419 housing units, and of these 427,572 are classified as "dilapidated or deteriorating."

[5] Peter S. McGhee, "From Pasture to Squalor," *Nation,* March 23, 1964, p. 295.

full rent − to themselves − even though the city had reduced rents. The money went into a fund to pay the janitor and buy coal. The old janitor was discharged and a new one hired by the tenants. There was some emotional debate about what should be done with six rent-delinquent tenants, and eviction was threatened.

It was midwinter, and people were cold. They wanted action. Groups everywhere began to organize. The East Harlem CORE chapter, working in the Triangle, was one of the first groups. "Landlords in the ghetto are really a class of terrible people," said one twenty-year-old CORE (Congress of Racial Equality) organizer. "They're irresponsible, and that's a nice word to use."

It is hard to get to the actual owner of the buildings, organizers said. "There are so many fronts you have to go through to get to him. But I'll bet you something like 1,000 people own the 20,000 buildings in this neighborhood. They never repair. And if they do, they have someone slap some plaster on the walls that comes down in about two months. And that's after three months of fantastic pressure."[6]

Putting a building on rent strike and holding it there is hard work. "The court procedure is a whole lot of trouble. The courts sometimes decide in your favor, and the landlord will be fined $25. And they won't follow through to find out if the repairs have been really made. The landlords have power on their side. They pay the taxes and they pay the lawyers. The landlord is in and out of the building and he scares people. Many of the Spanish people see an official paper, which is the dispossess, and they'll pay him. Or they won't communicate. Sometimes the tenants don't speak to other tenants."

CORE teams were composed of ten organizers and a captain. The team took one block, and three of four people went into each building. They got violation forms filled out and heard tenant complaints. Tenant meetings were held to voice complaints and plan action. "In case one landlord owns several buildings, you try to get them all on rent strike at once. That works much more effectively. We may hit one side of a block and get all those buildings organized. You try to get them interested in your philosophy and in the civil rights movement. It's one of our basic aims to do that."

Even more than the school boycott that preceded it, the rent strikes engaged East Harlem's citizens in the civil rights ferment. It engaged the "grass

[6]Daniel M. Friedenberg's answer to the question "Who owns New York?" is that ownership "is an overlay of shared interests − interlocked, interwoven. These interests are the life insurance companies, the commercial banks, the powerful old and the ascendant new families, certain churches, institutions and corporations, the union finance committees, the pension funds. New York is owned by perhaps one hundred men who sit on the right committees and who say yes or no when questions of leasing and sale, of temporary construction money and permanent financing come up." The Hundred Men on the Right Committees," *Herald Tribune,* February 21, 1964.)

In New York there is a far greater concentration of land and property ownership than is generally known. Samuel J. Lefrak, for example, has more tenants in his buildings than the city itself has in public housing (half a million).

roots" and called up indigenous leaders, male as well as female. It was led by Negro and Puerto Rican residents rather than white social workers.

The rent strike's course is familiar. It began with a legal breakthrough (as in the schools) and a court decision. Then it proceeded to direct action to enforce the law and publicize its breach. Now, more and more, it is moving into political action, self-help, and outside aid programs.

The City's Not for Burning*

Robert Conot

Los Angeles in the summer of 1965 was the scene of the opening skirmish. That is the reason why the August riot has importance and implication far beyond the turmoil of a few days.

It was a rebellion by the Negroes against the economic power the whites retain in the ghetto — in essence, the Negro city. Once the motif of the rebellion became established it was not upon the white person that violence was committed, but upon white property — and only in the ghetto! Although, at first, it may not seem so, it was an exercise of political power by the Negro — in this particular case political power in raw, physical terms. Twenty years from now the youths who threw rocks and burned will have learned more sophisticated use of such power. What they failed to do in 1965 with the torch they will succeed in doing in 1985 with the vote.[1]

They will succeed unless white reaction is even more aggressive than Negro action. In 1965 the reaction came in the form of the National Guard. By 1985 it may be in the form of a full-blown White Backlash, with all its attendant perils.

That there is already a white backlash can hardly be doubted by anyone analyzing political trends, or sampling the opinion of the groups that feel most threatened by the Negro — the small property owner and the middle-class white whose income and education straddle or are below the median. While the Negro and white at the top of the ladder are in many respects working to reduce the separation that exists between them, there is a growing polarization of the races and hardening of existing prejudices at the bottom.

It is almost impossible for the white to comprehend the alienation the Negro feels in American society. When, as happened recently, a Negro contends he is not subject to the draft because service in the armed forces is the duty of a citizen, and he has been denied the rights of citizenship; and another claims that

---

*Robert Canot, *Rivers of Blood, Years of Darkness*. New York: Bantam Books, 1967. Chapter 59, "The City's Not for Burning," pp. 454-465.

[1] It is clear that the incidents which are sparking the riots in the cities are so insignificant as to give credence to the white contention they are "senseless." In Chicago, in the summer of 1966, the riot began over the refusal of the fire department to let Negro kids turn on fire hydrants on a hot day. In Cleveland, over an altercation between Negroes and a white bar owner regarding a funeral collection. Only when one realizes there is a single *theme* — that of rebellion against white authority and control over the Negro's life — does a pattern emerge.

U. S. courts lack jurisdiction over him because, as the descendant of persons brought to this country against their will, he is an involuntary resident, the general white reaction is to laugh at what seem utterly specious arguments. But to many a Negro they are not specious, and certainly no laughing matter.

A Negro signing himself *C.M.A.* wrote an eloquent letter to the Los Angeles *Times* following that newspaper's series on Watts.

> As an American Negro I must say to someone who has shown basic understanding, that the present attitude of the white community — newspaper columnists, radio commentators, reporters and ordinary citizens — toward all Negroes is creating a bitterness and resentment which is becoming overwhelming.
>
> I do not know the answers. I was reporter and editor of Negro newspapers in the affected communities for 10 years and served with the information office of a government agency for two years, during which time I became conversant with a few of the problems. Even I was unprepared for the revolution.
>
> I have never harbored hatred, because I have always believed that it is an emotion more harmful to the hater than to the hated. I have always abhorred violence; yet in the past two weeks the kinds of comment to which I have been subjected have brought me to the point where I actually resent being included among 'our fine, responsible Negro (colored) citizens who make up the vast majority of our population.'
>
> Such condescending phrases make me gag.
>
> I feel a deep sense of responsibility for what happened. I feel that somehow I should be able to do something — what, I don't know — to alleviate the situation. But generally speaking, there seems to be very little real desire on anyone's part to understand that down through the ages when men have been oppressed and denied the simple necessities enjoyed by other men, they have revolted.
>
> Whether such revolts are justified has no bearing on the fact that they have occurred and will continue to occur. They are inevitable.
>
> For 300 years the black man in America has tried desperately to adjust to the white man's society. Until two weeks ago I thought, like hundreds of thousands of other Negroes, that I had done so. Now, it seems that there is no hope of my ever becoming a full-fledged American citizen, because every act committed by any Negro becomes the responsibility of all Negroes.
>
> Yet the white man accepts little responsibility for the acts of other white men and anyone who expected him to do so completely would be considered a stupid oaf.
>
> I am afraid that . . . if politicians pursue their present course of denying facts which every Negro knows but cannot prove in court, and if recriminations go on much longer with no attempt to seek solutions, the result will be a greater or complete separation of the Negro and white communities. This would be a disaster.
>
> I view this not as a Negro riot, but as a revolution of men and women who are tired of too few jobs, too little food and no hope for the future.

Even if, for the sake of argument, it is granted that many Negroes are incapable of pulling their full share of the load in this great white society, some effort must be made to help the weaklings make some adjustment.

After all, if one-tenth of the money spent for foreign aid, one-tenth of the money spent to free the Vietnamese, one-tenth of the money spent to explore the outer reaches of space, had been spent on a constructive program to help train these American citizens to live in our complicated society, the revolution would not have been attempted.

As an individual who has managed to exist on the fringes of your society, support his family, educate his two sons and abide by the rules you have set up — which I had little if any part in making — I am becoming desperate.

I have always considered myself an American, although it was quite obvious that I am an American Negro — one can never quite forget that — but if the present attacks on my race as a whole continue, I'm going to have to become a NEGRO, with little identification with the total American community.

If the present trend continues, those of us who believed that we had made a beginning, but now find ourselves a part of an isolated, condemned group, must adapt ourselves to the attitude of the group to which we have been arbitrarily assigned. We won't like it, but all of us will be forced to defend the actions of any of us.

Only if honesty replaces hypocrisy; only if expediency gives way to enlightenment; only if policy is made paramount to politics, may a genuine beginning be made to solving the interwoven racial and economic problems of America. And the problems must be solved, for they present a threat to the very survival of this nation on the concepts upon which it was founded.

When a politician cries "Communist!" every time he is embarrassed by Negro violence, the principal danger is not that he is adding a few persons to the ranks of those convinced of the ubiquitous Communist menace; nor that he is inflating the egos of a few generally ineffective agitators, giving them stature among the disaffected that they did not have before; but that by thus "solving" a complex problem with a simple panacea — *get rid of the Communists* — he is like a police chief pinning the murder on the first person who comes up and cries "Guilty!" Thus preventing the bringing of the real culprit before the bar of justice.

When political delicacies prevent a McCone Commission from coming to grips with the fact of prolific and indiscriminate procreation, the tragedy is not that this is a dereliction of the assigned analytical task; but that in avoiding the issue the commission prevented its inclusion in the problems to be solved.

When the citizens of a nation, both individually and collectively, would rather subsidize despair and pay billions of dollars as tribute in order to maintain order than to acknowledge that there is a sickness in the body, they are like a man who uses alcohol to escape the reality of a tumor. And the end result will be just as fatal.

It is not necessary to convince the white American that he must *love* the Negro in order to make him realize that he has a stake in raising the Negro's standard of living to a comparable level with his own. It is in fact folly to attempt to do so — the folly of one piece of legislation after another carrying a pseudo-altruistic ring, so that it seems the Negro suddenly has come into special favor, and is being granted that favor as a result of the pressure exerted by the civil rights movement.

Americans did not *love* the Germans and the Japanese after the end of World War II. They had, in fact, been taught for years to hate them. Yet within a very short period of time Americans became reconciled to the fact that they must pay taxes to help the erstwhile enemy. They accepted it not because they had suddenly been brainwashed to *love* the perpetrators of Pearl Harbor and mass murder, but because they were convinced that it was essential to American *self-interest* to help pull the enemy back to their feet. Self-interest must replace love and other abstract concepts as the motivating reason in the drive for full equality for the Negro.

It is, most assuredly, to the self-interest of the property owner not to have the property he owns turn into a ghetto, and then into a slum. It is to the self-interest of the suburbanites not to have the cities in which they work become bastions of black hatred. It is to the self-interest of the police to eliminate the hives of crime. It is to the self-interest of every city's civil servants to have reasonable racial balance maintained in the central city. It is to the self-interest of the metropolitan newspapers to have a literate population. It is to the self-interest of business to add millions of persons to the ranks of customers. And it is to the self-interest of every American tax payer, no matter what his race or occupation, to convert the millions of underemployed and unproductive into self-sustaining, positively contributing elements of the population.

To attempt to do this by fiat alone is as futile in the 20th century as it was in the 19th. If, after the white American becomes convinced that it is to his self-interest to have Negro children attending school with his own, he finds that the Negro children bring with them a deterioration of the standards of the school and have a pernicious effect on his own children, the human reaction will be for him to say "to hell with it!" If, after the white home owner has been convinced it is to his self-interest not to set up bars to a Negro's moving into the area, the result is, nevertheless, that the area deteriorates, he will be of the opinion that he has been conned. If, after industry has been convinced of the benefits of an open hiring policy, the Negro who is hired is unable to compete with the white, both industry and the Negro will be disillusioned — the Negro rationalizing that the reason he is unable to keep up is because he is discriminated against, the white reaffirmed in the stereotyped belief that the Negro is of a lower mental capability.

If Negroes and whites are to mix successfully, their standards will have to be approximately equal. Where such equality exists, integration tends to work.

Where it does not, the measures to achieve integration by law usually turn out to be a perverse hoax. For an underprivileged minority to impose its concepts upon a nation's power-holding majority, against the will of that majority, is a practical impossibility.

To raise the standards of the poverty classes will take an effort as intense, massive, and integrated (in the generic, not the racial, sense) as any in the history of this country. It will have to be a true war, not simply a *war* of semantics. The U. S. has shown its capability to wage such a war. The space race is one brilliant example. Another is a 20-year-old project that has been unqualifiedly successful, and which might well serve as a pilot study.

The contributing role the G. I. Bill of Rights has played in the unprecedented prosperity of the postwar era is deserving of a separate study. But there can be no question that it enabled millions of ex-servicemen to purchase homes, thereby stimulating the boom in the construction industry. That hundreds of thousands of men who, otherwise, would not have been able to obtain a higher education, became college graduates. These college graduates became the base material for the electronics revolution. Their purchasing power is high. They have provided the impetus that has raised the standard of living of the U. S. far above that of any other country. They are raising children better fed, better housed, better educated than any previous generation in history.

Yet the G. I. Bill of Rights, quite inadvertently, turned out to be a measure that grievously discriminated against the Negro.

It discriminated against him because his educational level – as well as physical condition – was so low that the armed forces would not take him in the first place. In the South, where by far the greater number of Negroes still lived 20 years ago, two thirds were rejected by the armed forces because they failed the mental test, a passing grade on which is the equivalent of a seventh- or eighth-grade education. This was four times the rate of white failures.

That this is a result of educational failure and not of innate ability is demonstrated by the fact that in the Western states the Negro failure rate of 31 per cent – although still two and a half times that of the white – was less than half that in the South. And, in fact, came very close to the white failure rate of 26 per cent in the Northeastern states.

It may now be better understood why white median income increased by $407 more than Negro in the decade between 1950 and 1960.

*　*　*

The government of the U. S. would do well to consider enactment of an economic bill of rights for the poverty classes – whether Negro, Mexican, or white. This should not, and must not, be viewed as a welfare or a giveaway program, but a capital investment in human resources that may be expected to repay, ultimately, many times the initial investment.

Such a program should embody, and be planned for, both short-term and long-term goals. If it does not view all of the problems as a unit, but attempts to solve them by a piece-meal approach it is very likely to fail. For to protect a population from smallpox is not the same as insuring its health.

The short-term program must aim for the alleviation of immediate pressures. Perhaps the most difficult, yet essential, task will be to provide jobs for people who, basically, lag a generation behind the economy of this country.

Dead-end make-work programs are not the answer. Neither is a training program in simple skills that are already obsolescent. The only real hope, though one encompassing great difficulties, is to launch a massive effort to raise the people to the level required by modern-day technology. This can only be done with the full participation of American industry. Just as the government has, in the past, subsidized certain industries, such as airplane manufacturers and airlines — not to speak of agriculture — which provide essential services, and has granted special tax incentives for capital investment, so it should now subsidize and provide incentives for industries participating in long-term training programs for previously unskilled workers. A small start has been made in this direction. But is is only a small start.

A major stumbling block to the inception of such a program is the fact that large proportions of the unskilled are functional illiterates. Industry should not be asked to cope with persons who cannot fill out orders or understand written instructions. (Often they cannot even understand *spoken* instructions, because of their lack of verbal skills.) It is ironic that the world's greatest industrial nation, which has sponsored literacy programs in underdeveloped countries everywhere, should exhibit such little concern for the illiterates in its own back yard.

It is essential, therefore, that the government initiate a program of adult literacy education whose theoretical aim is to bring every person in the U. S. up to at least a seventh- or eighth-grade reading and writing level.

A study should be made of the police practice of keeping permanent records of every arrest, no matter what the disposition. However theoretically innocent such a practice may be, the practical effect is the conviction of persons without a trial. It is, in truth, inimical to the operation of the police itself, since every person who, as a result, finds it difficult or impossible to obtain a job becomes a potential police problem. If the police deem it essential that arrest records be retained, and the courts support the police, then the records should be classified and made available to no one except the police authorities themselves.

Legal and consumer counseling offices should be established by the government where they are easily accessible to everyone in the poverty areas. Laws should be passed placing additional restraints on the rate of interest that may be charged, and on sales practices that, if not strictly illegal, are morally reprehensible.

Whereas the doctrine of *caveat emptor* may be one that can be lived with by the middle class, which has learned to protect itself to some degree against sharp business practices, it is too much to expect a semieducated, virtually illiterate lower-class person to do so, and there should be a reduction of an individual's responsibility to protect himself. In fact, the experience of such suburbs as Larkdale, near Chicago, where 40 per cent of the residents went bankrupt in recent years – as a result of such follies as buying food freezers, worth an estimated $250, for $700 under a contract calling for an additional $500 in interest charges over a period of five years – seems to indicate that the middle class is almost as much in need of protective legislation as the poverty class.

Consumer counseling should be directed toward teaching the people the essentials of comparative shopping, how to tell a good bargain from a bad, and how to resist the pitches of unscrupulous salesmen.

The aftermath of the Los Angeles riot revealed that people in the poverty areas have all kinds of legal problems they are incapable of solving for themselves, and that, as a result, they fail to obtain the protection that the law presumably provides for all. Other problems stem from the expense of legal advice and court procedures. A woman may be "living in sin" for no other reason than that the $500 to $700 required for a divorce is more money than she has ever had all at once in her life. And, if she did have it, she would want to spend it for something of more material benefit to her than a divorce decree.

Welfare codes should be revised to stimulate rather than stifle individual incentive, and to induce the exercise of individual responsibility in the practice of birth control. While complex and difficult issues are involved, it is believed that it would have a salutary effect to permit women on welfare who go to work a total income considerably higher than those who do not. Consideration should be given to raising the bare-necessities-of-life allowance – which, in actuality, does not even suffice to provide the bare necessities – but sharply reducing the amount of money granted for each additional child born after a woman goes on welfare. While in theory this might have the effect of "punishing the children," in actuality, since each additional child would reduce a woman's standard of living (and there must be no doubt that she understands this), it is quite likely to have a profound effect on the attitude of "what's the difference if I have another one or not?"

These should be the short-term programs. Some of the long-term programs are of a parallel nature, but they will be vastly more difficult and expensive to achieve.

Since it is elementary that one cannot build a dam in the midst of a flood, one of the first long-range programs that will have to be tackled is that of bringing some discipline to the conception of children. With 30 million Americans in the poverty classification reproducing at a rate only slightly lower than that found in some countries of the Far East, it is evident that a program, if it is to succeed, cannot be of a half-hearted or piecemeal nature, hamstrung by the kind of specious morality that has prevented the Office of Economic

Opportunity's birth control attempts from being effective. (OEO was prohibited from actively promoting birth control, and from providing contraceptive devices to unmarried women, who, of course, are the principal problem in the ghetto.) That the program will come under severe attack — from Catholic conservatives, on religious grounds, on the one hand, and Negro Nationalists, on the argument that it is a white scheme to exterminate the Negro, on the other — is inevitable. But every program of preventive medicine aimed at social improvement — from smallpox vaccination to the fluoridation of water — has faced such opposition in the past.

Since nothing is being done to lift the children out of the morass of the ghetto, the troubles of the parents are more than likely to become the troubles of the child. The scope of the problem may be understood when it is realized that it is not beyond the realm of possibility for an unmarried woman having six children to be responsible for 36 illegitimate grandchildren.

The only real hope for the children of the ghetto is education. To raise the standards of their education to the level enjoyed by middle-class children will take money and effort unprecedented in the educational field. It is not enough, as the McCone Commission suggests, to increase the intensity of academic education in poverty area schools by such measures as decreasing class size, and the like. The schools must be operated under the concept — entirely new on a mass basis — that they are responsible for every phase of a child's life. They must take over the functions the parents are either incapable of, or derelict in, performing.

This means that they will have to operate on a schedule of 12 or more hours a day, providing not only basic education, but a continuing program of sports and cultural activities, as well as study halls. They must take responsibility for the children's health and nutrition, and must provide the intensive counseling — not confined to educational matters — in those cases where the parents appear incapable of doing so themselves.

Clearly this will involve massive outlays of money that only the Federal government is capable of providing. To those who balk at the expense, one can give a simple answer. *Whether* or no the money is going to be spent is not in dispute, only *where* and *when*. If it is not spent in the schools, then it will be spent in the correctional institutions — at a cost of $4,000 per person per year — and for the support of uneducated people who are unable to support themselves.

Scholarship programs for higher education should be expanded so that college is not denied any person mentally capable of a college education, but they should be done so on a *quid pro quo* basis. If the government is to pay for four years of college, then the graduates should be committed to serve the government for an equal period of time — a policy that has been in effect in the service academies. Thus the skills acquired could be channeled back to aid in raising the standards of the poverty areas.

The government must undertake a large-scale program of property renewal in the deteriorating areas. It is incongruous that the poorest people should have to pay the highest prices for the essentials of life because, under the profit system, it does not pay large-scale firms to locate in these areas.

Industrialist H. C. "Chad" McClellan believes the government should, and will have to, provide insurance and financing for industries, supermarkets, and the like, since private rates are prohibitive. A study should be made of the advisability of creating tax incentives similar to those that have worked well in inducing industry to build in Puerto Rico, a previously underdeveloped area in many ways alike to the ghetto districts of the cities.

To stimulate the purchase of homes by people living in the ghetto, the government should provide home-loan insurance to the same extent it has done for ex-servicemen, since, again, the risks are too high for the setting of reasonable rates by private companies.

Finally, the government should put the weight of its prestige behind a reeducation of the American public regarding racial myths. The forms such a program may take are varied. They range from revision of textbooks to present a more balanced view of the Negro's place in history, to the encouragement of greater recognition by the media of mass communications that the Negro represents 10 per cent or more of the American population.

(It is ironic that the American sense of fair play insists on equal time on the air waves for political candidates, but has had no concern for the proportional representation of its minority people.)

*   *   *

Studies reported by Gordon W. Allport in *The Nature of Prejudice* have shown that prejudice tends not to be so much specifically directed as a general attitude; that the prejudiced person tends to be biased against any *number* of races, religions, cultures, or customs — anything that seems foreign. Yet it has been similarly demonstrated that prejudice may be tempered by education. That, in fact, there is an inverse correlation between education and prejudice — the higher the education, the less the prejudice.

*   *   *

In a way, Bob Bailey, a Negro member of CORE, summed it all up when he described his emotions during the riot.

> When I saw the police, and they were standing off — way off and wouldn't come down — I felt free for the first time in my life. I felt like I was really part of America, and America was part of me. And that if this is what the white people have been feeling all these years, what a wonderful thing it must be!

I'd participated in the civil rights movement, but I'd never felt that way before. And it seemed to me that that was what America was all about. I felt like I had the Constitution in my brain and that my body and soul were part of the land — that I owned it and wanted to plant flowers and make it green and beautiful. And I ran in the park with the kids and shouted Hallelujah! Hallelujah!

Cleveland's Crisis Ghetto*

Walter Williams

The riot in the Hough section of Cleveland, Ohio, occurred in July 1966. Not much more than a year earlier, in April 1965, the Bureau of the Census had conducted a special census for Cleveland that showed unexpected social and economic changes in the five years since 1960. What was most significant was a sharp economic polarization among the city's Negroes. A substantial number had moved up to a more affluent life; but the group in the worst part of the ghetto was at a level of poverty that was actually *below* the one recorded in 1960. Who rose and who stayed behind, and why?

What is most startling about the changes revealed by Cleveland's special census is their magnitude. These five years saw rapidly rising real income and falling unemployment for the city as a whole — but not for the very poor. The gap between haves and have-nots widened strikingly; and the most rapid widening was among Negroes — between those outside the slums who were rising, beginning finally to cash in on the American dream, and those still in the hard-core ghetto, on limited rations of income and hope.

In the special census nine neighborhoods at the bottom economically were grouped together and called the "Neighborhood." (See map.) The rest of the city, in which the prospering middle and upper classes are concentrated, was called the "Remainder of Cleveland." In Cleveland, however — as in the Inferno — there are different levels on the path downward, and one area of the Neighborhood is especially bad. This is the "Crisis Ghetto." It is predominantly Negro. Hough is part of it — on the edge.

The group that rose most swiftly in the period 1960 - 1965 were the Negroes who did not live in the Neighborhood. In 1960 they numbered 22,000. By 1965 their number had almost doubled. In all Cleveland they had achieved the greatest economic gains, showing that the door of opportunity, for some at least, was opening wider. (And also providing a convenient, but unwarranted, rationalization against help for the less fortunate — for if some Negroes could rise so quickly through their own efforts, why not all?)

At the opposite end of Cleveland's economic spectrum we find a grim picture. The number of Negro children in poor female-headed households increased sharply. By 1965 nearly two-thirds of these poor Negro youths in

*Transaction, September 1967, Vol. 4, #9, pp. 33 ff.

female families were in the Crisis Ghetto. Further, the Crisis Ghetto's average
resident was in worse economic straits than in 1960. Unemployment was higher,
income lower, and a larger percentage of the population was poor.

In relative terms the Crisis Ghetto was further away from the rest of the
city than in 1960 in terms of major economic indices. For instance, the income
gap between the Crisis Ghetto and the next economic stratum (the other five
sections of the Neighborhood) had spread visibly. The range of median real
incomes for the four sections of the Crisis Ghetto and the five sections in the
rest of the neighborhood was as follows:

Range of Median Incomes	1960	1965
Crisis ghetto	$3,170-4,900	$3,000-4,160
Rest of neighborhood	$5,450-6,230	$5,460-6,500

Hence the top of the Crisis Ghetto income range is now $1,300 short of the next
economic tier, in contrast to $550 in 1960. And that next tier itself had suffered
in income terms over the five-year period relative to the Remainder of Cleveland.

Thus, at least in Cleveland, the census validated our fears of the emerging
"two Americas." If this portrays what is happening in other cities, it is most
disturbing.

The Crisis Ghetto's potential for generating earned income has declined a
great deal since 1960. Those economic units with lowest earning potential –
female-headed families and aged people – have increased in absolute numbers,
while those with the greatest earning potential (younger male-headed families)
have diminished sharply. The Crisis Ghetto has become a concentration point
not merely for the poor, but for the hard-core poor – those with least hope
or opportunity of being anything else.

THE WIDENING GAP

The increasing distance between Cleveland's majority and its disadvantaged
segment is frequently hidden in the overall economic indices of the city.
Averaging the increasingly prosperous and the stable poor seems to give a "rise"
to everybody. But the almost unchanged poverty rate between 1960 and 1965
masks within different groups large movements that have further split the
population. Between 1960 and 1965, the poverty rate:

- — declined markedly among male-headed families while it increased
  among female-headed families;

- — fell for white people, but remained almost unchanged for Negroes;

- — yet showed a much greater decline (almost 40 percent below the
  1960 level) for non-Neighborhood Negroes than for any other

group (the whites outside the Neighborhood experienced a 12 percent decrease);

— and rose sharply in the Crisis Ghetto while it fell in the Remainder of Cleveland.

Another important change was in the *kinds* of poor families and poor people in the Crisis Ghetto. Between 1960 and 1965, the number of poor people fell by roughly 14,000. But members of Negro female-headed families increased by almost 12,000 persons (all but the merest handful of whom were found in the Neighborhood) while persons in families headed by Negro males and white males and females decreased by 26,000. As a consequence of these population changes in the five-year period, members of Negro female-headed families increased from one-fifth to one-third of Cleveland's poor. And in 1965, 60 percent of these poor, Negro, female-headed family members lived in the Crisis Ghetto.

Changes in the structure of industry have hurt the Crisis Ghetto. As Louis Buckley notes in discussing the plight of the low-skilled city laborer:

The changes in the demand for labor in our central cities have been in the direction of expansions of industries requiring well educated white collar workers and a relative decline in the industries employing blue collar unskilled and semi-skilled workers.

Many of these modern industries have fled to the suburbs. Unfortunately, public transportation has not followed, so ghetto residents have difficulty getting out to suburban jobs.

Further, an increasing percentage of the Crisis Ghetto's residents are in families whose heads have the least likelihood of increasing materially their earned income. In general, the two groups with the most limited economic potential are family units (our definition of unit includes single persons living alone) headed by women and by the aged. These groups rose significantly over the five-year period as a percentage of the Crisis Ghetto population. (See tables) Not only do these two groups seem *least* likely to earn much more than at present — but they seem the *most* likely group to suffer an actual as well as a relative decline in earned income. In short, they have the lowest chance to improve their financial position, and the highest probability of declining. Once a unit in this limited potential group becomes poor, by definition, it is likely to remain so. This persistent poverty is the eroding evil. Real income in the Crisis Ghetto declined by 2 percent for male-headed families and 15 percent for female-headed families between 1960 and 1965. At the end of the five-year period unemployment rates for both men (14.6 percent) and women (17.2 percent — up over one-third since 1960) were higher, standing at nearly three times the city's average; and the poverty level had risen from 36 to 40 percent. In 1965 the average Crisis Ghetto inhabitant was worse off than he had been in

1960, both absolutely and relative to others in the city. (The pattern of deterioration is shown in the tables.)

These facts have major implications. On the one hand, those with economic strength or potential *can* flee the Crisis Ghetto. (True, if Negro, they may only be allowed to escape to a better Negro area.) But it is also clear that entrapment in the Crisis Ghetto springs directly from poverty. The price over the wall is primarily money, not skin color. However, once poverty has locked one into the Crisis Ghetto, the chances of being forced to remain — and the bad consequences of remaining — are greater than if one lived in any other area of the city.

POPULATION DECLINE

The Crisis Ghetto population declined by about 20 percent during the five years (from 170,000 to 134,000 persons), and this exodus might seem to imply an explanation for the decline and the change. After all, if the more able, above-average people leave, averages should move down.

But exodus, by itself, cannot explain enough. Certainly the population decrease cannot be used to explain the absolute *increases* since 1960 of a few hundreds in the number of female-headed families, and of some 3,000 poor persons in such families. Yet that is what happened; and we have no pat explanation for it.

Nor does the population decrease necessarily counterbalance the possible adverse effects coming from the declining economic situation, particularly the rise in weak economic units as a part of the total population. These people seem likely to face the Crisis Ghetto over an extended period of time. What are the consequences?

The deleterious effects of a hard-core ghetto spread beyond the economy to the total environment — to schools, to street associations, to the preservation of life itself. This last point was driven home when three Washington medical schools threatened to pull out of the D.C. General Hospital because the meager budget provided almost medieval services. Even to be sick in the Crisis Ghetto is far more dangerous than in the suburbs. So, from birth to death the ghetto marks each person, and cuts his chances either to escape or survive. The Crisis Ghetto lacks the precise boundaries and imposed restrictions of the European ghettos of the past; but it is, nevertheless, an existing reality that limits and blights the lives of its inhabitants as effectively as did the old ghettos and pales.

Is this pattern confined to Cleveland? Only in Cleveland was a special census made for the city as a whole. But figures available for 1960-65 for South Los Angeles (which includes Watts and in an economic sense is like the Cleveland Neighborhood) also show a decrease in real income per family, a small increase in the percent of poor people, and a decrease in the male and increase in female unemployment rates (the Crisis Ghetto differs only in that it shows a very small male unemployment increase). Further, Negro female family members became a far more significant proportion of South Los Angeles poor (we do not have city-wide data) increasing from 37 percent to 48 percent. While the number of poor people in Negro female-headed households rose by 9,500 (roughly 25 percent) the number of poor among white male, white female, and Negro male-headed families all decreased.

At the national level poor Negro female-headed family members have increased both absolutely and as a proportion of the total poor population. For 1960 and 1966, the number of poor persons (in millions) for these categories was as follows: (Data furnished by Mollie Orshansky.)

	1960		1966	
	Number in Millions	Percent of Total Poor	Number in Millions	Percent Of Total Poor
Negro female-headed family members	3.2	8%	3.8	12%
All other poor persons	35.7	92	28.9	88
Total poor persons	38.9	100	32.7	100

The non-Neighborhood Negro has advanced greatly in the five years between the two censuses — more, as noted, than any other Cleveland group. Of course, this great improvement can be partly explained by residential segregation. The white on the rise goes to the suburbs — and out of the Cleveland census area — while his Negro counterpart must stay in the city. Still, there is no doubt that the Negroes escaping the Neighborhood are advancing as a group more rapidly than any within the city limits, and closing in on the Remainder of Cleveland whites. Even more striking than their increasing prosperity were their increasing numbers — from 22,000 to 41,000. They now account for 15 percent of the Negro population.

The Cleveland data indicate that economic discrimination has declined in Cleveland since 1960. Is this only in the upper and middle level jobs or has discrimination lessened across the board? I believe it may have lessened somewhat across the board; but this may not help the Crisis Ghetto Negroes unless direct action is taken to overcome their difficulties. Any decrease in overt economic discrimination, of course, is encouraging. However, it is absurd to think that this change *alone* — even if the reduction in discrimination had been far greater than I expect it was in Cleveland — will set right all the damage of the past. The liabilities of the Crisis Ghetto Negroes caused by past discrimination — poor education, lack of skills, poor health, police records — would still hold them back in the job market. In fact, the reduction in discrimination *alone* may exacerbate the split between the various strata of Cleveland Negroes.

Earlier discrimination possibly served as a lid for the advancement of *all* Negroes, squeezing them closer together in income and opportunity despite

The City of Cleveland

West Central — Hough

East Central

Kinsman

[illegible] The Neighborhood   [illegible] Crisis Ghetto

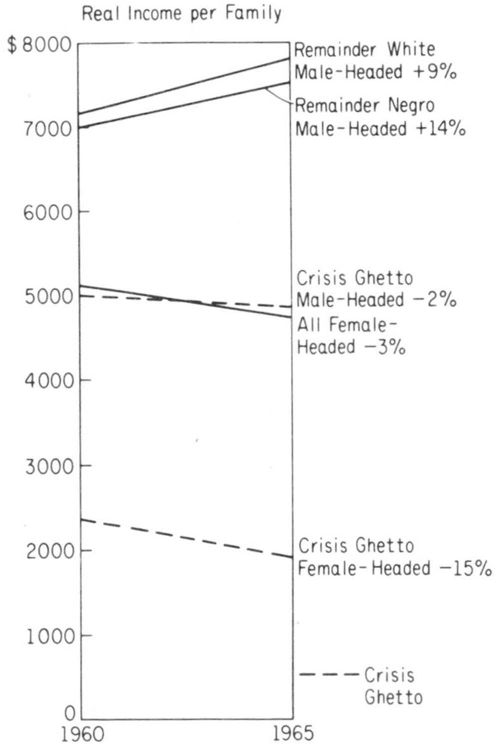

Real Income per Family

$8000

Remainder White
Male-Headed +9%

Remainder Negro
Male-Headed +14%

7000

6000

5000

Crisis Ghetto
Male-Headed −2%

All Female-
Headed −3%

4000

3000

2000

Crisis Ghetto
Female-Headed −15%

1000

— — Crisis
Ghetto

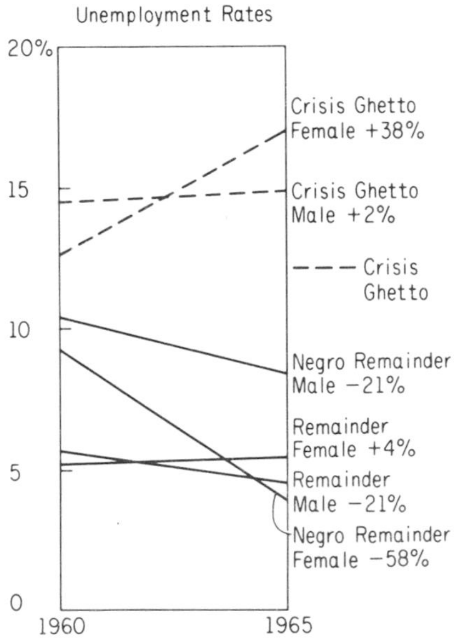

0

1960   1965

Unemployment Rates

20%

Crisis Ghetto
Female +38%

15

Crisis Ghetto
Male +2%

— — Crisis
Ghetto

10

Negro Remainder
Male −21%

Remainder
Female +4%

5

Remainder
Male −21%

Negro Remainder
Female −58%

0

1960   1965

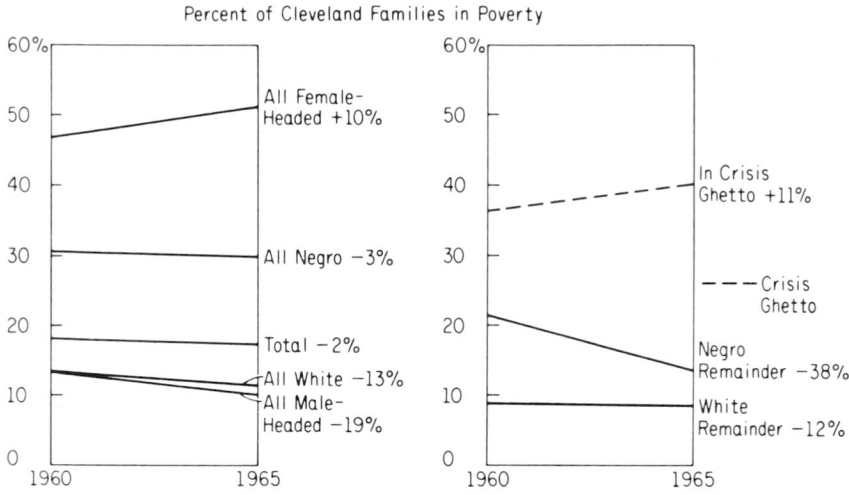

Percent of Cleveland Families in Poverty

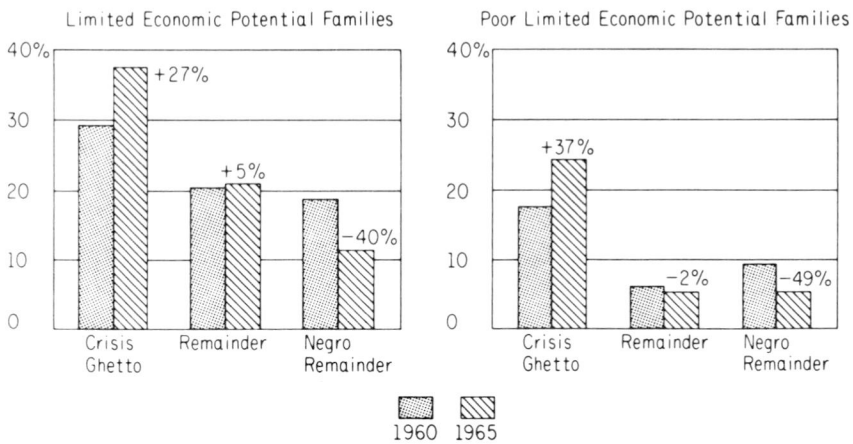

Limited Economic Potential Families

Poor Limited Economic Potential Families

differences in skills and potentials. But once the lid was lifted, especially during boom years, the more skilled, educated, and able rose much more rapidly than the others. So the gap widened. Unless something is done the more able Negroes should continue to widen their lead until they too become part of the symbols of success that have so far evaded the Crisis Ghetto Negroes and make failure ever more visible and disturbing.

At the opposite pole, though population in the Crisis Ghetto declined by one-fifth, Negro female-headed families increased by 8 percent, children in these families by 25 percent (16,900 to 21,000), and children in *poor* Negro female-headed families by 30 percent (13,100 to 17,000). Of the 21,000 children of female-headed families in the Crisis Ghetto, 17,000 are living below the poverty level. And it is this increasing group of female-headed families that suffered the largest real income decline of the five-year period, falling from $2,300 to $1,950 per family per year. That is, at the later survey date (1965), the average Crisis Ghetto female-headed family had an income *per week* of just over $37.50.

The implications of these statistics are appalling. There were 3,900 *more* poverty-stricken children in the ghetto in 1965 than 1960 — in a population 36,000 less — and there is no reason to believe that this trend is not continuing or accelerating. These children can do least to improve their condition — yet they must have a tremendous influence on the future of the Neighborhood, and of all Cleveland.

Poor Negro children in female-headed families are the great tragedy of the Crisis Ghetto. They constitute 13 percent of all persons there, 30 percent of all the children. They make up over half of the members of the poor limited-potential families.

There has been tremendous movement in and out of the Crisis Ghetto — at least four out of every ten departed or died in the five years. But the option of movement is not a random phenomenon affecting all equally. It seems available at will to some and almost completely closed to others — and most tightly closed to adults with limited economic potential, and their children.

Although the percentage of people with limited economic potential in the Crisis Ghetto is about twice as large as the population in the Remainder of Cleveland, the percentage of poor among them — standing at nearly 25 percent — is about *five* times as large. (See tables.)

Recent prosperity has removed many from the rolls of the needy, but those remaining may be far more discontented than when most of their neighbors were also poor. "Relative deprivation" is a very real force. For example, the classic study of this phenomenon made during World War II showed that there was more jealousy and dissatisfaction in an Air Force fighter squadron noted for rapid promotions ("boy colonels") than in a military police unit with few promotions. This feeling of being ignored, discriminated against, and isolated, while all around others rise, may create a far more explosive situation than when many are in the same boat, as during the Depression.

The Cleveland Census reveals the city's contrasting prosperity and decay. Sharp differences emerge within the Negro population. The rapid income increase for non-Neighborhood Negroes probably indicates less economic discrimination. Also, while residential segregation remained strong, the white flight to the suburbs opened up some of the desirable Cleveland residential areas. For example, Lee Miles, an area with many expensive dwellings, changed from 28 to 72 percent Negro in five years (21,000 Negroes by 1965). Many strong economic units fled the ghetto.

As many fled to better circumstances, others became more ensnarled. And by 1965 the most disadvantaged group had grown to a very significant portion of the total Crisis Ghetto population. Particularly depressing is the increase of poor Negro young people in the economically weak female-headed homes — young people whose bondage becomes more oppressive as the rest of the city grows more prosperous.

INCOME AND INCENTIVE

What can be done? What can be our long term goals?

The ghetto male, frequently with limited skills, enters the job market with grave liabilities. Often the job does not pay him enough to support his family and has little prospect of leading to a living wage. The longer the man works, the longer he fails as a provider. His marriage will frequently deteriorate. As Elliot Liebow has suggested in *Tally's Corner,* the unprovided-for family becomes a continuous symbol of a man's inability to fulfill the demands of his society — to be a man. So he opts out, and the sparse existence of the female-headed family has begun.

Job and training programs for men in the Crisis Ghetto are thus a first order need. Employment that yields a living wage over time seems to be the best bet for *preventing* family break-up, and *re-establishing* stable families.

Many broken homes, however, are not going to be re-established. Consequently, the female-headed family, as the Cleveland data show so starkly, will face a particularly exposed financial position. The mother may well seek a relationship with a man that has some prospect of offering family stability and also additional income. Unfortunately the "eligible" males are often the failures from prior marriages. The woman enters a tenuous relationship with the very unrealistic hope that it will work into a real family situation. The result is often another child.

Programs thus must be aimed at providing greater economic stability to the female-headed family. Job programs should be readily accessible for women as well as men. This means that major efforts for establishing day care centers are needed. Yet, work is not the answer for all these women. Also needed are better programs of income maintenance which will provide the family a reasonable income.

It is clear that our long run goals should be to prevent the breakup of families. But, many families are beyond the prevention of this sort. Further, the Negro mother has shown remarkable strength as a family head. Her great weakness has been in producing sufficient income, and the resultant poverty has had an adverse effect on the family. If these deficiencies can be overcome by work or transfer income, many of these mothers may be able to properly motivate their children. If freed from poverty, the inner strength of the matriarchal Negro family may begin to assert a positive effect upon the Crisis Ghetto.

Income increases from work and transfer payments are vital, but I believe that we must go beyond income programs to effect basic institutional changes in both the larger community that includes the Crisis Ghetto and the ghetto itself. A city must provide adequate education, health, and other services for all its residents. Further, direct community action must help Crisis Ghetto residents end the growing social decay in that area. As Richard A. Cloward and Lloyd E. Ohlin observed in *Delinquency and Opportunity*, the hard-core ghetto community must be structured to provide both social control and legitimate avenues of social ascent. That is, the neighborhood community – the Crisis Ghetto – must be a sound base of opportunity. The resident of the Crisis Ghetto must be able to form a realistic belief in a decent life.

We see the alternative in current trends. The poor in the Crisis Ghetto are falling further behind. Not only distance is building up between the two poles, but tension as well – as with electrodes approaching a sparking point.

If what is happening in Cleveland is also happening in other cities, we must multiply this tension, and the danger signals, by a large factor. If by inaction we consign the misery of the parents in the Crisis Ghettos to their children, the sickness of the central cities must fester and grow worse. Hough may be a pale prelude to other, greater Houghs – a short dramatic prologue, announcing that the tragedy has begun.

The New School System[*]

Herbert J. Gans

When the first Levittowners moved in they knew that the school was ready, but they knew nothing about what their children would be taught or by whom. Questionnaire data collected before they came indicated that they were not concerned; they were sure that the new schools would be as satisfactory as their new neighbors. As I noted in Chapter One, the builder had hired a national consulting firm to develop the physical plan for the new school system. This firm, having no parent or student constituency for whom to plan, developed a standard architectural program adaptable to whatever curriculum would eventually be created and left the determination of that curriculum up to the local Board of Education. The board, a group of elected, unpaid residents then running Willingboro's lone school, was also restrained by the absence of a constituency, and one of its members later reported that "since we had no Levittowners yet, we tried to give them a plan for the finest school system in the county." They decided that this system would be best achieved by giving the responsibility for course content, teaching methods, and staff recruitment to the county superintendent of schools.

Since that official was by state law also head of the township school, the board was familiar with his ideas and methods and trusted him to design a school system it would find acceptable. Indeed, its members were pleased that after the Ford Foundation plan could not be funded, the builder expressed no further desire to bring in an outsider; they were even more pleased that the county superintendent was very much interested in establishing the new system. Shortly before Levittown was opened for occupancy, he became its first Superintendent of Schools. Although much of the plan was fixed by state and county legislation and administrative regulations, the superintendent had some leeway on course content and was free to hire his own staff; most important, he could determine the priorities to be given to bright, average, and slow students. As a result, the school system was initially shaped by the superintendent's own goals.

The county superintendent had been in office for about ten years; before that he had headed the schools in one of the larger towns in the county. The system he developed in Levittown, however, reflected less his adult experience

---

[*]Herbert J. Gans, *The Levittowners,* New York: Pantheon Books, 1967. Chapter 5, "The New School System," pp. 86-103.

than his background and student years. An Irish Catholic of lower middle class origins, he was personally torn between enforcing discipline to maintain traditional restrictiveness and permitting more freedom to encourage expansiveness and individual development. He had been taught by rote, and had evidently suffered considerably at the hands of incompetent and petty teachers who punished for the slightest infractions of rules. Nothing was more important to him than to liberate the new generation from these bonds. Like many Levittowners he wanted the children to grow up under better conditions than he had experienced. He was not in favor of progressive education, which struck him as totally permissive, but sought to combine what he called "the teaching of traditional skills with individual treatment of the children." Hard-and-fast course outlines would be replaced by projects, and high school students would be free to choose their own courses, although they would be closely advised by guidance counselors and held responsible for their choices by a strict grading policy.

Reading was to him the most important of the traditional skills, and he planned a comprehensive elementary school reading program complementary to other coursework. Its aim was to teach children to read well, but — equally important — at their own grade level. When he interviewed a prospective teacher, he asked what the teacher would do if a child in the second grade had finished the second-grade reader. Candidates who suggested a supplementary second-grade reader were considered for a job; those who suggested a third-grade reader were not. As the reading expert whom he later hired to run the program pointed out, "A sixth-grade child should not get seventh-grade reading; that would get him into adolescent reading . . . a child should not start reading too quickly . . . that would take his childhood away from him."

Because the superintendent had spent his life in rural education, he was intensely concerned with average students, retarded children, and slow learners. Although he realized that many of today's high school graduates would go to college, the colleges he had in mind were not Ivy League types, but state schools and small private colleges in New Jersey and adjoining states — schools like the one he had attended. He determined that, in Levittown, the public school system would devote extra energies and its additional resources to the retarded, with lowest priority given bright students. Not only did he feel that the latter needed little help — much less than retarded students — but he found their motives and their behavior undesirable. In his view they were pushed too hard by their parents, who wanted them to advance beyond grade level, and they were often a burden to teachers, especially if parents demanded too much individual attention "to make sure that they all get college scholarships." An overemphasis on college preparation in the curriculum would ignore, he said, "the great unwashed who can't go to college; the girls who become typists." In line with his own lower middle class outlook, he insisted that Levittown would not copy Brookline and Scarsdale, and rejected such "Brookline ideas" as teaching foreign languages in elementary schools and allowing liberal skipping of grades. He liked to poke fun at a neighboring upper middle class community whose school system prided itself on a a high percentage of college scholarships, arguing that it ought to pay more attention to athletics so that average students could obtain scholarships. This justified his advocacy of varsity sports, although he also wanted to bring county athletic leadership to Levittown and end the virtual monopoly of county championships that had been held by a predominantly working class community for many years.

Rather naturally, the superintendent selected assistants who agreed with his basic philosophy. The elementary schools were assigned to a veteran county educator who shared the superintendent's preoccupation with discipline. Known as a "starter," he was an energetic man who thrived on the round-the-clock job of opening new schools. He too said publicly and more than once, "I won't stand for a Brookline education," and reinforced the emphasis on the average student by rejecting IQ tests and academic competition of any kind, whether among parents or children. He also believed that if the school staff took the initiative in shaping the school system, it could set standards which would be observed by students and parents alike. On the first day of school, he welcomed his charges at the front door and laid down his rules. Likewise, he personally initiated the organization of a PTA, choosing it because its bylaws demanded support of school policy and moving quickly to prevent parents from organizing home-and-school groups which could question it. Moreover, he personally recruited the actual PTA founders from people he already knew and trusted, taking strangers only if he could check with their previous communities on their loyalty to the school system. He also demanded that his teachers "belong to the system." Teachers were instructed to pay close attention to parents, for dissatisfied parents would create pressure groups, and these the elementary school official described as "cancers." His self-righteous authoritarianism was overlaid by an expansive idealism, that he or anyone else could do what he wanted provided he wanted it badly enough. This viewpoint not only served as a rationalization for his methods, but also blinded him to the difficulties of his task, making him an efficient starter and encouraging the beginnings of a common "school culture" in all the schools he set up.

For the first year, Levittown's high school students were farmed out to other communities, but in 1959, when it came time to plan a local high school, the superintendent selected a principal who was similarly seeking to balance discipline and freedom. Although he came from a school where 80 per cent of the graduates went on to college, he looked forward to being in Levittown, where preliminary estimates showed that no more than half would continue their education. He too argued that average students were being "robbed" by too much curriculum emphasis on college preparation, and he also resented the demands of "college prep students, who give you a harder time." He wanted to reduce the status hierarchy built into the academic, commercial, and general (a euphemism for vocational) divisions in the country high schools; he hoped that by permitting students to choose courses in all of them, college prep students would come into more contact with the business trainees and the general division students. He had a genuine interest in the last, who he felt were being neglected because of inferior or nonexistent vocational courses and were ostracized by their fellow students. As it turned out, however, not all Levittowners shared the principal's and superintendent's priorities and their belief in compensatory support for the intellectually disadvantaged.

THE DEFINITIONAL STRUGGLES

Voluntary associations and churches, being private agencies with sorting functions, could end definitional struggles by extruding people with divergent views. The school system, however, like all public agencies served the entire community and had to provide for its diverse demands within a single institution. As a result, it was soon embroiled in definitional struggles aimed at revising the superintendent's original goals.

When the Levittowners arrived, they were delighted that the first elementary school was open on schedule, and were pleased with the new, modern facilities and the young, energetic teachers. They seemed satisfied with their children's performance, joined the PTA and crowded its meetings, and even helped the schools by working in a variety of PTA fund raising and other projects. Some Catholics felt that the public school was lax — too much "play" and not enough discipline – and these parents (like most other Catholics) enrolled their children in the parochial school as soon as it opened. Other parents may have been uneasy about one or another aspect of the program, but they decided to be patient with the new system, arguing that "it was too early to heckle." As a result, the administrators and teachers received very little criticism during the first two years – or for that matter, little feedback of any kind. Although the principals maintained an open-door policy so that parents could air complaints at any time, relatively few did so. One man, who had run two Levittown elementary schools, reported that the only curriculum complaint he ever received came from a well-educated mother who wanted more work for her talented daughter. What complaints there were concerned the lunch schedule and overly severe discipline. On one occasion, when a teacher had a near-breakdown in class and upset many children to tears, almost every parent turned out that night at the school board meeting to protest. Beyond that, most parents seemed content to leave education to the school, assuming that the teachers knew best what was good for the children.

Some of the plans made by the superintendent and his associates had to be changed to respond to unexpected conditions. The elementary schools functioned pretty much as their starter intended – but then their students were a captive audience, too young to make choices or to object to adult demands. At first the parents, too, were pleased with him, particularly since he spoke to them idealistically, well, and often, never forgetting to praise their children. Once all the schools had been started, however, and a routine had been established, his flowery speeches began to grate, especially on parents and teachers who disliked his oppressive methods and his way of using rhetoric to avoid confronting disagreement. He resigned before opposition had a chance to become visible and widespread.

When it came to the organization of the high school, the initial plans had to be adapted to the diversity and choice-making ability of the students. Reducing the barriers between the three divisions assumed a fairly equal proportion of choices in each, but 50 per cent of the students opted for the academic track, and general students were a small minority. Consequently, the school had to emphasize "college prep" after all, and even initiated an honors program, but could not mount a vocational program. To prevent the possibility that the general students might become resentful and cause trouble, the principal tried to make them feel part of the school through extracurricular activities and sought, unsuccessfully, to have one elected as a student council officer. Even so, he could not counteract their hostility, and later they ranked high among the dropouts and serious delinquents.

Plans to give all students more freedom of course choice and class attendance were frustrated by the poor marks some had earned while attending neighboring schools the year before. Evidently treated as unwelcome outsiders, one third had to make up work that summer, and their poor records, as well as the initial stirrings of juvenile delinquency just before the high school opened, frightened the school board members. Teenage vandalism and delinquency had been unknown in the township previously, largely because its few adolescents had had to go elsewhere for recreation. Not knowing what to expect from the Levittown youngsters, the board and the administration were reluctant to trust their new charges, and because they were then engaged in a struggle with upper middle class parents on another issue, they were not eager to initiate freedoms that might well engender protests from restrictive parents. Instead, the high school principal sought to instill more "school spirit," particularly by encouraging the immediate formation of a varsity football team. Even though he believed it to be premature, he gave in to the demands of some residents and the wishes of the superintendent, hopeful that it would make for a peaceful and cooperative relationship with the student body. Needless to say, this was too much to expect of a football team, and although students maintained order – except for a rash of bomb scares one spring – the desired feeling of cooperation and trust was not achieved in the early years.

The Revolt of the Upper Middle Class

Highly educated Levittowners with bright children did not take long to realize that the new school was not giving their children high priority. There were relatively few such parents, and those who could afford it transferred their children to nearby private schools, but these did not provide kindergartens. Just as the superintendent had augured, the parents began to "cause trouble" soon after they arrived in Levittown.

In the spring of 1959, the township Board of Education announced that in congruence with state Board of Education policy, it would only admit children into kindergarten if they had reached the age of five by October 1. This policy was at once questioned by a couple of lower middle class parents with children born a few days after the cut-off date, but school officials persuaded them of the wisdom of the policy. At the next school board meeting, however, the issue was reopened by two upper middle class professionals, and before long, they presented the board with a petition signed by 170 parents asking for a change in the cut-off date to December 31. When that petition was rejected, they collected 200 more names, and with it a small but vocal group who kept the issue alive for several months.

The board members had never before been confronted with a petition and reacted with resentment and fear. "If we listened to all the wishes," one said, "there would be government by petition and that is not desirable." Protests would cast aspersions on them and mean longer working hours to deal with the protests as well. They wanted neither, particularly since they knew that they would lose their positions to Levittowners as soon as the latter had fulfilled the two-year residence requirement. A change in the cut-off date would bring more children into schools that were already full, violate state policy as well as the wishes of the superintendent, and force the board members to support a policy they themselves considered undesirable. The questions now at issue — responsiveness to the constituents, the justification of local innovation in county tradition, and the role of the school in the community — would come up again and again in the years to come.

The proponents of the date change were almost all upper middle lass people, eager to get their children into school, the sooner to qualify for college competition. The board members and the school staff believed, however, that children should not be asked to sacrifice their childhood or jeopardize their "natural" social adjustment. Indeed, some of them felt that a child should not enter the first grade until he was seven. The older he was at the time of graduation, the more mature he would be, and the more likely to obtain a good job. These were overwhelmingly lower middle class people, concerned only that the children would get good white collar jobs once they finished their schooling. To them, family came before school; in fact, they accused the proponents of the date change of wanting their children out of the house and of using the school as a baby-sitter. They could not understand that the proponents were already preparing their youngsters for professional careers.

The proponents of change were cosmopolitans and were thinking in terms of the nationwide competition for admission to "name" universities. The board members and the school staff, on the other hand, had spent all their lives in New

Jersey, and their allegiance was to the township, the county, and the local colleges. Finally the proponents fervently advocated innovation and argued that in a new community a fresh start should be made while conditions were still propitious – at the beginning, with consummate speed, and on the basis of expert advice. The board members retorted that they had no time for innovation, having enough to do just to get the routine established, and besides, as one pointed out, "The community is not like a Cadillac in which everything is finished before it comes out of the factory; it has to develop and the people have to put the finishing touches on it themselves."

In response to the board's call for more facts, the proponents consulted education psychologists all over the East Coast and superintendents of school systems with late cut-off dates. Agreeing that age was an arbitrary criterion for cut-off, they recommended a testing program by which children under five before December 31 would be admitted to the kindergarten upon a good showing on tests. To their amazement, however, the board rejected the proposal. It referred to other expert opinion on which state policy had been based, found studies which claimed that children's eyes would be damaged permanently if they started to read before age six or even eight, and sloughed off experience from schools in high-status communities. "We are not Brookline," said one school official, "and it cannot serve as our guide." They rejected tests as well, not only because they would force children to compete against each other but because of their political consequences. Anger from parents whose child had failed the test by a percentage point would be more intense than that generated by a birthday that came a day after the cut-off. But even as the board members tried to counter facts with other facts and turn the debate back to opinions which could not be argued so easily, they recognized a genuine community protest. The township government had recently rejected petitions on two issues raised by the newcomers and had roused the ire of many Levittowners. Even though they were elected on a nonpartisan basis, the school board members were Republicans, and yet another rebuff could only help the Democratic party. Conversely, they could not bring themselves to give in to "government by petition" or to cross professional educators. Indeed, the staff persuaded the board that "they [the proponents] are laymen; they don't really know what it's all about," but an argument that might have intimidated most Levittowners did not impress the proponents, some of whom were better educated and of higher occupational status than the school administration.

Caught in the middle, the board stalled, hoping that the controversy would abate over the summer. Although this did not happen, the stalling paid off, for as new purchasers streamed in, the lack of room for additional kindergartens served as an excuse to turn the proponents down without passing on the validity of their demands. Even then, another wave of pressure might have led to a reversal, particularly after the board met with the Levitt officials to seek their advice – and learned that they had no objection to the change – but also because all along the board had assumed that all Levittowners agreed with the proponents and might decide to petition en masse. Now, one board member who was active in the community and sat on other township boards, decided to sample Levittown opinion. To his surprise, he found that many Levittowners shared his own feeling that children should be kept at home as long as possible and that the proponents were most likely only a small minority. Once he communicated this to the board, it felt strong enough to resist further pressure.

The long struggle had unified the protesting parents and, a week after their defeat, they organized a Citizens' Committee for Better Schools, later renamed the Citizens' Association for Public Schools (C.A.P.S.), because some members felt the reference to "better schools" might cast aspersions on the Levittown system that would cost the group community support. Once organized, C.A.P.S. did not have to wait long for a new issue on which to oppose the school board: overcrowding and class size.

The schools had been planned on the basis of population data collected in Levittown, Pennsylvania, to permit classes of 25-30 pupils. But the new Levittown had attracted a higher proportion of larger families with school-age children, and the parochial school would not take as many Catholic students as had originally been expected. As a result, classes in the second neighborhood elementary school grew to 35 or more. Levitt altered his construction plans to build more four-bedroom and fewer three-bedroom houses in new "parks," but he was unwilling to plan more classrooms in the schools for these neighborhoods, arguing that the overcrowding would be temporary and assuming that there would be no objection to bigger classes in the meantime. C.A.P.S., supported by the neighborhood PTA, asked that classes be restored to their original size by busing the overflow to the first school (which served a smaller neighborhood). However, the superintendent, suspecting that the two organizations did not reflect majority opinion, conducted an attitude survey, asking parents whether they preferred busing or larger classes.[1] Three fourths of parents responding favored larger classes, and the C.A.P.S. proposal was rejected.[2]

The Attack on the School Budget

After this defeat, C.A.P.S., expecting to be permanently at loggerheads with the school system, started to draft what it considered to be a more desirable curriculum. The superintendent sought to reduce its antagonism, however, and asked several members to assist him on school board work, partly to coopt them,

---

[1] Despite the principal's careful screening of prospective PTA officers, this PTA regularly criticized school policy and, at one point, even proposed secession from the national PTA to enable it to fight the school system. The proposal was beaten by pressure from county and state PTA leaders and the lack of sufficient support from the neighborhood membership.

[2] My reanalysis of the survey suggested that parents who liked their children's teachers opposed busing; those who disliked them favored it, and class size was of lesser importance to them.

partly to take advantage of their research and their planning skills lacking in his own small staff. In working together, the antagonists discovered some shared goals. The superintendent actually supported the C.A.P.S.' desire for small classes, and a year later, he implemented a busing plan based on its original proposal. He also set up a testing system to enable children to enter kindergarten before the age of five if their parents requested it.

The sudden compatibility was, however, primarily a response to the development of a new and much stronger set of opponents to the school system: Levittowners who demanded less expensive schools devoted to little more than basic teaching functions, and who sought to prevent the establishment of additional educational services which both the administration and C.A.P.S. took for granted as absolutely necessary. By 1960, the rising school population and the hiring of auxiliary staff – for example, varsity coaches and a school psychologist – required a significant increase in the school budget. In Levittown, as in most other small New Jersey communities, this budget had to be approved by the voters, and in February 1960, the first election in which a sizeable number of Levittowners were eligible to vote, it was badly beaten. Even though the budget was then slightly cut, and even though Levitt was then paying about 40 per cent of all municipal operating expenditures, the tax rate rose 15 per cent, or about $25 a year.

When the new tax bills went out in the summer of 1960, widespread grumbling developed about school expenditures, too much expansion and innovation, and the high salaries of the school administration. To add fuel to the fire, a consultant hired by the Township Committee to help reorganize municipal government predicted that taxes in Levittown would eventually rise from about $275 per house to $645. Opposition to the rise in school taxes – which accounted for about three quarters of the total tax bill – came from families without school-age children and from less affluent Levittowners who were finding the cost of home ownership higher than expected. The most vocal attacks seemed to come from Catholics, who not only had lower incomes and more children than Protestant and Jewish Levittowners, but who were at that time also being asked to fund the building of a parochial school.

In the fall of 1960 the first Levittowners became eligible to run for the Board of Education, and leading Catholics in the Democratic party – whose leadership was largely Catholic to begin with – began to look for candidates for the 1961 board election who would vote for lower school budgets. As a result, C.A.P.S. rallied behind the school board and superintendent and, by the beginning of 1961, it had emerged as their principal defender in the community. The proposed budget for the 1961-1962 school year was again higher than the previous one, and because Levitt could no longer afford to subsidize school operations, except in new neighborhoods not yet on the tax rolls, another tax increase was threatening. Eventually, it came to about $100 per house. a 33 per cent increase over the previous year's tax bill.

By county tradition, school board elections were "above politics" and enough Levittowners agreed, thus discouraging the Democrats from forming a slate. Shortly before the mandatory public hearing on the budget and the election, however, three anti-tax candidates, two of them leaders of the Holy Name Society, were being talked up by many Levittowners as a so-called "Catholic slate." The year before, the public hearing had attracted only a handful of people, but in February 1961, more than 600, the largest crowd of Levittowners ever to meet together, jammed the auditorium in an angry mood to protest the proposed budget. The complaints of the previous year were repeated, and there was violent criticism of the superintendent's $18,000 salary and a newly suggested administrative post for curriculum planning. A group of engineers, constituting a Committee for Efficient Schools, argued that all the school really needed was teachers and that volunteers from the community could administer and plan. Others in attendance attacked the classroom size policy, pointing out that the parochial school was providing adequate education with 60 children per class; and a few people even objected to teachers' salaries, the highest of which — for ten years' experience — were then approaching the community's median income of $7500. The opposition to teachers' salaries came largely from a handful of working class Levittowners who had never before encountered teachers earning more than they. Most Levittowners were careful not to object to teachers' pay, however, and reserved their disapproval for "administrators."

The meeting was extremely bitter, with angry charges and exaggerated claims freely traded. The conflict was clearly between the haves and the have-nots, for when one lone budget supporter ended his speech, he was asked how much he was earning. There was also conflict, as in the voluntary associations, between the (few) advocates of rapid growth who wanted a fully staffed school system *now,* and the (many) proponents of gradual maturation, although they were only rationalizing their demand for tax reduction.

The protesting Levittowners resented particularly what they considered to be taxation without representation. Despite C.A.P.S. suggestions that the school board improve its "public relations," the budget was printed only in the classified advertising pages of the two county newspapers, as required by law — where, of course, few people saw it. Since attendance at board meetings had been minimal and the school board still had not become acquainted with many Levittowners, they did now know how to communicate with or represent their new constituents. At the public hearing itself, the board again objected to government by protest and petition, reinforcing the Levittowners' feeling that they lacked control over their own elected officials. As a result, the budget was voted down overwhelmingly at the election, and the so-called Catholic slate replaced three of the old residents on the nine-man school board. Subsequent interviews showed that blue collar and lowest income respondents rejected the budget in largest numbers. Unexpectedly, the most poorly educated parents were more favorable than high school and college graduates, as were mothers — not fathers — of school-age children, and 90 per cent of the Catholics turned down the budget as compared to 67 per cent of the Jews.

Once Levittowners had achieved even minority representation on the school board, the community's anger abated. In 1962, the school budget rose again, and the voters again rejected it, but they did not complain when the school board refused to cut it afterwards and levied another 15 per cent tax increase. Moreover, the voters elected to the board two C.A.P.S. leaders who had campaigned strenuously as a pro-budget slate, although they did poorly in the first neighborhoods and obtained their winning margin from the more recently settled ones. Thanks to rising house prices, the newer arrivals were somewhat more affluent; also, having come to Levittown after the initial tax hikes, they were not faced with so precipitous an increase in monthly payments.

After public concern over the budget had died down, the C.A.P.S.-administration alliance disintegrated. The main source of conflict now was the superintendent's unwillingness to plan for the future and to find some way of dealing with the growth needs of the system and the annual budget rejections by the voters. Indeed, the superintendent was too sluggish even for the remaining old residents on the school board who had originally appointed him, and in the fall of 1962, they joined forces with the two C.A.P.S. members in asking him to resign. Old differences with C.A.P.S. about what made for a good school, and the priorities for serving bright, average, and slow students also contributed to the superintendent's downfall, as did his reluctance to improve "public relations." Yet these factors were only symptomatic of a more basic problem — his inability to adapt his previously rural experience to the wishes of the suburbanites. He could, perhaps, not have avoided antagonizing the minority who wanted an upper middle class school system or the less affluent Levittowners who demanded economy above all and asked him to provide what he considered inferior education, but he did not really understand even the majority of his constituents. In a speech to the National Education Association, he mischaracterized Levittowners as "descendants of second or third generation immigrants whose national customs and mores are very slowly discarded," and compared them to his previous rural constituents, whom he eulogized as "descendents of early Colonial stock or the solid conservative descendents of the European farmer. . . .As our farms grow into neighborhoods, we [must] provide American, not foreign, education," he said, as if his role was to Americanize the Levittowners.

Ironically, and despite his ethnic misinterpretation, he differed little from the lower middle class majority in Levittown, and it agreed with most of his teaching policies. Indeed, the overall consensus between him and most parents about what class culture was to be transmitted by the school system had enabled him to implement his substantive educational ideas without much opposition. Conversely, if the Ford Foundation scheme for an upper middle class school system had been put into practice, and the school had consequently required what lower middle class students would consider excessive learning demands, they probably would have protested to their parents, who in turn might have forced the school board to transform the system into a lower middle class institution.

The superintendent's departure, and the ability of the two C.A.P.S.-affiliated board members to organize a coalition that outvoted the advocates of economy, now encouraged the twosome to believe that it could reorganize the school system closer to its wishes, but this hope was short-lived. The victory of the C.A.P.S. members appeared certain when a liberal Pennsylvania educator, who shared many of their standards, was found to replace the superintendent. Shortly before he was to take office, however, Democrats on the Township Council told him they would fight any policies that would result in higher taxes. He decided that it would be foolhardy to come to Levittown to face a continuous political battle, and resigned. The search for a new man took several months but, eventually, a more compatible New Jersey administrator was hired. Meanwhile, the Democrats then in control of the Township Council had decided that the traditional taboo against political party involvement in school politics was less sacred to their constituents than lower taxes, and put pressure on the school board for budget cuts. In this atmosphere, C.A.P.S.'s short-lived influence came to an end at the next school election. After one of the C.A.P.S.-affiliated board members had left Levittown for a better job in another state, the remaining member became the sole target for attacks on "better schools" and higher taxes. Although the newer neighborhoods provided some support, she trailed behind the other candidates and the brief reign of the cosmopolitans was over.

THE EVOLUTION OF THE SCHOOL SYSTEM

Recurring struggles over the amount and allocation of school funds did not prevent the rapid development of a functioning school system in Levittown. By September 1965 more than 8000 students were attending five elementary schools, two junior (or middle) ones, and a high school, the latter built entirely from public funds. These schools included all the curricular and extracurricular accouterments one would expect in a modern middle (but not upper middle) class suburb; the education they provided would prepare the students for about the same white collar, technical, and subprofessional jobs held by their parents and for the lower middle class culture that dominated the community. Perhaps the schools favored the restrictive subculture more than the expansive; the course offerings were quite traditional, and there was none of the "life adjustment" and "learning to get along with the group" approach that Whyte had found in Park Forest.[3] The teachers gave their students individual attention

3Whyte (1956), pp. 387-392.

and demanded neither superior intellectual achievement nor oppressive memorizing. As a result, the dropout rate was infinitesimal, and about 50 per cent of the graduates enrolled in college, although in 1963 a third of them chose junior colleges and teachers' colleges, and only 5 per cent went to "name" schools. It was, as one unhappy C.A.P.S. member put it, "the school system the community deserved." Interviews conducted in 1961 suggested, however, that the majority was pleased. Seventy-five per cent of all parents and 87 per cent of non-Catholic ones felt their children were either learning better or about as well as in their previous community, and 75 per cent of the parents considered the Levittown system superior to the one they had come from, praising it for better teachers and higher performance requirements from the children.[4]

A minority Catholic bloc had seemingly settled into the school board and opposed many majority decisions, but the conflict never reached the intensity or the longevity that had developed in Levittown, New York, where a large, predominantly Catholic group fought the budget and also accused the system of Communist leaning for many years.[5] Levittown, New Jersey still struggled with an increasing school population and rising budgets, requiring a 6 per cent tax increase in 1964 and a 16 per cent increase in 1965. In addition, insufficient classroom space continued to be a problem, possibly requiring an eventual enlargement of the elementary schools. However, it seemed as if the Levittowners preferred larger classes to rising taxes.

Actually, school expenditures could not have been considered unreasonable; in 1965, they amounted to $465 per student, less than in all but two of the seven townships surrounding Levittown. Even taxes were not exorbitant, amounting in 1965 to $425-$530, depending on the house type. The actual tax rate was only about 8 per cent higher than in 1959, and what had caused the precipitous tax rise, a total of 122 per cent since that year, was the withdrawal of the Levitt subsidies which paid for almost half of all municipal expenditures during the first two years.[6] Some Levittowners were undoubtedly hard pressed to pay the higher taxes, especially on top of increases in the cost of living and the rising expenses of maintaining their houses. For many, however, it was not so much the money as the idea of having to pay for a school their children did not attend — and then to have to fund the parochial school as well, and for others, of having to support a system with more "frills" than they wanted for their children. These parents were essentially objecting to a school that taught the culture of their more affluent and higher-status neighbors, a culture which they neither wanted to finance nor to have their children adopt. Since education

[4] Among Catholic parents with children in public school, 25 per cent reported improvement in school performance; 22 per cent, deterioration; and 53 per cent, no change. Among non-Catholics, the figures were 29 per cent, 13 per cent, and 58 per cent, respectively.

[5] Dobriner (1963), pp. 113-118. See also Wattel, pp. 306-311, and Orzack and Sanders.

[6] Altogether, the builder contributed about two million dollars between 1959 and 1963. See League of Women Voters, Willingboro, New Jersey, p. 14.

is supposedly not only above politics but also classless, the class conflict — for that is what it was — never came to the surface, but it pervaded the definitional struggle nevertheless.

Even so, the less affluent Catholic population was not quite as threatened either financially or in terms of status as its equivalent on Long Island — where half the people were blue collar workers and the cosmopolitan opposition, as well, was larger. This probably explains why the panic, the anti-Communist hysteria, and the witch-hunting never developed.[7] In 1963, a Birchite group did attack the school board for Communist sympathies but it received no support from other Levittowners and quickly faded out of the picture. Dobriner describes Levittown, Long Island, as "bimodal" in class, and Catholic blue collar anger there may have been heightened by relative deprivation vis-a-vis a single class enemy, whereas Levittown, New Jersey, was more "trimodal," and on some issues, working class residents found allies among lower middle class ones. The Long Island community was almost ten years old when the conflict reached its peak, and it may also be that the relative newness and the concurrent reservoir of residents' patience muted it in the New Jersey community.

[7]Dobriner (1963), p. 100. Also, the tax rate in Levittown, Long Island, rose a full 784 per cent between 1947 and 1962.

Additional Reading

Banfield, Edward C. and James Q. Wilson. *City Politics.* New York: Vintage Books, 1963.

Berry, Brian J. L. and Jack Meltzer. (eds). *Goals for Urban America.* Englewood Cliffs, N. J.: Prentice-Hall, 1967.

Gordon, Mitchell. *Sick Cities.* Baltimore, Maryland: Penguin, 1965.

Haworth, Lawrence. *The Good City.* Bloomington, Indiana: Indiana University Press, 1966.

Hoover, Edgar M. and Raymond Vernon. *Anatomy of a Metropolis.* Garden City, N. Y.: Doubleday Anchor, 1962.

Lowe, Jeanne R. *Cities in a Race with Time.* New York: Vintage Books, 1968.

Vernon, Raymond. *Metropolis 1985.* Garden City, N. Y.: Doubleday Anchor, 1963.

Weaver, Robert C. *Dilemmas of Urban America.* New York: Atheneum, 1967.

chapter 2

Youth

Without sympathetic understanding of disadvantaged urban youth it is impossible for many middleclass teachers to perform effectively. What prospective urban teachers clearly need are: (1) an understanding of the diversity of children and youth found in urban areas; (2) an awareness of social, ethnic, and individual differences which exist; (3) more exposure to the variety of peer group, family, and community influences which affect the behavior of urban youth in school; and, (4) a conviction that the situation is not hopeless and an understanding that there are ways of reaching almost all youngsters regardless of their backgrounds and environments. It is hoped that the selections in this section might contribute to this four-step process.

Professor Jean Grambs in "The Self-Concept: Basis for Reeducation of Negro Youth" looks at the literature dealing with this important theory and agrees that prior to any increase in achievement for black disadvantaged youngsters must come an improvement in self-concept. Paul Goodman in the selection from his now classic book, *Growing Up Absurd,* urges that young people including both disadvantaged and middleclass youngsters deserve to be taken seriously. He argues that the society at present dismisses their concerns and until this attitude changes the "youth problem" cannot be solved. Mary Frances Green and Orletta Ryan in their controversial book, *The Schoolchildren, Growing Up in the Slums,* describe the difficulties of dealing with disadvantaged and in some cases disturbed youngsters in the urban school setting. Charlotte Mayerson compares the lives of two adolescent boys, Juan Gonzales and Peter Quinn, who live as her title indicates, *Two Blocks Apart.* The youngsters' taped interviews, from which she edited the book, describe their families, neighborhoods, and schools. Jonathan Kozol in his best selling *Death At an Early Age,* describes vividly the disastrous and destructive effect which inadequate schools and school systems can have on children.

The Self-Concept: Basis for Reeducation of Negro Youth*

Jean D. Grambs

The human personality is a bundle of dynamic forces about which we have many conjectures and few certainties. Like the inner particles of the atom, which are seen only by the shadows they cast, so we have only the shadows of the workings of the human psyche. We are not always sure, and certainly not always in agreement, as to what these shadows represent. But whatever components there may be to personality, in the words of Park and Burgess, "it is an organization of traits and attitudes of which the individual's conception of himself is central."[1]

There are unresolved differences of opinion among psychologists as to the sources of behavior. Whatever it is that impels an individual to act or not to act, a significant role is played in this determination by what the person thinks about himself.[2] He may be able to tell us something about his view of himself, or he may be able to tell us very little. What he tells us may be what he really thinks, or it may be a selective version for a particular public; on what appears to be safer ground, he may reveal a different version of what he thinks he is. Or he may be completely unaware of what his true feelings about himself are. We are assuming, however, that the person acts and can only act, in terms of what he thinks about himself in a given situation, and he cannot assess that situation and its action requirements except in terms of his own view of himself.

Comtemporary research in child growth and development has highlighted the central significance of the individual's concept of himself.[3] The way a person views himself is the way he will behave. If he sees himself as successful, as

*Negro Self-Concept; Implications for School and Citizenship, The Report of a conference sponsored by the Lincoln Filene Center for Citizenship and Public Affairs, New York: McGraw-Hill, 1965, pp. 11-34.

[1] Bingham Dai, "Minority Group Membership and Personality Development," in Jitsuichi Masuoka and Preston Valien (eds.) Race Relations: Problems and Theory, Chapel Hill, N.C., The University of North Carolina Press, 1961, p. 183.

[2] Ruth C. Wylie, The Self-Concept, Lincoln, Nebr., University of Nebraska Press, 1961, pp. 1-22.

[3] Authur T. Jersild, "Emotional Development," in L. Carmichael (ed.), Manual of Child Psychology, 2d ed., New York, John Wiley & Sons, Inc., 1954, p. 837. "Selective Bibliography on Self," Childhood Education, vol. 35, October, 1958, pp. 80-81.

someone whom others like, as good-looking, then his behavior will reflect these views. If the person considers himself to be inadequate, as someone whom others probably won't like, as unattractive, then again his behavior will reflect these valuations. The factual truth of any of these statements is irrelevant. A very beautiful girl may consider herself unattractive; children with adequate intellectual endowment may do poorly in school because they perceive themselves as not able.[4]

The source of one's self-image, is, of course, not internal; it is learned. The way a mother responds to her newborn baby — with delight or with weary acceptance — will be apparent in the behavior of the baby before very long. A child whose parents trust and love him will be a loving and trustful individual who will tend to go out to greet the world and its many new experiences.

We have some research insights into the differential treatment that parents accord their children from the very beginning.[5] It is true, too, that different cultures produce different personality types. The ways in which children are reared, the things that they are told to do or not to do, the rewards for various kinds of competencies or their lacks, differ from one culture to another.[6] This produces, as Kardiner has pointed out, what might be termed a basic personality type consistent for a given culture.[7]

Venturing outside the family provides the child with additional clues to his self-worth. As he meets teachers, policemen, and storekeepers, he is told what these powerful persons think of people like him. He learns about himself from other children on the block who report to him how they feel on seeing him and playing with him. Out of countless messages, the individual contrives a picture of who he is.[8]

It is obvious that individuals develop different concepts of themselves and that the concept of self is always in terms of degrees of *adequacy*. Everyone must have some sense of adequacy, no matter how minimal, or he cannot cope with his own existence and then must escape into psychosis or suicide. *"We can define man's basic need, then, as a need for adequacy,"*[9] Jersild refines this further: "The needs associated with a person's idea and appraisal of himself include both desires for enhancing his self-esteem and also striving to preserve the integrity or consistency of the self."[10]

[4]M. B. Frink, "Self-Concept as it Relates to Academic Underachievement," *California Journal of Educational Research,* vol. 13, March, 1962, pp. 57-62.

[5]Robert R. Sears, Eleanor E. Maccoby, and Harry Levin, *Patterns of Child Rearing,* New York, Harper & Row, Publishers, 1957.

[6]John W. M. Whiting and Irvin L. Child, *Child Training and Personality: A Cross-Cultural Study,* New Haven, Conn., Yale University Press, 1953.

[7]Abram Kardiner et al., *The Psychological Frontiers of Society,* New York, Columbia University Press, 1945.

[8]Helen G. Trager and Marian Radke Yarrow, *They Learn What They Live: Prejudice in Young Children,* New York, Harper & Row, Publishers, 1952.

[9]Arthur W. Combs and Donald Snygg, *Individual Behavior* (rev. ed.), New York, Harper & Row, Publishers, 1959, p. 46.

[10]Jersild, *op. cit.*

There is agreement that the contemporary situation of the American Negro is deplorable. A nationwide, continuing debate is concerned with ways of ameliorating this condition. As educators, we need to develop strategies for change which will aid the individual in achieving more adequate adjustment to and control of his environment. The role of the concept of self in achieving this sense of adequacy thus appears to be central. The questions that must be considered are these:

1. How do Negro children and youth now achieve a sense of who and what they are?
2. What is the role of education in the school in developing this sense of self?
3. What is the potential within the educational setting of achieving a desirable shift in self-image?

These questions can only be answered by further research. Our purpose here is a brief review of the relevant research and speculation.

THE QUESTION OF DIFFERENCES BETWEEN NEGROES AND WHITES

One of the clearest differences between Negro and white is that society in the contemporary United States continually tells the groups that they are different. Not only are the groups different, but the Negro group is considered inferior to the white group. This message has been communicated in different ways via different social media ever since the Negro was first brought to America. It is obvious that this kind of differential social communication is going to have a differential impact on the personality. As Allport asks:

> ...what would happen to your own personality if you heard it said over and over again that you were lazy, a simple child of nature, expected to steal, and had inferior blood. Suppose this opinion were forced on you by the majority of your fellow-citizens. And suppose nothing you could do would change this opinion – because you happen to have black skin.[11]

Or, stated in the words of the late President Kennedy:

> If an American, because his skin is dark, cannot eat lunch in a restaurant open to the public; if he cannot send his children to the best public school available; if, in short, he cannot enjoy the full and free life which all of us want, then who among us would be content to have the color of his skin changed and stand in his place?[12]

The self-concept of the Negro is contaminated by the central fact that it is

[11] Gordon W. Allport, *The Nature of Prejudice,* Reading, Mass., Addison-Wesley Publishing Company, Inc., 1954, p. 142.

[12] John F. Kennedy, "A Time to Act." an address to the American people, June 11, 1963. Reprinted by Anti-Defamation League of B'nai B'rith, New York.

based on a color-caste complex. The American color-caste system was evolving at the same time that the brave concepts of the American and French revolutions about human equality were also born. It was thus almost inevitable that the racial situation would cause trouble. The first drafts of the Declaration of Independence contained a clause objecting to the imposition of slavery upon the American colonies by the English power. The clause was stricken from the final version for fear of alienating Southern support. Shades of contemporary political maneuverings over civil rights legislation in Congress!

In order to cope with the obvious discrepancy between Christian beliefs about the oneness of the human family, slaveholders had to resort to the idea of the supposed inferiority of the Negro, preaching in some instances that he really was a subhuman breed of animal. Even today there continue to be strenuous efforts to convince those who require scholarly evidence that the Negro is, in fact, inferior.[13]

The social system that emerged out of the need to rationalize the owning of slaves and, following the Civil War, refusal to accord the Negro full citizen status was a clear development of a caste system. Unlike the caste system of India based on religious beliefs, the caste system in the United States was based on color and on the assumption of inferiority due to color. The Brazilian melting pot, unlike that in the United States, classifies anyone with any amount of white ancestry as white; in the United States, the smallest amount of Negro ancestry classifies an individual as Negro.

In the evolution of institutions, those provided for the Negro in the United States, therefore, had to be *separate,* but also *unequal.* It is possible that there are caste systems in which parallel caste-class groups exist without any presumption of superiority or inferiority for one caste over another; this certainly has not been true in America.[14] Of course, the South had to refuse to provide equal educational opportunity for the Negro; the Negro was *not equal.*

THE IMPACT OF INEQUALITY IN VALUATION

It does not take much imagination to understand what generations of being told one is unworthy do to a group's own valuation of its worth. From the first slave revolts, Negro leaders have continually fought against this self-view; but there have been relatively few leaders, a condition also produced by the effect of inferior caste status. Only in recent decades have there been enough Negroes who have overcome these multiple barriers to challenge the general valuation of the Negro.

[13]Robert D. North, "The Intelligence of American Negroes," *Research Reports,* Anti-Defamation League of B'nai B'rith, vol. 3, no. 2, November, 1956; Melvin M. Tumin (ed.), *Race and Intelligence: A Scientific Evaluation,* New York, Anti-Defamation League of B'nai B'rith, 1963.
[14]John Dollard, *Caste and Class in a Southern Town,* 3d ed., Garden City, N.Y., Doubleday & Company, Inc. 1957.

To quote Dollard, whose original study of caste first focused general attention on this problem:

> Nothing has happened since 1936 [the date of the original study] which has served to unconvince me about what I saw. It seems as real now as then. We are still in the hot water of conflict between our democratic ideals and our personal acceptance of caste status for the Negro. We are still deliberately or unwittingly profiting by, defending, concealing or ignoring the caste system.[15]

Interestingly enough, a recent comprehensive review and evaluation of the research in the area of self-concept does not include any discussion of research that considers race as an aspect of self-concept, though research relating to other factors, such as sex, religious affiliation, social-class status, is discussed.[16] Blindness to, or avoidance of, the implications of the caste system on the self-concept of the Negro, and of the white, which is thus seen to occur at the most- and least-sophisticated levels of society, is symptomatic of the difficulty of dealing with color discrimination in American life and thought.

The Negro personality *cannot* be unmarked by the experience of caste discrimination based upon color.[17] One of the first family learnings of the Negro child has to do with his color. The more white a Negro child is, the more he will be accepted by his family, the greater his opportunity will be to use his talents, the more likely it is that he will be able to make the most of the limited opportunities of his environment. The love that his family will accord him can be calibrated on the same scale as one calibrates color differences. To be most loved as a Negro child, one has to appear least Negro.

In one of their cases, Kardiner and Ovesey describe the reactions of a middle-class Negro woman, herself light, on giving birth to a dark baby. She was sure she had been given the wrong baby; later she tried to bathe it in bleaches of various kinds; she refused to appear in public with it. She reacted almost the same way with a second baby.[18]

In the early drawings and stories and dreams of Negro children appear many wishes to be white. Negro children have a harder time than white children in identifying themselves correctly in terms of race.[19] This identification is also related to color: the darker Negro is able to see himself as a Negro earlier than a light-colored one. In the latter instance, is the nearness to being white such as to make the acceptance of being Negro that much harder?

---

[15]*Ibid.*, p. viii.

[16]Wylie, *op. cit.*

[17]Abram Kardiner and Lionel Ovesey, *The Mark of Oppression: Explorations in the Personality of the American Negro,* Cleveland, The World Publishing Company (a Meridian Book), 1962.

[18]Kardiner and Ovesey, *op. cit.,* pp. 252-253.

[19]Kenneth Clark and Mamie P. Clark, "Racial Identification and Preference in Negro Children," in Eleanor Maccoby et al. (eds.) *Readings in Social Psychology,* New York, Holt, Rinehart and Winston, Inc., 1958, pp. 602-611.

The self-esteem of the Negro is damaged by the overwhelming fact that the world he lives in says, "White is right; black is bad." The impact on the Negro community is to overvalue all those traits of appearance that are most Caucasian. Evidence is clear that in almost every Negro family, the lighter children are favored by the parents. It is interesting to note that most of the Negro leadership group today are not Negroid in appearance, many being almost completely Caucasian in terms of major physical appearance.

What effect does this have on the child? Of course, his own color becomes extremely important to him. As Dai points out, "... the color of one's skin, which does not occupy the consciousness of children of other cultures, is here made an issue of primary importance, and the personality problems thus created are almost as difficult to get rid of as the dark skin itself."[20] The Negro press is replete with advertisements for skin lighteners and hair straighteners. It strikes some Negroes as ironic that, while they strive to become lighter and to make their hair less curly, whites go to great pains to stay out in the sun in order to become darker and spend endless amounts of money on getting their hair to curl! Unfortunately, the efforts of the whites do not assume an acceptance on their part of the features of the Negro which appear to be desirable: darker color and curly hair. But the efforts of the Negro do spring from a deeply ingrained view regarding appearance: it is better to be more white.

One interesting feature of the current Negro revolution has been a small but persistent insistence that the Negro cease trying to make himself white. The Black Muslim group is an almost pure expression of the need to reject all that is white and replace Negro self-hatred with justified hatred of whites, including the dominant white Christian religion.[21] With some Negroes, it is now considered a matter of racial pride to refuse to straighten the hair or to use cosmetics to lighten the skin. It is possible that this movement will reach other Negroes, and with it will come a lessening of the rejection of color and the personal devaluation that this has carried. But unfortunately it hardly seems possible that a reversal of the value system will occur for many, and certainly not for a long time to come.

Thus we see the central ambivalence that makes the world of the Negro so baffling, frustrating, confusing, and demeaning. On the one hand, he is told that white is better, and he relates this to his own social system in which the Negro who is most white, but still a Negro, has highest status. But to *be* white is not good. Whites are not to be trusted: they are, in fact, hated as much as they are feared.

[20] Bingham Dai, "Problems of Personality Development Among Negro Children," in Clyde Kluckhohn and Henry A. Murray (eds.), *Personality in Nature, Society and Culture,* New York, Alfred A. Knopf, Inc., 1953, p. 560.

[21] C. Eric Lincoln, *The Black Muslims in America,* Boston, The Beacon Press, 1961; E. U. Essien-Udom, *Black Nationalism,* Chicago, The University of Chicago Press, 1962; James Baldwin, *The Fire Next Time,* New York, The Dial Press, Inc., 1963, pp. 61-120.

Hatred breeds aggression. Aggression seeks an outlet. A major focus of the hatred of Negroes is the white group, but this group is almost completely protected because of the potency and immediacy of white retaliation.[22] One must remember that the antilynch laws are quite recent. Pictures of burning buses, fire hoses, mounted police with electric cattle prods, and attacking police dogs show only too well that the Negro is still not protected from the quick and vicious reactions of the white group when this power is challenged in any way. Incapable of attacking the white group, the Negro has several psychological alternatives: to hate himself, to act out his aggressive needs within his own group, and to escape into apathy and fantasy. All these paths are utilized, and often by the same individual, depending on the situation. As Combs and Snygg point out, responses to feelings of inadequacy range from the neurotic through perceptual distortions and may result in actual psychosis. The production of "multiple personalities" is, as they see it, one response to feelings of loss of self-esteem.[23] This splitting of the personality in response to the social disvalue placed on being a Negro is graphically stated by Redding:

> From adolescence to death there is something very personal about being a Negro in America. It is like having a second ego which is as much the conscious subject of all experience as the natural self. It is not what the psychologists call dual personality. It is more complex and, I think, more morbid than that. In the state of which I speak, one receives two distinct reactions – the one normal and intrinsic to the natural self; the other, entirely different but of equal force, a prodigy created by the accumulated consciousness of Negroness.[24]

As the gifted Negro writer James Baldwin puts it, in commenting on his own childhood:

> In order for me to live, I decided very early that some mistake had been made somewhere. I was not a "nigger" even though you [whites] called me one. . . .,I had to realize when I was very young that I was none of those things I was told I was. I was not, for example, happy. I never touched a watermelon for all kinds of reasons. I had been invented by white people, and I knew enough about life by this time to understand that whatever you invent, whatever you project, that is you! So where we are now is that a whole country of people believe I'm a "nigger" and I *don't*.[25]

It does not escape the Negro observer that Negro crimes against Negroes are

[22] Baker M. Hindman, "The Emotional Problems of Negro High School Youth Which Are Related to Segregation and Discrimination in a Southern Urban Community," *Journal of Educational Sociology,* vol. 27, November, 1953, pp. 115-127.
[23] Combs and Snygg, *op. cit.,* pp. 265-303.
[24] J. Saunders Redding, *On Being Negro in America,* Indianapolis, Ind., The Bobbs-Merrill Company, Inc., 1962, p. 12.
[25] James Baldwin, "A Talk to Teachers," *Saturday Review,* vol. 46, December 21, 1963, pp. 42-44+.

considered far less serious by the law in many areas than similar crimes of whites against whites, and certainly not nearly so serious as Negro crimes against whites. And white crimes against Negroes are the least serious of all. Again, these social symptoms report to the Negro that he is not valued as a person; he cannot, against such massive evidence, counter by his own feelings of self-esteem, since in truth he can typically show little factual support for a contrary view.[26]

CRUCIAL SOCIAL FORCES CREATING THE NEGRO SELF-IMAGE: THE FAMILY AND POVERTY

The potency of the family in producing the culturally approved person has tempted social manipulators since the dawn of history. Sparta intervened at a very early age in the child-rearing functions of the family. Recent attempts to supplant the family have been unsuccessful. The most enduring such contemporary situation, the Kibbutz of Israel, appears to have produced a rather special kind of person whose social potential can be questioned.[27] So far, no adequate substitute for the family has been found, despite Huxley's predictions.[28]

That there are unique stresses and strains in the modern family is agreed; but the stresses in a Negro family are qualitatively different from those in a white family, even when we hold socioeconomic status constant. The poor have never lived in comfort, and the struggle for material survival has certainly made psychologically adequate survival extremely problematical anywhere in the world. The situation of the Negro family today in the United States is qualitatively different on a number of important counts.

The Negro family is much more likely than the white family to be on the lowest economic rung. Furthermore, we could say that no more than a very small percentage of Negroes is more than one generation removed from abject poverty, so that "Negroes have [a] deeply ingrained sense of impoverishment."[29] It is a rather special kind of impoverishment, too; it is almost inescapable. Although we have seen in recent generations the rise of a Negro middle class, and even a few very wealthy Negroes, most Negroes remain in the "last hired, first fired" category of employment — and if not this generation, their parental generation. Most Negro children, then, inherit a family which is economically insecure from the very start. Most of them live at the edge of survival; and those who have moved a little bit away have a constant fear of a future which may reduce them, too, to desperation.

[26] Walter Reckless et al., "Self—concept as Insulator Against Delinquency," *American Sociological Review,* vol. 21, no. 6, 1956.

[27] Abram Kardiner, "When the State Brings up the Child," *Saturday Review,* vol. 44, August 26, 1961, pp. 9-11; Albert J. Rabin, "Culture Components as a Significant Factor in Child Development: Kibbutz Adolescents," *American Journal of Orthopsychiatry,* vol. 31, 1961, pp. 493-504.

[28] Aldous Huxley, *Brave New World,* New York, Harper & Row, Publishers, 1932.

[29] Kardiner and Ovesey, *op. cit.,* p. 366.

It is almost impossible for one not reared in a slum to understand its awfulness. Middle-class America flees from a true picture of slum degradation.[30] But as Riessman points out, children reared in these environments will soon constitute 50 percent of all children enrolled in schools in large cities.[31] Most of these children will be Negroes unless something drastically changes the housing situation which exists in urban centers.

The Negro slum child is far more liable than a white slum child to experience also an unstable home.[32] The self that the Negro child learns early in life is one exposed to the most difficult of all situations for the human being to cope with: an inadequate family living on the edge of economic insufficiency. The impact of family disruption is accentuated by the incapactiy of those involved in the rearing of the children to do an adequate job of it because they have had few experiences with family stability and adequacy to guide them.

The circle is indeed a vicious one. The case studies, reported by Riese provide appalling accounts of generation after generation of defeat in Negro familes.[33] Often neither mother nor father is able to provide the minimum of affection and attention that an infant needs in order to grow into a person able to like himself and others, because, of course, his parents do not like themselves. Too many of these marriages are the result of implusive escape wishes and lack a secure base in personal regard for the marital partner.[34] Poignant testimony to the difficulties facing the Negro wife and husband is given by talented Negro singer Lena Horne.[35]

As she describes it, her marriage was an effort to get away from the miseries of being a Negro singer in a white man's world. Yet she was not able to accept her role as a Negro wife. The needs her husband brought home from his work, mainly with white colleagues, she felt quite unable and unwilling to deal with. Not only had she to cope with the ordinary problems of running a home and rearing children, she had to absorb the anger and hurt her husband bore on his job, the countless humiliations and degradations that he a Negro, experienced daily in his contact with white people.

What Lena Horne tells us provides a needed window into the inner reality of Negro family life. The normal hazards of the working world are multiplied many

[30] Michael Harrington, *The Other America: Poverty in the United States,* New York, The Macmillan Company, 1963, Chap. 4, "If You're Black, Stay Black," pp. 61-81.

[31] Frank Riessman, *The Culturally Deprived Child,* New York, Harper & Row, Publishers, 1962, p. 1.

[32] Martin Deutsch, *Minority Group and Class Status as Related to Social and Personality Factors in Scholastic Achievement,* monograph 2, Ithaca, N.Y., The Society for Applied Anthropology, Cornell University Press, 1960; E. Franklin Frazier, *The Negro Family in the United States* (rev. ed.), New York, The Dryden Press, Inc., 1951; Nathan Glazer and D. P. Moynihan, *Beyond the Melting Pot,* Cambridge, Mass., The M.I.T. Press and Harvard University Press, 1963, pp. 25-85.

[33] Bertha Riese, *Heal the Hurt Child,* Chicago, The University of Chicago Press, 1962.

[34] Kardiner and Ovesey, *op. cit.,* pp. 345-349.

[35] Lena Horne, "I Just Want to be Myself," *Show,* vol. 3, September, 1963, pp. 62-65+.

times over by the pervasive insecurity attendant on almost all of the Negro's economic activities. Not only is the Negro the last to be hired and the first to be fired, but he pays more for insurance premiums, he has a much harder time obtaining home mortgage money and any kind of bank or credit loans. Even the slum store preys upon the poor with higher prices for shoddier stuff. In such an environment, it is hard indeed for the Negro male to achieve a sense of self-worth as a breadwinner and provider for his family.

The woman typically is aggressive and hostile; the man is hostile and dependent. Because his economic situation is so insecure, the husband-father cannot be sure that he will provide the economic base for a family; and in a majority of cases, he is right. He cannot assure his wife of support or his children of food and shelter. Who can feel pride of self in such circumstances, and who can pass on feelings of adequacy to anyone else?

The economic security of the Negro family rests primarily with the mother. This is one outgrowth of slavery, when at least the mother could keep the children with her until they could be physically independent and able to work, while the father was often not even accorded the recognition of paternity. Certainly the family as the white population knew it was prohibited for slaves. The patterns of employment in today's urban centers have continued to make economic stability more available to the women than to the men. The significance of this family situation appears in study after study.

The home life reported in many case studies of Negro youth is one of constant bickering and fighting. One father leaves; a stepfather or father substitute appears. The family conflict continues. Because of death or illness or desertion, children often are left with grandparents or other relatives. If an attachment occurs, it may not last until adulthood. Thus many Negro children have few experiences with stability, warmth, attention — all of the things that are taken for granted as part of the necessary environment for healthy personality development.

The important point, of course, is that while many of the conditions reported are a result of acute and continued poverty, a major ingredient is also the color-caste of the Negro. One of the child's early racial learnings is that he cannot turn to his parents for help and retaliation if he is hurt.

> A white man yanked me off a streetcar because I got on ahead of a white woman. He shook me good and tore my clothes. I walked home crying, knowing that my father would do something about it. (But his father could do no more than remark, "You should have known better.")[36]

The denial to a parent of his role in protecting his own child is deeply destructive, not only to the parental feeling but to the possibility that the child

[36] Robert L. Sutherland, *Color, Class and Personality*, Washington, D.C., American Council on Education, 1942, p. 41.

will look to his parents as adult models. Nor will the growing child be able to internalize the parental feeling without which having children of one's own is a dangerous enterprise.

What the Negro child is likely to learn is that no one is to be trusted. He is given such small ingredients of affection and attention that he has too meager a hoard to share with anyone else. He learns, too, that his family is only partly responsible for the horrors of his existence; it is the whites who have created this situation, and it is they who keep him in abasement. The burden of hatred for the whites is increased because he is also told that he cannot be anything about that hatred; in fact, he must be particularly careful and watchful in all his relations with whites. These persons hold the key to all that is desirable and good. It only one were white, too!

The earliest learnings, then, of the Negro child, particularly one in the rural or urban slums, is that the family is not a source of basic nurture and support. He seeks his gratifications, therefore, on the street and among peers.[37] But as Kardiner and Ovesey point out, at no time are these relationships such as to produce a feeling of comfort and safety. No one can find in the street a substitute for parental and adult guidance and parental affection. If the child does not necessarily become antisocial, he is asocial.[38]

The damage to the child's self-esteem appears greater for Negro boys than for girls.[39] Though it is debatable whether, in general, it is more or less difficult to grow up as a boy or as a girl in our culture,[40] it seems clear from the evidence that during early childhood and school years, the Negro girl accommodates better to the circumstances of existence. Certainly in school performance the Negro girl exceeds the Negro boy. In most measures of social disorganization, the Negro boy appears to be far more vulnerable. This can be accounted for in part by the fact that the male models available for the growing boy are themselves demoralized. A father who feels defeated by the world is not in a good position to give his son a sense of optimism and a feeling that he can achieve something himself. The fact that the father is most likely to be the absent member of the family and often is replaced by a succession of fathers or father substitutes also tends to militate against the establishment of a view of the male as a reliable, responsible individual. If the boy sees around him men who are unable to sustain a consistent and positive social and economic role, it is hard for the youngster to build a different pattern out of his limited experiences.

Recent efforts to equalize educational opportunities for Negroes in the South should not obscure the fact that these efforts are indeed very recent, and

---

[37]David and Pearl Ausubel, "Ego Development Among Segregated Negro Children," in A. Harry Passow (ed.), *Education in Depressed Areas,* New York, Bureau of Publications, Teachers College, Columbia University, 1963, p. 113.

[38]Kardiner and Ovesey, *op. cit.,* p. 380.

[39]David and Pearl Ausubel, *op. cit.,* pp. 127-128.

[40]Walter Waetjen and Jean D. Grambs, "Sex Differences: A Case of Educational Evasion?"*Teachers College Record,* December, 1963.

still fall far short of providing, even on a segregated basis, an adequate education for all Negro young people. The fact that even today many Negro children and youth have far from adequate schooling, whether they live in the rural South or the urban North, Midwest, West, or Southwest, should not make us forget that, with few exceptions, the story of Negro education to this day has been one of gross lacks.[41] As Horace Mann said over a hundred years ago, "No educated body of men can be permanently poor"[42]; and the obverse is that no uneducated group can expect to rise out of poverty.

Although the Ausubels state that "Negro girls in racially incapsulated areas are less traumatized than boys by the impact of racial discrimination,"[43] further evidence is needed to support such a statement. On the surface, Negro girls seem more able to cope with some of the demands of middle-class society: going to school, behaving in school, keeping out of serious trouble with the law, showing responsibility for child rearing, and keeping a job.[44] It is nevertheless possible that the impact of their situation is just passed on to the men in the household. Certainly a mother is a prime source, as we have stated, of the child's self-concept. It is communicated to Negro boys, somehow, that they are less wanted, less able to deal with their world, bound to fail in their efforts to be men. We cannot lay the major blame for the way Negro boys develop on the lack of adequate male models. It is highly probable that the trauma suffered by Negro females is passed on and displaced upon the males in the situation. Certainly the case material of Kardiner and Ovesey shows much personal trouble experienced by female as well as male Negroes.[45] The fact that so many Negroes become contributing and stable members of society is an extraordinary tribute to the resilience of the human psyche.

EDUCATIONAL PROCESSES AND SELF-CONCEPT

It is clear that the life experiences of the Negro child are not such as to aid him in developing a positive sense of himself or of his place in his world. What does this suggest to us? It would seem that a very compelling hypothesis is that *the Negro child, from earliest school entry through graduation from high school, needs continued opportunities to see himself and his racial group in a realistically positive light. He needs to understand what color and race mean, he needs to learn about those of his race (and other disadvantaged groups) who have succeeded, and he needs to clarify his understanding of his own group history and current group situation.*

[41] Virgil Clift, Archibald W. Anders, H. Gordon Hullfish (eds.), *Negro Education in America,* New York, Harper & Row, Publishers, 1962.

[42] Marjorie B. Smiley and John S. Diekoff, *Prologue to Teaching,* Fair Lawn, N.J., Oxford University Press, 1959, p. 286.

[43] David and Pearl Ausubel, *op. cit.,* p. 128.

[44] Albert J. Lott and Bernice E. Lott, *Negro and White Youth,* New York, Holt, Rinehart and Winston, Inc., 1963.

[45] Kardiner and Ovesey, *op. cit.*

At the moment, these are missing ingredients in the American public school classroom. Numerous studies of textbooks have shown them to be lily-white.[46] Pictures do not show Negro and white children together; when Negroes appear they are usually either Booker T. Washington, George Washington Carver, or foreign.[47] Neither whites nor Negroes have an accurate picture of the American Negro and his history.[48] One observer noted that a commonly used contemporary civics book had no index entry for *urban renewal, transporation, transit, or Negro.*[49] The lily-white nature of text materials is true also of other visual aids used in the schools. If Negroes appear in school films, they are in stereotyped roles. One film, for instance, showing "community helpers" illustrated the work of repairing the street with a Negro crew and a white foreman. The educational consultant, incidentally, who worked with the film company to produce the film was surprised at his own blindness. This kind of presentation merely reinforces the many communications to children that Negro work is inferior work.

That these materials can and do have a strong impact on the child's perception of himself and others was well documented in the study by Trager and Yarrow. When a story describing a Negro child as a funny savage (Little Black Sambo) was read aloud to young children, white and Negro children's feelings were affected, particularly when the white children pointed this out in the schoolyard.[50] The only thing that is surprising about these findings is that educators and others have consistently ignored them. It is interesting that the Trager-Yarrow research report is probably the only study made of the differences in education (textbook) content that is reported in the literature. As a matter of fact, it is claimed by one of the very knowledgeable experts in the field, that *no* experimental study has been done of differences in textbook content, despite the fact that the textbook is the most consistently and constantly used educational aid in the classroom, other than the teacher.[51]

If teaching materials present a slanted view of him and his place in the world to the Negro child, what does the teacher tell him? It is no very startling

[46] Abraham Tannenbaum, "Family Living in Textbook Town," *Progressive Education,* vol. 31, no. 5, March, 1954, pp. 133-141; Martin Mayer, "The Trouble with Textbooks," *Harper's Magazine,* vol. 225, July, 1962, pp. 65-71; Otto Klineberg, "Life is Fun in a Smiling, Fair-Skinned World," *Saturday Review,* February 16, 1963; Albert Alexander. "The Gray Flannel Cover on the American History Textbook," *Social Education,* vol. 24, January, 1960, pp. 11-14.

[47] Lloyd Marcus, *The Treatment of Minorities in Secondary School Textbooks,* New York, Anti-Defamation League of B'nai B'rith, 1961; Jack Nelson and Gene Roberts, Jr., *The Censors and the Schools,* Boston, Little, Brown & Company, 1963.

[48] Melville J. Herskovits, *The Myth of the Negro Past,* Boston, The Beacon Press, 1958.

[49] Atlee E. Shidler, "Education for Civic Leadership: The School's Responsibility," an address presented to the 68th National Conference on Government, The National Municipal League, Washington, D.C., November 16, 1962, mimeo.

[50] Trager and Yarrow, *op. cit.*

[51] A. A. Lumsdaine, "Instruments and Media of Instruction," in N. L. Gage (ed.), *Handbook of Research on Teaching,* Chicago, Rand McNally & Company, 1963, p. 586.

piece of news that teachers, too, bear the majority version of the Negro. Studies of their attitudes toward children show that the Negro child is rated lowest in all rankings of groups on a Bogardustype social-distance scale.[52] The original study was completed thirteen years ago; teachers in training in 1963 give the same responses. Attempts to change teachers' attitudes through human relations workshops and special courses have reached very few. In formulating some guidelines for the education of the culturally disadvantaged, Niemeyer stated:

> Our hypothesis is that the chief cause of the low achievement of the children of alienated groups is the fact that too many teachers and principals honestly believe that these children are educable only to an extremely limited extent. And when teachers have a low expectation level for their children's learning, the children seldom exceed that expectation, which is a self-fulfilling prophecy.[53]

Nor is the situation made easier where Negro teachers are employed. The Negro teacher represents a middle-class position, and there is evidence that virulent anti-Negro feelings are expressed by middle-class Negroes for lower-class Negroes. Unfortunately, most Negro children come from lower-class homes. Dai makes the point that, denied access to other rewards in life, the Negro tends to put an overemphasis upon status.[54] The Negro professional, who may have many contacts with white professionals, must even in these professional relationships maintain an etiquette which prevents showing resentment or rage; but this is not necessarily controlled to the same extent when dealing with fellow Negroes. Children, particularly, are available targets of all the displaced self-hatred of the professional middle-class Negro teacher. If they are lower-class children, they typically will demonstrate everything the middle-class Negro most despises about the race from which he cannot dissociate himself. The warmth, welcome, and support which children should find, particularly in the early elementary school grades, and which the Negro child needs in abundance because of so much deprivation at home, is exactly what teachers, Negro or white, as presently oriented, can least provide.

In this necessarily brief discussion of the factors that enter into the development of the self-concept of the Negro, we have utilized only a small sampling of the wealth of research literature and other documentation which bears on this subject. We have merely tried to suggest some of the crucial situations which help to mold the Negro child. It is these of which educational practitioners must be aware.

[52] Jean D. Grambs, "Are We Training Prejudiced Teachers?" *School and Society,* vol. 71, April 1, 1950, pp. 196-198.

[53] John Niemeyer, "Some Guidelines to Desirable Elementary School Reorganization," in *Programs for the Educationally Disadvantaged,* Washington, D.C., U.S. Office of Education Bulletin 1963, no. 17, p. 81.

[54] Bingham Dai, "Minority Group Membership and Personality Development," *op. cit.*

EDUCATIONAL INTERVENTION

The child with a negative view of self is a child who will not be able to profit much from school. Once a child is convinced that school is irrelevant to his immediate needs and future goals, the task of education becomes almost impossible. As one junior high student said, after having failed all his subjects for two years:

> I just don't like it. It seems to bore me. It seems silly just going there and sitting. And most of the time it is so hot and they don't do anything about it and the teachers just talk, talk, and you never learn anything.[55]

Deutsch's research points out that the lower-class Negro child probably received about one half to one third less instructional time in the primary grades than did white children from the same slum environment: "our time samples indicated that as much as 80% of the school day was channeled into disciplining, and secondarily, into ordinary organizational details. . . ."[56]

In 1951, it could be said:

> It is difficult to conceive of a more hopeless and dispirited group than a high school class of Negro adolescent girls; nor a more bored and resentful group than a high school class of Negro boys. Both seem equally aimless and befogged. They do not assume these attitudes through choice. The fault is society's, not theirs.[57]

Recent research indicates that Negro youth are responding to their caste position and selecting lower goals and lower standards for themselves, even when their family, socioeconomic position, and innate capacities would indicate higher achievement motivation: "lower caste and lower class status go hand in hand and . . . even when some lower caste members have achieved a more favorable class position, their caste restrictions continue to be perceived and to influence their behavior, both overt and implicit."[58]

Negro youth are almost totally ignorant of the community in which they live and the vocational and educational opportunities available.[59] They have a very restricted view of their community because their contacts via parents and other Negro adults are also limited by patterns of discrimination and selective reporting. Although many Negroes may today be aware of the outstanding few Negroes in sports, entertainment, and diplomacy, few know of the middle group of Negroes working in skilled trades, businesses, and other ordinary

[55] Kardiner and Ovesey, op. cit., p. 264.
[56] Deutsch, op. cit., p. 23.
[57] Kardiner and Ovesey, op. cit., p. 72.
[58] Lott and Lott, op. cit., p. 163.
[59] Dennis L. Trueblood, "The Role of the Counselor in the Guidance of Negro Students," Harvard Educational Review, vol. 30, no. 3, Summer, 1960, p. 252-269.

occupations. As Ginzburg and others so eloquently put it, persons of "exceptional accomplishments may not be as helpful a guide to the average Negro youngster as the knowledge that individuals not too different from himself have risen one or two rungs on the ladder."[60]

This point is amply supported by the research by Lott and Lott, who state that "we would predict a real change in the level of academic accomplishment among Negroes would be one of the major consequences of a greater availability of Negro models who could illustrate that such achievement 'pays off' and thereby increase the expectation that the Negro youth, too, might reap tangible benefits from his academic labors."[61]

It is not our purpose here to provide a blueprint for educational innovations which might be the object of experimentation. What is significant, however, is that the school has not as yet been used deliberately to change the self-concept of students. As Combs and Snygg state it: "To be really effective, education will have to accept the task of dealing with the whole phenomenal field of the individual, of producing changes in perception of himself as well as in his perception of his environment."[62]

Some interesting experimentation does indicate that the self-concept of the learner can be affected by deliberate school practices. Brookover and associates[63] explore a number of possible approaches that might be taken with early adolescent youngsters. Significant results were obtained when special methods were introduced for working with the young people and with their parents. There are many comments about the role of self-concept in achievement, but very few deliberate experimental studies aiming toward changing such an image.

Can the self-concept of the Negro child be changed in a positive direction by education? The study by Campbell, Yarrow, and Yarrow suggests that an integrated camp experience did have a significant effect on the self-perceptions of children, in particular of Negro children.[64] The permanence of this change, however, the authors state, would depend in large part on the support for such change on the return home. Studies of school desegregation have shown tendencies toward better school achievement on the part of Negro youth, but so far relatively little has been done to explore either the changes in self-concept

[60]Eli Ginzberg, James K. Anderson, and John L. Herma, *The Optimistic Tradition and American Youth,* New York, Columbia University Press, 1962, p 107.

[61]Lott and Lott, *op. cit,* p. 155.

[62]Combs and Snygg, *op. cit.,* p. 374.

[63]Wilbur B. Brookover and Associates, "Improving Academic Achievement Through Students' Self-concept Enhancement," Report of Symposium at the 1964 Meeting of the American Research Association, Chicago.

[64]John D. Campbell, Leon J. Yarrow, and Marian Radke Yarrow, "A Study of Adaptation to a New Social Situation"; "Acquisition of New Norms: A Study of Racial Desegregation"; "Personal and Situational Variables in Adaptation to Change"; and "Leadership and Interpersonal Change," *The Journal of Social Issues,* vol. 14, no. 1, 1958, pp. 3-59.

that might have occurred or the causes for such change. In fact, some indications are that integration actually lessens the Negro child's view of himself; that is, Negroes growing up in segregated communities and attending segregated schools tend to have a higher appraisal of Negroes in general, according to one study.[65] This supports, too, the finding of Campbell, Yarrow, and Yarrow that in the initial stages of the camp experience, Negro children were highly tentative and withdrawn, expressing most often the fear that the *other* Negro children would not behave properly.

The situation facing the school is exceedingly complex, and the problem is not one that is amenable to easy solutions. A number of approaches have been suggested. The Special Guidance Project in New York City has been described as an effort to change the perception of Negro and other disadvantaged youth regarding their own potential and opportunity.[66] Essentially, most proposals relating to school programs strive toward giving the Negro child more of what the average white child has been having all along — a good school environment.[67] It is our contention that this is not enough. Arguing from the data on self-concept, we would suggest that it is the view of self that has to be the focus of specific attention.

We are suggesting that education *can* make a difference. One difference, so far cited, as far as Negro youth are concerned, is the deliberate provision in guidance procedures to demonstrate to Negro youth that other Negroes have succeeded in moving up and out of the ghetto, becoming skilled and white-collar workers.

Other kinds of educational intervention might be utilized. For instance, in his reports of observations of classroom behavior, Deutsch found that only during Negro History Week did the majority of the students appear to be making a real effort to learn, and in some classrooms this was the only time at which some semblance of order was achieved and maintained for any length of time.[68] Arguing on theoretical grounds, Lewin claims that the child who has insight into his group status, particularly if it is a disadvantaged one, is better equipped to cope with this status in a positive manner, though he was speaking with particular reference to the problem of the Jewish child.[69] In the Campbell, Yarrow, and Yarrow study, one of the most effective counselors was a Negro

[65]Joshua A. Fishman, "Childhood Indoctrination for Minority-Group Membership," *Daedalus,* vol. 90, no. 2, Spring, 1961, pp. 329-349.

[66]J. Wayne Wrightstone,"Demonstration Guidance Project in New York City," *Harvard Educational Review,* vol. 30, no. 3, Summer, 1960, pp. 237-251.

[67]For example, Horace Mann Bond, "Wasted Talent," in Eli Ginzberg (ed.), *The Nation's Children, 2: Development and Education,* New York, Columbia University Press, pp. 116-137; Dorsey Baynham, "The Great Cities Projects," *NEA Journal,* vol. 52, April, 1963, pp. 17-19.

[68]Deutsch, *op. cit.*

[69]Kurt Lewin, "Bringing Up the Jewish Child," in *Securing Our Children Against Prejudice,* New York, Community Relations Service.

who dealt forthrightly and frankly with the question of race and did not attempt to evade and avoid it as did other counselors.[70]

As James Baldwin has so eloquently stated it:

> If . . . one managed to change the curriculum in all the schools so that Negroes learned more about themselves and their real contributions to this culture, you would be liberating not only Negroes, you'd be liberating white people who know nothing about their own histroy.[71]

In the fifth, eighth, and eleventh grades, when schools typically tell the story of American history, supplementary materials could be provided which show accurately the place and role of the American Negro during the historic periods being studied. For the eleventh grade, some fairly sophisticated material might be organized, including some documentary sources. It would be important to draw on such sources as *The Myth of the Negro Past,* by Herskovits,[72] and other recent historical findings. The superb collection of materials from the Federal Writers Project, the Slave Narrative Collection, available in the volume, *Lay My Burden Down,* edited by Botkin,[73] is another example of the kind of material that might well be more widely known by Negro youth. Trueblood suggests[74] that files of the Urban League be perused and actual case reports of successful Negro workers be made available. *Ebony* magazine regularly runs articles about the unusual, and some usual, successes attained by Negroes.

Material for kindergarten and primary grades is more difficult to produce and to define. It is possible that some cartoon-type booklets could be made which would show integrated and nonintegrated real-life situations with opportunities for the youngster to complete the action sequence himself. The sequence would focus in part on normal interaction among children but also would include the typical "race" situation in which children ask questions about differences, respond to racial attack ("nigger"), and so forth. It is possible that some comparative-culture material could be introduced earlier than is usually done, showing vividly contrasting ways of life, including that of the segregated American-Negro community.

It is clear that considerable exploration must be done before any decisions are made regarding what kinds of materials would be most appropriate. It would be useful to gather a panel of Negro and white social scientists knowledgeable in the fields of child psychology, education, history, psychiatry, and sociology to help explore and plan the development of materials.

Pilot materials might then be developed and tried out in several situations: a large northern city, Negro and white schools predominantly; suburban white

[70] Campbell, Yarrow, and Yarrow, *op. cit.*

[71] Baldwin, "A Talk to Teachers," *op. cit.,* p. 44.

[72] Herskovits, *op. cit.*

[73] B. A. Botkin (ed.), *Lay My Burden Down: A Folk History of Slavery,* Chicago, The University of Chicago Press, 1945.

[74] Trueblood, *op. cit.*

schools; and southern Negro and white schools (if possible), both city and rural. These trial runs would not only test the materials but would provide evidence as to the impact on self-concept of such materials on the part of Negro youth. It would be highly important also to see if any modification of white students' attitudes could be achieved. Workshops of teachers and administrators would be valuable in helping to understand what it is these adults would need to know in order to use the materials with competence and acceptance. The Campbell and Yarrow research, as well as our own experience, suggests great adult confusion when it comes to dealing directly with the problem of race with an integrated group of children or youth.

The analysis by Riessman regarding the kinds of instructional materials and instructional situations which are educationally effective with culturally deprived children suggests some of the kinds of materials to be developed.[75]

A study of the differences between good and poor achievers from severely deprived areas found some differences with significant educational implications:

> From the findings of this study, the hypothetical good achiever from an underprivileged environment emerges as a child who is relatively controlled and cautious, often stereotyped and constricted, but who still retains a degree of originality and creativity. He seems more willing than his less successful classmates to conform to adult demands, has a more positive view of authority figures and greater self-confidence. In cognitive functioning he excels chiefly in tasks requiring memory, attention and verbal abilities. He is also superior in analytical and organizational abilities and generally in processes that require convergent thinking.
>
> In contrast, the composite picture of the poor achiever is that of a child burdened by anxiety, fearful of the world and authority, and lacking in self-confidence. He is more apt to be impulsive and labile with relatively poor controlling mechanisms. His defenses against anxiety and feelings of inadequacy may be expressed in talking and in uncritically favorable surface attitude toward self and others. Nevertheless, the poor achiever still seems to have sufficient potential for adaptive behavior which the school could build upon. His cognitive activities are often quite similar in content, approach and process to those of the good achiever and in fact, he demonstrates greater facility in divergent production. Many of his reactions give evidence of creative capacity which might be directed and controlled. From his behavior in the testing situations and in tasks requiring social comprehension, the poor achiever seems to possess substantial understanding of the world around him, although he seems less able to act upon this understanding than the good achiever.[76]

[75] Riessman, op. cit.; Frank Riessman, "Cultural Styles of the Disadvantaged," Integrated Education, vol. 1, April, 1963.

[76] Helen H. Davidson, Judith W. Greenberg, and Joan M. Gerver, "Characteristics of Successful School Achievers from a Severely Deprived Environment," unpublished research report, The School of Education, The City University of New York, October, 1962, p. 18, mimeo.

As this research indicates and as other studies substantiate, the beginning scholars of any race or socioeconomic condition tend to start school at somewhat the same level.[77] But they soon diverge. Those who are not going to succeed are soon exposed to failure of various kinds. After a few years in school, the culturally deprived child may show an actual decline in tested intelligence.[78] Again, however, it must be noted that what may be tested may not be native endowment, and the test instrument may be measuring success plus knowledge, rather than innate capacity. As Hunnicutt and his associates point out, primary grade teachers may assume an oral vocabulary that just may not exist among the deprived children and thus fail the student for lacks that he cannot help, instead of diagnosing the problem and teaching to fill the gaps.[79]

Diagnosis of learning lacks is essential. These may be restricted oral vocabularies, poor speech habits, or lack of auditory discrimination skills.[80] Beyond that, to meet the requirement of effective education, we would suggest other kinds of educational materials that capitalize on divergent thinking and the immediate environmental experience of the student. These would probably be open-ended, problem-centered, realistic presentations. The use of short films, six minutes or less in length, which defined a problem that would lend itself to role playing as a class sought a solution, should be explored. Semiprojective pictures, such as those used in the "Focus" series of the National Conference of Christians and Jews,[81] might be further developed to stimulate discussion of the problems of racial self-identity. Recordings of stories, poems, or dramatic skits could be used to convey a particular sense of immediacy. Anthologies of stories, biography, and commentary might also be useful, particularly where these focused on the perception of the Negro in society and his ways of coping with his world.

The development of appropriate instructional materials for children with backgrounds which differ substantially from the middle-class norm is urgent; there also exists a need to modify the standard classroom procedure. For example, we do not know what are the real effects of overcrowded living. Recent research on the effect of overcrowding on laboratory animals demonstrates that these kinds of living conditions foster many pathological behaviors. The parallel between the pathology that develops among overcrowded

[77]Gordon P. Liddle, "Modifying the School Experience of Culturally Handicapped Children in the Primary Grades," in *Programs for the Educationally Disadvantaged.* Washington, D.C., U.S. Office of Education Bulletin 1963, no. 17, p. 59.

[78]C. W. Hunnicutt et al., *Survey of the Croton and Washington Irving Elementary Schools of the City of Syracuse,* Syracuse, N.Y., Syracuse University, Bureau of School Services, June, 1963, pp. 19-21, mimeo.

[79]*Ibid.,*pp. 28-34.

[80]Joseph M. Wepman, "Auditory Discrimination, Speech, and Reading," *Elementary School Journal,* vol. 60, March, 1960, pp. 325-333.

[81]*Focus on Problems Facing Youth* (a picture packet), New York, National Conference of Christians and Jews, 1954.

animals and the social pathology of the slum seems obvious.[82] A psychiatrist notes that slum children are exposed to continual overstimulation, which results in behavior not conducive to learning in the standard school situation. This kind of "over-loading of the perceptual apparatus," in the words of Sarvis, can be an extremely disorganizing experience — so much so that the children so exposed may, in school,

> ... often act as if they were under the influence of one of the overstimulating drugs. Their thinking is scattered, their attention span is short. Frequently they talk in an excited, irrepressible way without regard for whether anyone is listening or not. Conversation may be almost unknown. Distractibility and hyperactivity may be marked. Teachers become frustrated because efforts to calm such a child are transient; moments later he has returned to his previous wild and distractible behavior.[83]

The schools are not prepared to deal with such children. We have suggested that the attention of these children may be attracted by different kinds of instructional materials. We also may suggest that different kinds of learning situations may be required. How large a group, for instance, can such children tolerate and for how long? When does the group become too small? Can these children bear to be alone, and if so, for how long? Sarvis suggests that many small-group activities, carefully scheduled and structured, may be one answer.[84] The work of Reger[85] with hyperactive, distractible children suggests that some of these youngsters need more rather than less stimulation.

It is imperative, however, that one take care in developing both special materials and special procedures to use with the culturally deprived Negro child. He may differ in many ways, as we have noted, but only some of these may be significant to a given child. He may have all the handicaps of massive and continued poverty and defeat, or he may only be struggling with a problem of adequate self-identity. It would be a mistake to assume that because some slum dwellers are particularly rich in some kinds of vocabulary that all are and that all are creative in nonintellectual ways because many are. In fact, the need to meet such individual differences may actually boomerang against programs to speed up school integration, which are probably the best method for ultimate solution to our problem. As one writer observed:

> Teachers talk at length about the "cognitive difficulties" of the economically, socially deprived, disadvantaged child. Whether or not

[82] "Sociology: A Self-corrective for the Population Explosion?" *Time,* vol. 83, February 28, 1964, p. 56.

[83] Mary A. Sarvis, "Reactions of Children from Crowded Areas," *Childhood Education,* vol. 39, May, 1963, pp. 413-415.

[84] Sarvis, *loc. cit.*

[85] Roger Reger, "Stimulating the Distractible Child," *Elementary School Journal,* vol., 64, October, 1963, pp. 42-48.

Dr. Frank Riessman, who has written eloquently about different learning styles, realizes it, many parents in my neighborhood use his thesis to "prove" that children must be educated differently. It is so easy to make the erroneous assumption that all poor children have one style of learning and all middle-class children another.[86]

It is hypothecated that no one kind of material nor one kind of program will suffice. Children respond to materials differently; what will produce insight in one child may merely baffle another. A multiple approach using as many media as possible is therefore more promising. Research may be helpful in identifying the approach and the medium which seem to be most effective with most youngsters at a given age and in a given cultural setting. More work, following the lead of Hoban,[87] could be done to find these "bridges" which aid children in understanding and accepting the "message" of a given communications medium.

CONCLUSION

If today we note a change of tone, a militancy and impatience on the part of Negro youth, it is not because schools are any different. For the first time, the Negro, via TV, is beginning to see that the world of comfort, luxury, and fun is all around him. He wants some of it, too. As Hayakawa pointed out in a speech at a recent American Psychological Association convention in Philadelphia, the ads that beckon one to join the fun on the picnic do *not* add "for whites only."[88]

But the militancy, welcome as it may be, cannot erase the burden of self-hatred that has accumulated through so many generations. And many who most need to hear the call to challenge the racial status quo may already be too deeply sunk in despair and apathy. These fellings are so quickly communicated to the infant and child that intervention by the school even as early as kindergarten or the first grade may be too late. But if many older adolescents can respond to a new concept of their role in the world, then certainly the younger child can be reached, too, by deliberate efforts to change the way in which he views himself. These, then, are the challenges we must meet.

[86]Ellen Lurie, "School Integration in New York City," *Integrated,* vol. 2, February-March, 1964, pp. 3-11.

[87]Charles F. Hoban, Jr., *Focus on Learning,* Washington, D.C., American Council on Education, 1942.

[88]*Washington Post,* September 10, 1963.

Being Taken Seriously *

Paul Goodman

1.

The simple job plight of these adolescents could not be remedied without a social revolution. Therefore it is not astonishing if the most well-intentioned public spokesmen do not mention it at all. In this book we shall come on other objective factors that are not mentioned. But it is hard to grow up in a society in which one's important problems are treated as nonexistent. It is impossible to belong to it, it is hard to fight to change it. The effect must be rather to feel disaffected, and all the more restive if one is smothered by well-meaning social workers and PAL's who don't seem to understand the real irk. The boys cannot articulate the real irk themselves.

For instance, what public spokesman could discuss the jobs? The ideal of having a real job that you risk your soul in and make good or be damned, belongs to the heroic age of capitalist enterprise, imbued with self-righteous beliefs about hard work, thrift, and public morals. Such an ideal might still have been mentioned in public fifty years ago; in our era of risk-insured semimonopolies and advertised vices it would be met with a ghastly stillness. Or alternately, to want a job that exercises a man's capacitites in an enterprise useful to society, is utopian anarcho-syndicalism; it is labor invading the domain of management. No labor leader has entertained such a thought in our generation. Management has the "sole prerogative" to determine the products and the machines. Again, to speak of the likelihood or the desirability of unemployment, like Norbert Wiener or J. K. Galbraith, is to be politically nonprofessional. Yet every kid somehow knows that if he quits school he won't get ahead – and the majority quit.

During, let us say, 1890-1936, on Marxist grounds, the fight for working conditions, for security, wages, hours, the union, the dignity of labor, *was* mentioned, and it gave the worker or the youth something worth while. But because of their historical theory of the "alienation of labor" (that the worker *must* become less and less in control of the work of his hands) the Marxist parties never fought for the man-worthy job itself. It is not surprising now if workmen accept their alienation, and are indifferent also to Marxist politics.

*Paul Goodman, *Growing Up Absurd.* New York: Random House, 1956. Chapter II, "Being Taken Seriously," pp. 36-51.

2.

When the objective factors cannot be mentioned, however, other rhetoric is used instead, and in this chapter let us examine its style, as applied, for instance, to juvenile delinquency, on which there is a good deal of oratory.

In our times the usual principle of such speech is that the others, the delinquent boys, are not taken seriously as existing, as having, like oneself, real aims in a real world. They are not condemned, they are not accepted. Instead they are a "youth problem" and the emphasis is on their "background conditions," which one can manipulate; they are said to be subject to "tensions" that one can alleviate. The aim is not to give human beings real goals that warrant belief, and tasks to share in, but to re-establish "belonging," although this kind of speech and thought is precisely calculated to avoid contact and so makes belonging impossible. When such efforts don't work, one finally takes some of the boys seriously as existing and uses force to make them not exist.

Let me give a childish but important illustration of how this works out. A boy of ten or eleven has a few great sexual adventures — *he* thinks they're great — but then he has the bad luck to get caught and get in trouble. They try to persuade him by punishment and other explanations that some different behavior is much better, but he knows by the evidence of his senses that nothing could be better. If he gives in, he lives on in a profound disbelief, a disbelief in their candor and a disbelief even of his own body feelings. But if he persists and proves incorrigible, then the evidence of his senses is attached to what is socially punished, explained away; he may even be put away. The basic trouble here is that they do not really believe he has had the sexual experience. That objective factor is inconvenient for them; therefore it cannot exist. Instead, this is *merely* a case of insecure affection at home, slum housing, comic books, and naughty companions: tensions and conditions. My hunch, as I shall discuss later, is that this kind of early sexual adventure and misadventure is fairly common in delinquency. It is called precocious, abnormal, artificially stimulated, and so forth — an index of future delinquency. In my opinion that's rubbish, but be that as it may; what is important in a particular case is that there is a stubborn new fact. Attempting to nullify it makes further growth impossible (and *creates* the future delinquency). The sensible course would be to accept it as a valuable part of further growth. But if this were done, they fear that the approved little hero would be a rotten apple to his peers, who now would suddenly *all* become precocious, abnormal, artificially stimulated, and prone to delinquency.

The sexual plight of these children is officially not mentioned. The revolutionary attack on hypocrisy by Ibsen, Freud, Ellis, Dreiser, did not succeed this far. Is it an eccentric opinion that an important part of the kids' restiveness in school from the onset of puberty has to do with puberty? The teachers talk about it among themselves, all right. (In his school, Bertrand Russell thought it was better if they had the sex, so they could give their undivided attention to mathematics, which was the main thing.) But since this objective factor does not *exist* in our schools, the school itself begins to be irrelevant. The question here is not whether the sexuality should be discouraged or encouraged. That is an important issue, but far more important is that it is hard to grow up when existing facts are treated as though they do not exist. For then there is no dialogue, it is impossible to be taken seriously, to be understood, to make a bridge between oneself and society.

In American society we have perfected a remarkable form of censorship: to allow every one his political right to say what he believes, but to swamp his little boat with literally thousands of millions of newspapers, mass-circulation magazines, best-selling books, broadcasts, and public pronouncements that disregard what he says and give the official way of looking at things. Usually there is no conspiracy to do this; it is simply that what he says is not what people are talking about, it is not newsworthy.

(There is no conspiracy, but it is *not* undeliberate. "If you mean to tell me," said an editor to me, "that *Esquire* tries to have articles on important issues and treats them in such a way that nothing can come of it — who can deny it?" Try, also, to get a letter printed in the *New York Times* if your view on the issue calls attention to an essential factor that is not being generally mentioned.)

Naturally, the more simply true a statement is in any issue about which everybody is quite confused, the less newsworthy it will be, the less it will be what everybody is talking about. When the child in the story said, "But the Emperor has no clothes!" the newspapers and broadcasts surely devoted many columns to describing the beautiful new clothes and also mentioned the interesting psychological incident of the child. Instead of being proud of him, his parents were ashamed; but on the other hand they received $10,000 in sympathetic contributions toward his rehabilitation, for he was a newsworthy case. But he had a block in reading.

Where there is official censorship it is a sign that speech is serious. Where there is none, it is pretty certain that the official spokesmen have all the loud-speakers.

3.

But let us return to our theme of vocation and develop it a step further. Perhaps the young fellows *really* want to do something, that is, something worth while, for only a worth-while achievement finishes a doing. A person rests when he has finished a real job. (The striking illustration of this is that, statistically, the best mental health used to be found among locomotive engineers, and is now found among air-line pilots! The task is useful, exacting, it sets in motion a big machine, and when it is over, it is done with.) If the object is important, it gives structure to many a day's action and dreaming — one might even continue in school. Unfortunately our great society balks us, for it simply does not take seriously the fact, or the possibility, that people want this; nor the philosophic truth that except in worth-while activity there is no way to be happy. For instance, in a standard questionnaire for delinquents, by Milton Barron, in a hundred headings there do not appear the questions, "What do you want to be? What do you want to work at? What do you want to achieve?" (But Donald Taft's *Criminology,* which Barron is adapting, has the sentence: "Absence of vocational interest at the age when it is normal . . . is tell-tale of a starved life.")

In despair, the fifteen-year-olds hang around and do nothing at all, neither work nor play. Without a worth-while prospect, without a sense of justification, the made-play of the Police Athletic League is not interesting, it is not their own. They do not do their school work, for they are waiting to quit; and it is hard, as we shall see, for them to get part-time jobs. Indeed, the young fellows (not only delinquents) spend a vast amount of time doing nothing. They hang around together, but don't talk about anything, nor even – if you watch their faces – do they passively take in the scene. Conversely, at the movies, where the real scene is by-passed, they watch with absorbed fantasy, and afterward sometimes mimic what they saw.

If there is nothing worth while, it is hard to do anything at all. When one does nothing, one is threatened by the question, *is* one nothing? To this insulting doubt, however, there is a lively response: a system of values centering around threatened grownupness and defensive conceit. This is the so-called "threatened masculinity," not in the sense of being called a girl, but of being called, precisely, "boy," the Negro term of insult. With this, there is an endless compulsion to prove potency and demand esteem. The boys don't talk about much of interest, but there is a vast amount of hot rhetoric to assert that oneself is "as good as anybody else," no more useless, stupid, or cowardly. For instance, if they play a game, the interest in the game is weak: they are looking elsewhere when the ball is served, there are lapses in attention, they smoke cigarettes even while playing handball. The interest in victory is surprisingly weak: there is not much glow of self-esteem. But the need for proof is overwhelming: "I won you, didn' I? I won you last week too, didn' I?"

During childhood, they played games with fierce intensity, giving themselves as a sacrifice to the game, for play was the chief business of growth, finding and making themselves in the world. Now when they are too old merely to play, to what shall they give themselves with fierce intensity? They cannot play for recreation, since they have not been used up.

The proving behavior is endless. Since each activity is not interesting to begin with, its value does not deepen and it does not bear much repetition. Its value as proof quickly diminishes. In these circumstances, the inevitable tendency is to raise the ante of the compulsive useless activity that proves one is potent and not useless. (This anaylsis applies equally to these juveniles and to status-seeking junior executives in business firms and on Madison Avenue.)

It is not surprising then, that, as Frederic Thrasher says in *The Gang,* "Other things being equal, the imaginative boy has an excellent chance to become the leader of the gang. He has the power to make things interesting for them. He 'thinks up things for us to do.' "

At this point let us intervene and see what the Official Spokesmen say.

4.

Last summer, after a disatrous week when there were several juvenile murders, the Governor of New York made the following statement (*New York Times,* September 2, 1959):

> We have to constantly devise new ways to bring about a challenge to these young folks and to provide an outlet for their energies and give them a sense of belonging.

The statement is on the highest level of current statesmanship — that is why I have chosen it. It has been coached by sociologists and psychologists. It has the proper therapeutic and not moralistic attitude, and it does not mention the cops. (The direct appeal to force came a couple of weeks later, when there were other incidents.)

The gist of it is that the Governor of New York is to play the role that Thrasher assigns to the teen-age gang leader. He is to think up new "challenges." (The word could not have been more unfortunate.) But it is the word "constantly" that is the clue. A challenge can hardly be worth while, meaningful, or therapeutic if another must constantly and obsessively be devised to siphon off a new threat of "energy." Is not this raising the ante? Solidly meeting a real need does not have this character.

("The leader," says Thrasher, "sometimes controls the gang by means of summation, i.e., by progressively urging the members from one deed to another, until finally an extreme of some sort is reached.")

My guess is that in playing games the Governor will not have so lively an imagination as the lad he wants to displace as leader; unlike the grownups, the gang will never select him. One of the objective factors that make it hard to grow up is that Governors are likely to be men of mediocre humane gifts.

The psychology of the Governor's statement is puzzling. There are no such undifferentiated energies as he speaks of. There are energies of specific functions with specific real objects. In the case here they might be partly as follows: In adolescents a strong energy would be sexual reaching. For these boys, as for other adolescents, it is thwarted or imperfectly gratified, but these have probably not learned so well as others to cushion the suffering and be patient; so that another strong energy of the delinquents would be diffuse rage of frustration, perhaps directed at a scapegoat. If they have been kept from constructive activity making them feel worth while, a part of their energy might be envious and malicious destructiveness of property. As they are powerless, it is spite; and as they are humiliated, it is vengeance. As they feel rejected and misunderstood, as by governors, their energy is woe; but they react to this with cold pride, and all the more fierce gang-loyalty to their peers. For which of these specific energies does the Governor of New York seriously plan to devise an outlet? Their own imaginative gang leader presumably does devise challenges that let off steam for a few hours.

What is the sociology of "belonging" here? In the great society they are certainly uprooted. But in the gang their conformity is sickeningly absolute; they have uniform jackets and uniform morals. They speak a jargon and no one has a different idea that might brand him as queer. Since they have shared forbidden behavior, they are all in the same mutually blackmailing plight and correspondingly guilty and suspicious toward the outsider. It is a poor kind of community they have; friendship, affection, personal helpfulness are remarkably lacking in it; they are "cool," afraid to display feeling; yet does the Governor seriously think that he can offer a good community that warrants equal loyalty?

5.

More aware of what challenging means, the New York Youth Board has had a policy more calculated to succeed. Its principle is provisionally to accept as *given* the code of the gang and the kids' potency-proving values and prejudices; and then, as an immediate aim, to try to distract their overt behavior into less annoying and dangerous channels. This immediate aim is already valuable, for it diminishes suffering. For instance, there is less suffering if a youth's addiction is changed from heroin to alcohol, so long as heroin is illegal and alcohol is legal; the youth is less in danger and the store that he would rob to pay for the criminally overpriced narcotic is out of danger.

Then there is the further hope that, accepted by the wise and permissive adult, the adolescents will gradually come to accept themselves and the spiral of proving will be arrested. Further, that the friendship of the trusted adult will evoke a love (transference) that can then be turned elsewhere. I take it that this is the Youth Worker philosophy. In many cases it should succeed.

I am skeptical that it can widely succeed. For here again the young people are not taken seriously as existing, as having real aims in the same world as oneself. To the Youth Board, in their own real world (such as it is), the code is *not* acceptable, and the teen-age vaunts and prejudices cannot lead to growth in any world. To pretend otherwise is playing games and continuing to exclude them from one's own meant world. How then can the boys be trusting and feel they are understood? Not being morons, they know they *cannot* be understood in their own terms, which are empty to themselves. They know there is another world beyond, as square and sheepish as they might please to rationalize it, but which is formidable and enviable. (Actually, apart from the code itself and the sphere of their delinquencies, the kids are models of conventionality in their tastes, opinions, and ignorance.) And though they have a childish need for sympathetic attention and are proud of having compelled it — "We're so bad they give us a youth worker" — they are too old not to demand being taken seriously.

There is a valuable nondirective approach which makes no judgments or interpretations and gives no advice, but which simply draws the patient out and holds up a mirror; and this is no doubt also part of the philosophy of the Youth Board. But then, it must be a therapy, it must hold up the mirror and risk the explosion of shame and grief, or the impulsive defenses against them, violent retaliation or flight. In youth work this is very impractical. It is a different thing to go *along* with the patient, or worse to seem to go along with him, and provide only the reassurance of attention.

The philosophy of the Youth Board can succeed only if the worker can hold out some real objective opportunity, something more than "interpersonal relations," and make the boy finally see it. (E.g., at P.S. 43 in New York there has been an experiment of simply urging the kids to go to college — a far-off goal — showing that it is economically possible for them, and promising that the school will follow up. This alone has resulted in rapid academic advance, increases in I.Q., and less truancy.)

My hunch is that the occasional spectacular success occurs not because of the "accepting" method, but because the youth worker does not really belong to the world of the Youth Board either, and his acceptance is bona fide. For whatever motive, he confronts the young people as real. He may be a covert accomplice with the same inner dilemma as his gang, and can pass on a more practical worldly wisdom. He may be emotionally involved with some of them, so they are in fact important. He may be so deeply compassionate or so inspired a teacher that he creates new interests and values altogether, *not* the meant world of the Youth Board which is, after all, just what had proved unsatisfactory to begin with.

6.

Our society has evolved a social plan, a city plan, an economy and a physical plant, of which this delinquent youth is an organic part. The problem is *not* to get them to belong to society, for they belong a priori by being the next generation. The burden of proof and performance is quite the other way: for the system of society to accomodate itself to all its constituent members. But can it be denied that by and large the official practice is to write these boys off as useless and unwanted and to try to cajole or baffle them into harmlessness?

Suppose we look at it the other way. Like any other constitutional group, they exert an annoying pressure, but they are inarticulate. In some dumb way they are surely right, but what the devil do they want? Has much effort been made to ask them and help them find words? We can guess that they want two broad classes of things: changes in the insulting and depriving circumstances that have made them ornery, spiteful, vengeful, conceited, ignorant, and callous — unable to grow; and objective opportunities in which to grow.

Let us go back to the Governor. On the same occasion mentioned above, he issued to the press the following formal statement:

> The problem of juvenile delinquency has no easy remedy. There is no quick or overnight solution. It is compounded of neglect by parents, broken homes, poor living conditions, unhealthy background, economic deprivation, mental disturbance, and lack of religious training.

This is not a bad list of background conditions; it satisfies every popular and scientific theory of etiology. The question is, does the Governor seriously not understand how organic these conditons are in our society? They cannot be remedied by gimmicks or the busy kind of social work that offers no new vision or opportunity. He speaks of broken homes; has he some plan to improve the institution of modern marriage, especially among folk for whom it is hardly an institution? The present-day urban poor are largely Negro and Spanish, they are excluded from many unions, they often earn less than the minimum wage, they are unschooled; naturally there is economic deprivation, poor living conditions. How is their religion relevant if it is irrelevant to the basic community functions of vocation and war, and wrong on sex? There is no community and not even a community plan; naturally there is unhealthy background.

What great concerted effort is being led by the Governor to remedy these conditions, not overnight, but in the next five, ten, or twenty years?

Indeed, *official* policy has often worked to increase delinquency rather than remedy it. For instance, in a characteristically earnest analysis, our best authority on housing, Charles Abrams, has shown how the public-housing policy has had this effect. Slums have been torn down wholesale, disrupting established community life. By not building on vacant land and by neglecting master planning, our officials have created insoluble problems of relocation and have vastly increased the number of one-room flats, making decent family life impossible. (Suppose you were fifteen years old and returned home at 11 P.M., as the Mayor urges, to a room with Mama and Papa in one bed and two little brothers in your bed and a baby yowling; you might well stay out till four in the morning.) Also, families are ousted from public housing when their incomes increase, thus eliminating and penalizing the better models; and on the other hand, other families are expelled on irrelevant moral criteria, without thought of what becomes of them. And the original income segregation in large blocks was itself bound to increase tension, like any segregation. All of this has been *official* policy. The picture gets even grimmer if we turn to the quasi-official graft in Title I that for two- and three-year stretches has stalled either demolition or construction, while families pay rent in limbo.

The trouble with Abrams' analysis is that he, Mumford and others have been saying it aloud for twenty years, while the New York City Planning Commission has gone on manufacturing juvenile delinquency.

7.

Now finally (January 1960), the Governor's practical antidelinquency youth program is offered for legislation. Let me summarize its chief points: (1) Reduce the age of felonies to fifteen. (2) Space for 390 more in the forest camps (added to the 110 now there). (3) Admit a few older to these camps. (4) Establish "Youth Oppportunity Centers" — residences for youths "on the verge of delinquency." (5) Provide "halfway houses" for those in transition from institutions to freedom. (6) Certified boarding houses to which the court can direct youngsters. (7) Ease compulsory continuation school. (8) Permit after-school work from fourteen to sixteen. (9) Encourage work-and-study programs "to keep potential drop-outs in school long enough to prepare for employment." (10) Centralize probation services. (11) Increase probation staff.

Of these eleven points, eight seem to be aimed primarily at punishment or control: the boys are really unwanted, the problem is to render them harmless. Only two (8 and 9) envisage, very unimpressively, any substantive change whatever. What on earth has happened to the program of "constantly devising new ways to challenge these young folks"? But let me call attention to the forest work-camps (2 and 3). There is good evidence that these are excellent and have provided a rewarding experience. But then certainly they should be made available not for convicted delinquents as such, but for all kids who want to work there a year. Naturally, however, there is no money — not even for more than five hundred delinquent boys altogether. The question is whether or not such a program of camps for many thousand boys is less important than one of the Park Commissioner's new highways to Westchester. Until they will face that question, our public officials are not serious.

8.

Positively, the delinquent behavior seems to speak clearly enough. It asks for what we can't give, but it is in *this* direction we must go. It asks for manly opportunities to work, make a little money, and have self-esteem; to have some space to bang around in, that is not always somebody's property; to have better schools to open for them horizons of interest; to have more and better sex without fear or shame; to share somehow in the symbolic goods (like the cars) that are made so much of; to have a community and a country to be loyal to; to claim attention and have a voice. These are not outlandish demands. Certainly they cannot be satisfied directly in our present system; they are baffling. That is why the problem is baffling, and the final resourse is to a curfew, to ordinances against carrying knives, to threatening the parents, to reformatories with newfangled names, and to 1,100 more police on the street.

Into the School*

Mary Frances Greene and Orletta Ryan

It is now nearly 10:30 and no Mrs. Abernathy. I put the faster group on reading workbooks, her slower group on their assignment. Mrs. Abernathy is Corrective Reading Teacher. Mr. Yount is Reading Improvement Teacher. Both were very helpful for some time. Then Mr. Yount dropped off (he's been hiding out, studying for assistant-principal exams in his office most of the school day), and Mrs. Abernathy began coming late.

Mrs. Abernathy is conscientious, brings special teaching aids to her work, and knows the teaching of reading, but has become very uneasy toward the children since she began coming late. She has been in P.S. 200 for several years. She's hit the circle that awaits the sensitive teacher — can't take any more, will quit if she isn't let out of the classroom. She becomes a specialist or supervisor. A less competent teacher takes her place. My slower reading group is scheduled for 33J, a big classroom. Mrs. Abernathy is supposed to take them out of the room. But lately, her friends Miss Perez, Mrs. Rumstedt, Mr. Kaplan have taken to holding "curriculum meetings" (which develop into coffee and cigarette breaks) in 33J.

There is not much I can do. Mr. Zang drives Mrs. Abernathy to school in the mornings. She's also grown very critical. Amy Katz said, "She's been getting in on that coffeepot in 33J, that's all. That's why she's been so critical lately."

Amy found some fifth grade social science books in the basement this month — beautiful covers and illustrations, stacked to the ceiling, have never been opened. Sixth, seventh, even eighth grade will never read well enough to read them. Amy took them up to her fifth grade for her faster readers — they're at third-grade level but progressing rapidly. The maps and noble engravings would inspire any class with the excitement, the pleasure, of learning.

When Mrs. Abernathy's eye fell on the new treasure, she told Amy simply, *"These books are threatening, Miss Katz."* And back they went to the basement where, said Amy who accompanied them down, six A.D.N.S. (All Day Neighborhood Schools) teachers were busy unpacking more crates of new books, and next door to the book room the second grade was doing Dutch dances. (They do a lot of dancing in second grade, and when the lunchroom's occupied

*Mary Frances Greene and Orletta Ryan, *The Schoolchildren; Growing Up in the Slums.* New York: Pantheon Books, 1965.

by third grade doing square dances, second grade does its dancing next to the book room.) That same week I'd picked up second-hand copies of *National Geographic, Natural History,* and other magazines for our library shelf. "You're not being fair to them," said Mrs. Abernathy. "You must not make these demands. Stick to the books they can read."

"But I often read to the children from them. We talk about all the birds – see these fine color photographs of the swamp birds, scavengers, birds of prey. It's a reward for finishing work pages. The children's interest is so strong – you should see them struggling to read these magazines! Last week Carlos almost cried because he couldn't read the caption under a picture of a snowy egret."

"That's what I mean. You're not being fair."

"But then he went to work – he took the magazine home. Thursday he could read, 'This is a snowy egret.' "

"And will that help him in the reader? You're arousing desire in him for something he can't achieve. We try to treat the child as a decent human being." she concluded – as so often.

She's also been made Cultural Coordinator between "Higher Horizons" and the Reading Program. This week a sudden burgeoning – Abernathy's work – of posters and reading displays on first-floor walls. Some Puerto Rican area supervisors were due on a flying visit (though few of us will get to see them – they only go to the brightest classes). Friday she hurried into my room to get material for a display. "I want everything your room's been doing for Choral Speaking." said Abernathy. "Now how about those lovely big illustrations you had in Assembly last week for *Winnie-the-Pooh?*" I didn't really want to take time out helping Mrs. Abernathy deck up halls for supervisors. One group was reading; another group was on phonics workbooks. How about later? But Abernathy had now noticed "March 21" in cursive writing on the board, a sight which always seems to make her half lose her mind. She kept hold of herself this morning, just murmured, staring. "Oh . . . I'll wait. Please go right on with what you're doing. As you know, Miss Burke, you're not to teach them handwriting until they're reading on second-grade level. It's too confusing to a child."

"Mrs. Abernathy, many examiners have proved cursive is easier to learn than printing. In the Montessori and other methods, the children never learn to print."

"They simply can't do it, Miss Burke."

"Boys and girls, hold up this morning's class papers – they are doing it, Mrs. Abernathy. They're eleven years old."

But she wouldn't look at the papers. And even though her group is reading aloud because she is late, I expect trouble this morning.

It's still some minutes before we hear her calling from the door, "Good morning, children! Are we ready to take a trip?" Books slam shut – no trouble there — as she continues, gliding briskly to the back of the room, "Yes, we're 'going to the country' with Ted and Sally, where we'll see many wonderful things we can't in the city! And someone else is going today, I believe — Ted and Sally's puppy, who'll meet a friendly new animal in the country! Are we ready for the fun? All aboard! . . . Now, who'll bring Mrs. Abernathy her chair?" Big haul of chairs on all fours, rearward — new diversion, which gets everyone excited. "Don' you touch my a'm, man, I warnin you." "Don't curse my mother!" "I'm bringing the chair; you brought it yesterday."

"We're on a *train* now, boys and girls! Let's lock our lips and throw the key away out the window!" Mrs. Abernathy calls, putting up primer charts "The Puppy and the Rabbit" for these eleven-year-olds, most of whom were born in the United States and started kindergarten at five years.

The hubbub begins: emotionally shaky children who can't read doing phonics in front, even shakier but slower children being told in back, "Let's open to the picture of the train getting itself all ready to leave its home, the station. It's taking Ted and Sally and Tuffy *to the country!* It's a *happy* train. How can we tell? . . . well, just look at the big smile it's wearing on its engine! Who knows what the engine does?"

"Miz' Abby, we awready had dis story today."

"Mrs. Ab-er-nathy, Marshall."

"Mis' Abio, we had about that puppy-rabbit ina country today."

"No, no, Miguel, you're thinking of another puppy we had such fun with last month. That was another book. Who can tell the name of the reader we're reading now?" The fifteen children in front are now stirring, giggling, and twisting, trying to fishhook their friends' eyes out of the slow group in back. Abernathy's rimless glasses seem to rotate slowly before fixing themselves on me.

"You've been through the story, Miss Burke?"

"Well, we went as far as —"

"You've conducted them far enough that initial expectation can no longer be aroused?"

"Mrs. Abernathy, there *is* no — yes . . . we have been through it."

"Well, children . . . we'll just have to start over again. Could you give me the page number, Miss Burke?"

Meanwhile they've found the initial-expectation page all right. Resistance is shaping in a solid, muttering child wall. "*I* ain' readin dis story again." "I ain' *nevah* goin look at it again." "I hate Ted, I hate ol' Sally more. Who cares about that ol' red wagon and kitten they drag aroun' in it." "I rea' it today, and I rea' it in firs' gra'."

Fifteen minutes later, front: we're adding *ing* to root words. "If Ted rides, Roderigo, he is —?" "Riding." "Good. Call on another child, Roderigo." Rear: "*Frame* the word. Finger on each side. Now what do you see? What do you see? — Just a moment. Are you on the right page, Carmacita?" The room is suppressed uproar. Abernathy is wearing a smile like a tied-on bandage. No trouble about the noise, though. Noise doesn't exist. Interruptions permissively treated. "Marshall, what do *you* see?" "Mis' Abernath', Marshall took my pencil." "I *ain'* took, he *trade* for his yo-yo wi' me, Miz Abby." (Handbook: "We must give scope and understanding to that intense and growing êthique of the fourth-grader.") At times the back of the room seems to have swung around entirely with a big clatter of chairs, clockwise. To add to everything else, the hall door's been left open. Abernathy's girl friend, Svenson, and another teacher outside: "Yes . . . Ninety-first Street outlet . . . I hear they have some pretty good stuff there."

"Bianca, please close the door."

But Mrs. Abernathy rises, carrying today's glacial smile upward, and glides. "*Please,* Miss Burke." All the slow-group books bang shut behind her. Svenson leans in as her boss approaches. "So you need anything else, Mrs. Abernathy?"

"No, Mrs. Svenson, we're all aboard for the country — our train's just a little late pulling out. — No, I'll see you later about that whole problem. Thank you for waiting."

Teacher: "Workbooks, Mrs. Abernathy? We've needed them for a week."

Dirty look from Svenson, who lists it, however, and sends down Pablo with a note. Svenson-teacher conversation resumes outside. Carlos returns with the wrong workbooks.

"All right. We'll start with these, boys and girls. They're one grade behind us so they should be really easy. Monitors, see if you can pass these out quietly."

"We can' do this kin' work," they say immediately. "These too hard for us." "I ain' gonna work this workbook."

"No, these aren't the *right* workbooks, boys and girls, but let's use them as a little review. Let's settle down and be happy."

Mrs. Abernathy's hearing has suddenly returned to her. Long, gray raised eyebrows from the back. "Really, Miss Burke, they read *very* well. Beautiful reading experience in here one day last week — let me see — Wednesday! Let's not forget to priase them when it's due, Miss Burke."

"Mrs. Abernathy, these children have not really learned to read."

"They've been *well* taught, Miss Burke. All our teachers are doing their best."

"Their files said 3.1 when I started, you mean? Then why didn't they know *a, e, i, o,* and *u*?"

All the children are now out of their seats and talking; I've let my temper slip and it's too late. But Mrs. Abernathy arm-gathers materials and glides in perfect calm to the door. "Mrs. Abernathy, there *is* a certain resistance to learning here." I say to her through the din.

"We have one or two children that don't apply themselves, but really it's a beautiful class." she firmly answers. "I'll be back on Friday, boys and girls, to hear about the library books. But Roberto, let's remember, dear, to ask the librarian if she has some other kind of story than Bible books. The story of Moses finding the baby was very colorful and exciting, but we come from many different religious backgrounds. Let's find stories we can all share."

To me: "They're underprivileged but teachable, Miss Burke. We're here for the children and for no other reason."

Miss Moyle, an O.P.T. teacher (supplementary teachers who relieve the regular classroom teacher), comes in at 11:00 for social studies. These children are scheduled to study (the syllabus says they *do* study) math, social studies, science, music, and art, although they can't read. Miss Moyle is very amiable with teachers, recently engaged, salt-and-pepper gray in her hair, and happy.

For a month we had walk-ups and skyscrapers, multiple dwellings, and the subway. "You'd be amazed," Moyle would insist, "how many of the children just don't know what the subway is."

"But Miss Moyle, all the children go to every borough with their families over the week-end, visiting relatives, staying overnight. The little boys sneak on and ride the subway all day Saturday by themselves. They ride all over New York; they go to Coney Island, to Forty-second Street, and get themselves home on the subways."

Moyle: "Many of them have simply never seen a subway. Many of these children, dwelling in the world's largest metropolitan area, simply grow up without having learned what 'sub-way' means. We're here to teach them about their cultural environment, such as the subway."

February was Manhattan Island. "We're going to learn many wonderful things about Manhattan Island." "They don't know their street addresses," objected Miss Peruzzi when Moyle first hit 3B. "None of them know their birthdays; a few can't spell their names."

"Now put everything away and sit tall. How many children know what the Atlantic Ocean is? – Put that away. – Today we're going to play a game to learn many wonderful things about the Atlantic Ocean. Let's say that together, children . . . that's right . . . once again, rounding our lips when we say 'O-cean' – good! fine! – and about Manhattan Island on which we live. Manhattan Island is in the Atlantic Ocean. Now who knows what an eye-land is?" (Eyes not exactly where she wants them but wandering from sparkler, to dapper suited front, to graying hair.)

"Now some of us are going to come up front – no, no, not until Miss Moyle calls on just four *quiet* children who don't leave seats until she says – and join hands.

"Put that away. I want your eyes looking at *me*.

"All right: you, you, you, my dear, and you. Now a fifth child. That child is to have a very important part in our play. *We're going to make our own Manhattan Island.* I'm going to look for the very tallest and ready-est . . . Edwin! Very well, Edwin, you may come up front too. (Put that away. I don't want to speak to you again.) Edwin is going to be Manhattan Island.

" — I'm going to send you — this girl — back to your seat if you can't play your part gently. Edwin, haven't you got a hanky, dear? You should use a hanky for that.

"Again, mouse steps back and forth! Now what is it we're looking at, children in seats? What are Edwin and the four children pouring back and forth on him, showing us?"

Silence. Deep contemplation. Four answers are garnered from the room:

"Hol' hans'."

"Play house?"

"_____" (in Spanish which "elicits" big, general dirty laugh.)

"Ring-aroun'-a-rosy."

Last month, one solid month, was the Community. ". . . The Community is made up of many wonderful workers. Can anyone name a worker? No one? Surely someone knows the name of *one* kind of worker. Good, I knew you did! All right, that little boy."

"Policeman."

"Good, What does the policeman do?"

"He'p us."

"Good! *Fine! How* does he help us?"

"He our fren',"

"Yes, good but *how* is he our friend? *How* does he help us?"

Lots of trouble on this one. Much time consumed. Finally, something like "he'p a los' chil' fin' he way home," is "elicited."

"Good! *Very* good! Now let's think of some other kinds of workers. Who can name another kind of wonderful worker?"

"Policeman," answer several together.

"Yes, but still another kind! We'd have a funny kind of Community, wouldn't we, if we were *all* policemen?" Frowns, sulks, drop toward apathy again.

"Let's put on our thinking caps. *All* the kinds of wonderful workers we know. What about people who help us learn many wonderful things? What kind of workers are they?" Silence . . . "*There* goes a hand up. All right, little boy with the bandage. Can't you ask Mommy to change that bandage, dear? All right."

"Teach',"

"Good! And what good workers they are, too, your wonderful teacher here and me, and Mr. Zang and Mrs. Abernathy — how really *hard* we work, don't we?"

Fireman, Nurse, even Jim the Friendly Street Cleaner, each in turn is elicited. Then on to a cloudier side of the subject. "What about *our own parents,* who work so hard to care for us? What kind of work do *they* do?" Many children really don't know what she's talking about. A few have fallen to dreaming again. "Well, what about *our fathers*? Don't our fathers work so *very* hard, coming home at the end of day all tired but happy, too, because they've been working to earn money for our food and clothes?" This reminds them of lunch. "Good! *I* see a hand that knows the answer!" "Miss Moily, w'en bell time?"

"Quite soon, dear. Now everyone *think*. Thinking caps on tight, pulled *way* down for a cold, cold day, down to our *ears*. *What kind of work do our fathers do?*" Not six fathers in the room have jobs, as Miss Moyle might know if she kept her eyes open coming along ____ th Street in the morning. But on she goes, question, hint, probe. Finally lets it drop, provisionally.

But *someone* in our family works, or we wouldn't *be* here with our food and clothes, would we, we wouldn't have *any*thing! Who in our family works? Mommy. "But then, what does Mommy do, all day, what *kind* of work, when she goes away and doesn't come home until sunset time?" Three minutes produce two mommies who work in the garment district, one who works stringing jewelry, "Fine! *Very* good! How interesting and wonderful a talk we've had this morning, boys and girls. And now it's time for l ____ . . . for Miss Moyle to go.

"But first, Miss Moyle wants each child to do something for her. Each child is to go home and search in the newspaper tonight for a picture of a wonderful worker. Someone in our big wonderful city on Manhattan Island, who's doing some kind of work. For example: a picture of a worker in the *garment district* working: how wonderfully and carefully she's pulling her needle in and out of the cloth that will turn into trousers for a little boy or skirt for a little girl. Take notebook paper; use one side only; paste neatly just at each corner. And one more thing. How many think they can write a nice sentence, telling what the worker in the picture is working at?" (No child in this room could write a full sentence. But every hand flies up.) "Good, *good!* I knew that's what you'd like to do for Miss Moyle. And she'll be back tomorrow at eleven o'clock" — heading for the door — "to see how intelligent you are. I know we're going to have some won __"

"Miss' Zangy?"

"I'm Miss Moyle, dear"

"We don' have no newspaper." She has to return and wring this out. Magazines? No, no magazines. But surely a Spanish-language newspaper? That would be perfectly fine for a worker picture. No, no Spanish. "But then your next-door neighbor must have a newspaper he or she would gladly give you for your picture." Ignores the silence. (Some aren't sure what a neighbor is.) "Fine. How many are going to have the assignment tomorrow? Won-derful! Good morning, boys and girls."

Of today, third session on New York State, I will just say that Miss Moyle could not believe they didn't remember one fact from last week. Angel at last refused to answer. He laid his head down on his desk and went to sleep. It's because they're not interested. Angel is simply not interested — yet. "Our job is to help him be interested," says Miss Moyle. "He'll enter into situations creatively when they involve him. Learning's got to be fun."

When she'd gone, I woke Angel and we had a talk. I outlined to him his present and future in the class. He did get back his memory. And we found he was able to repeat back a dozen facts: New York State is bounded on the east by the Atlantic; the governor lives in Albany; Henry Hudson was an explorer; New York was called New Amsterdam, and so on. And this with messages winging between: Youth and Adult Center forms; Dental Control Sheet; check periodically that children are under treatment, completion date, etc.; cumulative records or transfer slips: "Be sure to enter grades in Academic Progress as well as in Personality Growth"; PTA forms; something from Mayor Wagner about registering to vote; and always the pleas or whinings: "Are we goin gym today?" "Miss Burke, when's Rumpelstilts?" and Angel sobbing in between facts, "My mudder'll get you in court for dis."

Teachers' lunchroom is empty today but for Miss Peruzzi who goes around with liberal Catholic groups, young couples who meet Friday nights in each other's apartments and wish to help the poor. And some of them do: her friends, Gerald and Susan, who drive her with her children to the country on Saturdays — people who never did things like that before. Others get lost in theory. Peruzzi is the quietest teacher in school, always thinking of what Saint Francis of Assisi wrote long ago about the poor or what Mr. Ephraimson, her supervisor, said yesterday on the same subject; or kissing her charges, trying to make up for all the ills of society. However, she's honest about where she stands ("Oh, I have a long way to go. . . . I wish the supervisor would spend more time in my room.") and a good teacher with her retarded children, who leave her in June still thinking life is magic, worth learning to read for. She also had Danny Aguilez (he kicked her in the stomach) in between Mr. Dion and Mr. Pickard, and Danny's poor mother on a bad day. Danny hung on the trembling mother's skirts, yelling "Gimme a quarter" in English and Spanish; then a policeman came in off the beat — all this in Peruzzi's room, during a class — looking for Danny. "My mind just went blank," says Peruzzi. "And I — I was trying to pray for all of them; but the words just wouldn't come."

She has the latest thing from the grapevine this noon. "Oh, Danny's not getting *out*. I don't know why Mr. Spicer implied that. In spite of that scene in your room — oh, everyone's heard about that! What was it? Was he trying to kill children? Really, you'd think that *now* they'd — but no, Danny's staying. Skally's going to take him. She made a deal with the office — she gets to teach that top sixth next year, she takes Danny now."

I take a sip of coffee, then it occurs to me, "Skally's quite good but she'll only teach bright children, not retarded in any way. Danny's a bit emotionally retarded, wouldn't you say? She tried to trade a kid in her room with me for

Roderigo when I first came here — she'd give me Israel as a throw-in. Roderigo is an artist. She shops around for a nice room. But wait a minute, what's wrong with the way Al's teaching top sixth now — what are they doing with Al?"

"Well, I suppose they'll do something else with Al," says Miss Peruzzi, who doesn't like to go into things too deeply. "I guess they think if she keeps Danny more than six weeks she *should* get a top class, sort of a strength prize."

"And he is going to sit here another semester, getting sicker?"

"Well, Skally will probably leave him out in the hall a lot," says Miss Peruzzi simply. And being a New Yorker at home with economic facts, she adds, "I think Skally's going to teach in the afternoon study center next term — know what I mean?" Which explains things a bit more. For that is the latest plum at P.S. 200 — eleven dollars a night from 3 to 5 P.M., teaching children phonics and the reading they didn't learn during the day. Peruzzi adds "Gee . . . that eleven dollars is a temptation. But Eineman wouldn't, I wouldn't. I mean, you're too tired, if you've had these kids all day." But here Peruzzi has gone far enough. She takes out some red grapes and begins to peel them, then inserts them dreamily, one by one, between her white teeth.

A special new sound is now rising from the far end of the building, a sort of low distant humming. Traffic boy Jose Cardona, age eleven, a fat, intellectual boy with solemn smile, appears in the door. He jerks his chin at the corridor: "Gonna be bad today, Miss Burke, Miss Peruzzi, due to the rain. Lotta subs. Get ready."

Peruzzi says across the table, "Let's see the hands, José," and he holds up beautiful, small hands that are so dirty that even washing (I've stood over him while he's washed them) doesn't get the dirt out of the cracks. Every line in the palms is etched in dirt. She had José in second grade, when he first came out of a long stay in Bellevue. She never found out why — he is as easy-going, always talking and chatting with you, as he is alienated — she heard he set things on fire in buildings. He thinks the worst of himself. "I don't get along with kids good," he says. "Oh, listen:" (spittle at his lips) "I'm not goin in the class for two days. The kids are layin low for me." This is not true; the children respect him, but he has few friends. Mrs. Bergens has him in sixth grade now, and sometimes he comes in with a note to me from her about coffee at four. I'll see him washing his hands in the drinking fountain in the corridor before he enters. Loves to stand around interrogating the children while I answer the note. "What book are you reading, children? — Hey, that's all? Primer level in this class?" "Yes, José, unfortunately it's all they can read." "Well, let's play something," he calls out. "Give me the names of two great American writers after 1850 . . . name two works by Mark Twain."

Once, José gave me the names of books that Enrico Fermi had in his library. He pulled a piece of paper out of his shirt pocket, which turned out to be a pajama top — a formula of Fermi's, could I explain it? Once, last term, I went with Mrs. Eineman to his home. She wanted to take him some tangerines. There had been some problem; she was told to send down his class folder, but she could never find out why. In his home he told her, "Oh, I got a home teacher now since I've been in Bellevue. I don't get along with children; you know that, Mrs. Eineman." "That's ridiculous. Who told you that?" He was spending the week-end with his mother and baby sister that day we visited him, in a flat whose walls were a grim but blinding steel blue. We'd walked in on a family quarrel. José had sneaked home to see his family, then refused to go, while his mother pleaded. It was pouring rain outside. He was soaked to the skin — had on pajamas under a leaky raincoat and wouldn't take the raincoat off. He'd say, "Hey, Mom, you know what a pinwheel is? It's an optical illusion if you paint it different colors." "Your're supposed to be at Gramma," she would tell him. "No room here." He kept laughing, crying, and refusing to leave. The ninety-pound mother repeated. "No room José, you a big boy. You must go to Mama." "Listen to that mother of mine, Mrs. Eineman. Hey, what do you think about this hair my sister's got herself?" he laughed, picking up a handful of one child's flaming red hair. "Wild, isn't it? I'll never forget this hair."

"Well, come on, read us the news, José," Miss Peruzzi tells him now and hands him a *Times*. He begins with dramatic pauses, "Heroic Major Gordon Cooper, conqueror of space — oh hey. Listen to that! Must get back to my post!" The distant drone is changing key — an intent muttering now, drawing closer. It's the approach of hundreds of children's feet. It detaches itself suddenly from any organ of sound and bursts into a free rumbling roar.

Lunch cook, a huge Negro woman with arms and hands like oars, materializes at the door to the children's lunchroom. Next to her, Burns, an aide, in the green tam. Only the toughest teachers will take lunchroom duty and few do — even though if you do, you're given a smaller class. The last child to call Burns a fucking bitch will not do so soon again. Burns has lately been put on guard duty and taken on trips. She said, "I went with 'em to that soap factory, but none of 'um knew the capital of New York." Cook is now swinging to and locking the door, so that only a single line can cram through and hurl itself on the food. The roar is rising — claps and crashes mingling into it — they're rounding the stairways. It mounts to a great wave of sound and breaks, lunging with a rush through the gym doors! Cardona disappears; a moment later his traffic badge flings up over the small rushing bodies. "Get back! Get back!" Burns is booming. One great arm becomes a bar to the half-door, the other she uses to encircle with a single flowing movement children who thrash or kick. Does something to the nerve in each child's arm — pinches or deadens it. You can tell it all the way from here — you can hear the yipes and even make out hungry faces bellowing up at her.

We salvage Cardona, help him find his badge and glasses, then for the next few minutes Peruzzi and I chat in low voices under the roar. Between us and the children lies the gym floor decked with basketballs.[1]

---

[1]Health class has been playing all morning directed by Mr. Zoller, who can't make them put the balls away, and this is our school in a nutshell. This month at practically any minute of the day you can find health classes playing ball in the gym, or the second grade

The noise going on behind the closed metal doors of the children's lunchroom is indescribable. Just to give an idea: it takes thirty minutes to feed most of 1200 children. Once fed, they're channeled out the other end onto the street. When Peruzzi and I walk through today, it's empty but a shambles. Only "slow eaters" — fifty or so — are still at tables covered with pools of slopped or hurled pineapple juice, some bloodied. Untouched liverwurst sandwiches are stomped onto the floor, some wrapped in wax paper and never opened. Smashed hard-boiled eggs, puddles of vegetable soup, quarter-oranges trampled into garbage. Sandwiches with holes in them (spit-through-the-hole game), sandwiches packed into baseballs. The slow eaters we pass are small or weak children whose first tray was torn from them. A few are hungry children who'll eat what they do not like. But few will eat carefully these well-balanced meals served to them each day; eight hundred or more, free of charge. "I can't eat sausage; I can't eat dark bread." "I ain't eatin this. I only eat beans, rice, and bananas." "I gonna puke." "My mother lets me drink coffee at home, so why do I have to drink milk here?" Milk once served, opened or not, must be poured out or drunk under the attendants' eyes. It's against the rule to tell a child not to take milk if he won't drink it. All uneaten food, touched or not, must be tossed into garbage cans under attendants' eyes. To exit, you must be in the garbage line. Many children take the tray and dump it without sitting down.

Women at the food end of the room are lugging the giant garbage cans, two women to a can, to the alley doors. Every day when the sanitation trucks have come to pick up, the rows of cans are Lysolized, hosed down, and polished by Puerto Rican women until they shine like silver. In the alley, we pass the first ten: loaded with sandwiches, eggs with one end ripped off, oranges, that taken from P.S. 200 alone would feed fifty people a day. One great can is flowing to the brim with milk. The children tear open the cartons, sip or spit the milk at one another. But they must pour away whatever's left.

Office notices: Last week of the Book Fair. Teaching Career Month. Pan-American Day. "Boys and Girls of Other Lands Week." From the Bureau of In-Service Training: Remember to file applications for salary differentials.

Teachers gathering again. "Sure, it's worth it if you care about culture at all. . . . You get your group of ten or more, group discount —" "Barbra Streisand?" "Yeah, but I don't know, I thought she'd be better than she was. . . . No, no, she's great — I just though she'd be better, that's all." ". . . down to Florida over Easter, but could we keep a sun tan more than a week back here? I hear those Florida tans —" "Oh I knew a kid in college kept a real even deep tan year round, she'd just fly down to Florida in vacation and keep it

---

dancing. Last month, in contrast, there were so many meetings – teachers' interest committees, meetings about what door the children would come in, Higher Horizons meetings, Teachers' Luncheon, pinata parties – so much frolicking of every kind going on, the gym had to be locked off for two weeks.

up with a sunlamp." "Yeah, but I have a funny kind of skin." Mrs. Moss found someone for lunch, though it was only Mrs. Rudge.

Moss: Mar-velous Picasso show on Fifty-seventh. I was fortunate enough to go with a very dear old friend of mine; it was an emotional catharsis. I love Picasso; if they were showing Picasso in Jersey, I'd go to Jersey; if Brooklyn, Brooklyn, but I will say frankly —
Rudge: Yeah, I don't blame you, you feel that way about it.
Moss: Well, what do you feel? About Picasso?
Rudge: Well, I like Picasso, sure, but —
Moss: Like? That's no way to talk about Picasso. Listen, I've always been interested in the arts —
Rudge: Yeah, I can see your point. I don't blame you.

Mrs. Feldman, a former teacher, now a supervisor, has been waiting at my mailbox. I was trying to see Zang again. She is deeply distressed that I'm not going to Europe this summer. Can she be of assistance in obtaining a bank loan? "If you *are* setting forth to that matchless continent, there is a certain aggregate that is entailed. . . ." In this same manner Mrs. Feldman addresses the fourth grade if she enters my room. The children stare at her elegant blue-tinted hair; they listen to the low melodic voice that seems to them to come from some long-ago fairyland: ". . . to grow up in the United States, to devolve from childish idleness into the heritage of thoughtful citizenship, we must apply ourselves diligently, boys and girls, through childhood as at every other period, to the problems at hand. I do not expect, boys and girls, when next I may have reason to enter this room, to see confusion and chaos. . . ."

Juan Gonzales and Peter Quinn*

Edited by Charlotte Leon Mayerson

JUAN GONZALES

I think about what I should do when I get out of school, and I just don't know. The people in my neighborhood, in Harlem, or downtown, they're all doing it wrong. And if one tries to get out, the rest laughs. Like they say that they tried and couldn't do it, so you're not going to do it either. And this guy feels, "Well, maybe I can't do it," and he comes back into the slum. You figure, you know, they failed, man, I might as well give up.

I mean, even someone like Adam Clayton. O.K., maybe he studied as a child. I guess to be a Congressman, it doesn't matter how much money you got, you got to be doing your stuff. But maybe that money his father had, helped him, because maybe his father gave him special things. You know, private school, things like this. Or maybe he never once had even to *go* to a slum area.

And that's the thing that gives a feeling of inferior. It tells a person that no matter how hard they try, they can't get out. That's the whole thing right there. I mean a rich person wouldn't have to go around mugging people, or robbing them. The trouble really is down at Harlem, because Harlem is a place where you don't get anything of anything. That's where, like you used to live when you didn't have nothing. And until you get something, you'll never get out of that place.

If I could start fresh, do anything in the world, I would like to live in a place where it wouldn't be crowded, where it wouldn't have 20 million people walking up and down the street. I don't like living in the city, I want to live in the country. I think when people are further away from each other they can have more peace. When you're crowded in like this, you're worried. You're worried that your child's going out into the street and he's going to get killed.

Living in a project, we can't do anything; it's not ours. With all of this, if you have a house in the country, that's your own. You have it for yourself. You have enough to keep you happy. You have enough food there and enough good food to get by. You could be out there feeling free and gay.

Two Blocks Apart; The Stories of Juan Gonzales and Peter Quinn. Edited by Charlotte Leon Mayerson. New York: Holt, Rinehart & Winston, 1965. (Published as Avon Book)

I mean you would be free. You would know that you're not in any political strife, that you have no segregated problem. I am alone and I am enjoying it. Because you don't want to be bothered with these problems, you don't want to be bothered like crossing the street, or walking somebody else's turf. You don't want to be bothered by anything. You just want to be left alone. Maybe a couple of people you'd like around — out there by myself with a couple of friends, maybe a girl, you still have enough fun with each other. You get along.

But when you put all the people up together under one roof, they just don't get along. They dispute and argue. If you could move wherever you want, and if there was no money and nobody to bother you, I would build my house in a nice spot in the country in the shade of the trees. You know everybody thinks of a paradise for themselves and I think that's mine.

But I know I could never have it. First, it costs too much and I don't have any money; and two, I don't think there's a place in the world where you can go and be alone and you can get away from all the troubles in the world.

I like a couple of friends, for company, but there's really nobody, like, you could say I look up to, I admire, in this world. Only Napoleon, or Hitler. Not so much because of what they did, but I admire the way they came to power. I admire the way they got their power. Just think of Napoleon, this small guy you have there, everbody around is real tall, real important, and this guy says he's taking over. Think of it. He's just a corporal and he took over the government. That's what I admire. I admire a person who, when he wants something, he goes after it. Me, I don't do it. I don't do it.

Of course what Hitler did was wrong, killing everybody, destroying people. But you saw what he could do, how he constructed the army and things like that. If he could have done that, why didn't he use his power to create good things? He wouldn't have to go out and kill everybody else so that then they could be best, because his people were the only ones alive. He could have done something to keep his people best fit. Or he could have created a paradise out of Germany because of the way the people followed him. He took over so quickly, he so arranged it, that the people were willing to do anything for him and when you have people like this, you have to use them. You don't put them into weapons. You give some people weapons, they go out and kill every Jewish, or they go out and kill every Negro. I would try something else, to construct something, if I was in power, like Hitler.

But I really think he was right on one point; that you can't trust the people with power. Here in the United States you can't tell the people who are not educated to take over the government, because look what they'll do with it. They'll just make so much turbulence and destruction that you're going to find yourself without a government, without any kind of nation. Like even now, the people don't know which way they're going. The Puerto Ricans and coloreds don't know, the whites don't know. Say you see two boys fighting or yelling at a movie or something like that. People don't even have to turn around. They say, "Oh, well, that's the Puerto Ricans or the Negroes."

Well, if I'm sitting next to them, I kind of feel sad. I mean, how can you blame *them*? How can you blame *everything*? You can't blame everything on Puerto Ricans and Negroes. Well, the Puerto Rican or colored kid they blame it on wrong, they punish, they get even. He doesn't go out and beat up another kind of kid. He comes and he beats up a Puerto Rican or a colored kid just like himself. They don't have any reason. It's just because they're looking at themselves, sort of like a mirror of themselves. They want to take it out on themselves, being colored, so they go out and hurt somebody just like themselves.

I mean they can't help it. They're stuck. I'm not accusing the whole group of whites. But you take a couple of whites and anything that happens to them, their house can be robbed, or their daughters can be raped, or their sons can be beat up, and they won't ever bother to ask the police who did it. Right away, they say it was a Puerto Rican or Negro.

The trouble is a lot of times they're right. But what do they think? The Puerto Ricans and the Negroes have to get even for what this man does to them, they have to resort to violence. If the white man likes to see a picture in the movies, they start rioting in the movies. To get even. They want their rights, and if the white man is stopping them, they are going to make sure that white man moves aside, so they can get by. It doesn't have to be the same white person that did one thing; it just has to be the same kind of person — white — and they want to make him suffer.

Then, the other side, the white man, he's got to hold off these groups, and it's pretty hard for him. So, since he has the law on his side and everying else, he uses it against them. The thing begins again.

Like of all the Negroes and Puerto Ricans I know, none of them know any whites except social workers. And a real tough guy, he wouldn't go near the social worker. Because he'd feel that he is going to be changed, and he doesn't want to be changed. He wants to be able to be the same way he is, so he can tackle the world.

Then there's another kind of kid, like a boy in our building, about ten or eleven years old. He walks around with those boys from the other houses, kidding around in the park with them, and he *thinks* like them. But when he comes to our side, he thinks like us. His father and mother, they taught this boy everything. You know that he used to be able to read an *encyclopedia* at the age of nine? He could pick up an encyclopedia and read it through with no problem. But the trouble is, the parents don't want him to be around us, or with the rest of the people in our building. They want him to go over to the other side.

In a way they're doing right, and in a way they're doing wrong. When you think of it, why should he stay on our side when it's really better for him to stay on the other side? I mean, he's very intelligent. What can he do with our groups that don't even know how to spell all the words he pronounces?

And the other thing, there's a lot of boys in my building that are like animals. When they start playing around, they aim to hurt you. And that boy, he's not that strong or that big. He can get hurt very easily. He should stay on the other side where the boys play silly games. The little games that they play, we've grown them out. We never play them since we were very little. You know that they have those big parks near our house? Even so, you know where those boys play? They don't go near those big parks, they play out against the buildings. And why? I would say they would play there like the little kids because they can't go across the street to our neighborhood. They think it's dangerous for them.

Ah – it is. They'd probably get beat up. Maybe if a boy is alone from across the street? They might stop him and ask him for a nickel or dime. And if they found he had it, they'd take the money from him and beat him up before they'd let him go, whether he had money or not.

I don't believe in that, to take money from a little boy. They used to do that to me a lot, you know. I was smaller at P.S. 305, the boys from 96 would come over and take all the money the little kids had, but I had a couple of fights and they started laying off. I never did it because I can't look into a little kid's eyes and ask for his money because I could feel him shivering and I don't like it.

But I don't know any boys from those big houses. As long as I'm living here, all the boys over there have been going to private schools and they're very snotty. They think they're way superior. They can't show it by a fight because they lose. They never fought, you know; they always had it easy. But if we went to the same school; they would show it. If I didn't have the answers to a question and I was wondering how to do a problem, Paddy boy wouldn't tell it. He would tell you, "Well, you're stupid. You don't know."

But we fix them up. We do the same thing they did to us. For once, we had something that they wanted and we wouldn't give it to them. Like questions, you know, girls' phone numbers, or to teach them how to fight, or how to make out. Things like that. They never had any girls. Those kids around there, they're locked up like in solitary. They don't even know what girls look like. Their mothers don't want them to get it because then, they will know. They want to get that little boy of theirs into a good family. They don't want to let him go around with the trash downstairs. I know that, but the boy, you know, he wants it. He still feels lonely, he wants to go around, wants to meet some of the girls.

And then you know something, the girls really go for him because he's different. At the same time some of them are disgusted with him, it depends. Like some girls that we introduced this one boy to, they generally went head over heels with him. But as soon as they heard him talk, they all walked away. Because he's snotty. He tries to make himself bigger than he really is. And it doesn't make sense. He's a nice-looking kid all right, but he should just keep it like that. As soon as he talks, he starts with the feeling, "I got more money than you have."

That's one good thing about it, I mean about the way things are with us. I get freedom, a lot more freedom than those other kids who live near us. If I want something, my parents will give it to me if they can. But if they can't give it to me, they know it's not going to kill me. Whereas with *those* boys, their parents would give him all kinds of different arguments on why they shouldn't have it.

Or another thing. I could go out any time of night, you know, if I felt up to it. I'm pretty sure that one of the boys in those houses couldn't go out as late as I could. Their parents think up excuses instead of just saying no. They want to tell the boy why he shouldn't go.

Let's say it's Friday night about nine o'clock, and I get all dressed up, and I say, "I'm going out to a dance," or to someplace like that.

This boy, if he was going, they would say, "Where are you going? How far is it away? How long are you going to stay away? Who are you going with? What are you going to do there? Are there gangs there? Bad girls?" And they might tell him when to come home, they might tell him not to drink. He wouldn't be able to do almost anything I would.

That boy, he doesn't go out much because they are not sure of him. They don't know what he is going to do outside. They are always walking with him. He has a lot of protection from his parents and then, when he is away from them, he doesn't know how to handle himself. I usually go all the time away from my parents and I do pretty well.

The way I see it, right now, I think I have it better than that other one. But when I was small, then he had it, and when I get *older,* he will have it still better. He will have a better education. He will have a better atmosphere.

Like I wouldn't be able to go to a rich night club, or hire a night-club singer, or have a good career. He might turn out to be a lawyer or a doctor or something, whereas I could only be maybe a mechanic or a machinist. I might make money, but I won't make the same kind of money he makes.

Even so, with the people that live in those houses, the parents tell their kids right from wrong, so the boy never knows right from wrong until he goes out into the world himself.

But with me, my mother always had affection, more affection than I think the women in that building. They just smother their kids. They make them like the Mama's boy. They say, "Well, don't go out too far. Be careful. Come back soon. Don't make me worry." So the boy might even be sixteen, seventeen, and he is still worrying about his mother. He still is hanging around her. Just taking all he can get. Not on his own, still living off his mother.

And about girls? With us, if a girl developed at twelve or thirteen years old, she was made. That's about the age. There were no girls belonging to the gang, but when a boy met a girl, she went around with other girls and the boys would know all of them. That's how we got around. We'd see each other like at private parties, something like that. Most of the time there were no adults around, and some of the boys would bring along something to get it going. Kids would be drinking and they'd go wild. At fifteen, I was something like what you would call one of those lovers. I was always walking around with the girls. That was the most exciting.

Sometimes I'd go to those Latin dances and sometimes I'd go to the dances at St. Mary's. I went there instead of Holy Family because I don't like that church or anything about it because of the priest there who did me. Even so, even at St. Mary's most every time there's troubles, fights. I mean, you know, you go over to dance with this girl you think is alone and the guy that brought her doesn't like it. Sometimes you push this one guy and you find out that he brought his whole gang with him. Your friends are not going to let you get beat up and disgrace the neighborhood. I mean, are you going to let this little gang beat you? Here you fought so many times?

Sometimes there are a couple of priests at a dance, but mostly there are men and women who are just watching out. When a fight breaks out, they get out of the way. At first, they tried to stop it, but I mean how could you stop it? Everybody is in a gang. That's how come they usually went to these places. Some went to fight, some went to drink, some went to find sex, others just went to see what was going on. Mostly, what turned out were fights, sex, and drinking.

Some guys went in couples, but I could never see myself bringing a girl there because you'd probably lose her halfway through the dance, you know. You had to be watching this guy wasn't fooling around with your girl while he was dancing with her, things like that.

I don't think the priests know how much goes on, and if they do know, they keep it quiet. If it got out in the papers or somewhere, they'd put up such a fight. They'd say, "No, no, it never happened." Because nobody wants to discredit the Church.

Except me. I don't care any more. My mother was Catholic, but she got divorced and remarried, so they took her off the Catholic religion. She still cries about it sometimes, even though she goes to some other place now that has all religions in it. Whereas I won't go to any of them, I wouldn't go near a church.

My brother used to go, too, but now he's got the same ideas as I do. All of a sudden I thought it was so meaningless. You know? It was nothing there. My mother says that I should go, but I tell her I believe in myself and I believe that there's a Supreme Being and that if anything goes wrong it's because He wants it to go wrong. Nothing else.

I can't help what life is, I can only live it. Going to church is not going to do anything for me because there's thousands of people who go to church and they all come out cursing and believing in all kinds of sinful things. Some people, they could be in there praying for years and they come out of church and they get run over by a car.

Then, something happened that really made me see it. My house was robbed and the boys that were robbing, they were all caught. There was a lot of money stolen and everything, but the parents of these boys, they went to the church and they said, "Father, please help us out. Get our children out of jail." So that priest went and he swore on the Holy Bible that these boys went to confession every week and they went to church every day, that they were holy and that anything that they were supposed to have done just wasn't true.

So, on the word of that priest, those guys were released. I went to see him. I went to confession and I went to see him, but you know, I didn't say anything. I just walked into the booth. I didn't even get down. I looked right at him and I asked him if he believed in God and he told me he did. Then he said, "Do you believe in God? That's the question."

I answered him, I told him, "I don't believe in God as long as you are a priest."

Then I went on and I told him everything, that he let some boys out of prison on false evidence and on false pretense. Those boys never went to church because I went to church and I never saw any of them. And because of him, who is never supposed to lie, they got away with it and they're probably going to hold up somebody else.

I said . . . right there in the confession booth I told him, "You lost yourself a customer. I'm never coming back here again. Because if *you* believe in God, *I* can't believe in God."

Oh, I used to believe in the Church. When I was a little boy I believed that when I did something wrong, the Church could cure anything. You know, by going to church and by praying to God, everything would be all right. It never turned out that way. It was always the same thing when I came out. Always lousy, always trouble.

Now I'm not going to bend to anybody's will. Now I see that when you pray, you're praying because you're scared, you're scared of what's going to happen, and you're scared of stopping from praying because you're afraid that the Lord might come down and strike you with a bolt of lightning or something. I feel really sorry for my mother in all this, her getting kicked out for remarrying, but I'm not going to go anyhow. I haven't gone at Easter and I guess that lets me out for them, too. My mother doesn't like it, but she doesn't like a lot of things.

Another thing that gives her worry with me is that she has a sort of pride about Puerto Ricans. When I first started talking English at home, my mother said, "You speak English outside, you talk Spanish in here!"

Well I spoke Spanish and English, and I had it all mixed up. It got so I couldn't talk either one. Finally, I just kept talking English and after a while she got used to it.

My mother called me an American. She says that first you've got to be loyal to your own race, and then to Americans. But I was practically *born* here, you know, so why can't I be an American? An American Puerto Rican?

Then, I don't go with Spanish girls much and she gets mad about that. I've got to say the truth about it. I don't tell her, but I like white girls better. White girls. I mean, did you ever see a Puerto Rican girl walk and talk? She looks like tomorrow the world is going to end and I better hurry home. But a white girl? She walks real slow. So slow.

I have Puerto Rican girl friends sometimes, but they are too old-fashioned. I mean, it's hard to say. See, like I have a sister. She's Puerto Rican, I'm Puerto Rican. But she's sort of like pure Puerto Rican. Her Puerto Rican ways are like from the old country. She believes the husband is ruler, that mostly what he says goes. She doesn't think she has to go to school, she only has to be a good housewife. Maybe, if I had a special kind of girl, I think a special kind of white girl, she wouldn't think so much about all that, she wouldn't think only about boyfriends. Maybe she'd talk about school, or politics, or some of that.

And that's what I want. Now, I want more. Oh, when I was thirteen, fourteen, all I wanted was to jump in a hall or behind the stairs and get from some girl what I wanted. Now, that's not it. I mean, if all you do is go outside and make love with a girl, you're not going to be interested for long. You can get anybody for that.

See, I'm not rich I'm limited. But what I want is another kind of action.

Sometimes, I've been hanging around for a couple of weeks, and I get tired of nothing. Then, I get some work here and there, and maybe my father will give me a pound (a five-dollar bill) and then I take that money and I hit the night life. I like to see how the other kind behaves, what makes them different.

Take eating. You know a Puerto Rican eats practically all he can eat with his hands. Most of them do that. And when they eat with their forks, they don't know how to hold it. And dressing? Some Puerto Ricans like to dress up, too. But they don't have the same atmosphere. I mean, I *am* a Puerto Rican, and I dress like a Puerto Rican, because, I mean, there's no change. But – well – I guess I like the other style.

I guess I'd like to be like white people a little more than a Puerto Rican, although I am Puerto Rican. Not so much because they're different, it's because the Puerto Ricans have not learned this way yet. I mean they're still the same way. Whereas the whites, they have everything, so they can civilize themselves.

Sometimes I think it's the Puerto Ricans' own fault. Because I try to improve myself and, I mean, if I can try, they can do it, too.

I mean, the whole thing's mixed up. One time I think the Puerto Ricans don't ever get a chance to do anything. The Puerto Ricans and the coloreds, they're just stuck. Another time, I say, why don't they help themselves?

Me, I'm Puerto Rican, colored, and I'm not going to turn my back on that, but if you ask me, if I could say, "Which would you rather be?" Well, I mean, you've got to face it. I mean anybody would. If you ask me, which I'd rather be, well, man, I'd rather be white.

PETER QUINN

The one thing I'd like is to be finished with college and have all that worry behind me — all the difficulty of whether I'm going to get in, how my marks are going to be and all that over with. I'd like to be settled down in a good job with enough money to buy all the necessities and some luxuries. The thing I'd like is a lot of clothes, an awful lot of clothes. I love buying clothes. Then I'd buy a car if I were old enough and a house of my own and, of course, a dog. I see myself in a life with a lot of friends around me and a good family.

You look around and you see that there are some people who've made it and some who are certainly going to. Like my best friend has that kind of character. I don't know how to explain the way he is, but he is a very determined kind of person. Once he starts something, he can't put it down until he finishes it, and even though he is a lot of fun to be with, he really pays attention and works hard on what he is doing. Of course, like all my other friends, he wants to go to college. That's the important thing to us and to our families.

I admire my friend John, but the person in the world I admire most is my brother. I really think he's great. He's twenty-six and he's all set for life. He's got an answer for everything, for everything about life. He's got a good job, good standing in the community, a nice house, a beautiful car. My brother has everything he needs and he's got a wonderful personality, too. The thing about him is that he's very smart, but, more than that, he can handle difficult things. Nothing comes up in his life that my brother doesn't know the answer for and doesn't know how to take care of.

My mother would like to see my brother married and starting a family, but he wants to wait awhile. I think he's right, that twenty-seven or twenty-eight is a good time to get married. I see myself with two or three children whom I can take care of financially, physically, and in every way. And the kind of girl I'd want to marry would be well-mannered, respectable, and good-looking, with a good personality. The important thing is to have a refined girl who knows how to speak, act. My sister is like that. She might have come from any very wealthy home.

Then, after I'm settled, I never want to live anywhere but in New York. My father says that San Francisco is a great collection of the most comfortable people he has ever seen in his life. He says that there are very few poor people there and it's a wonderful city because of that, and almost as good as New York in other respects. Of course, he likes New York better and I really don't see moving myself, certainly not to the suburbs, where I'd have to travel back and forth all the time.

If I had enough money, I'd have a good house or apartment here in New York and a place in the country. I wouldn't like to have too much money, and if I did, I'd get rid of it through charities and that kind of thing. I guess I'd live pretty much like my parents do.

Then, I would bring my children up pretty much the way I've been brought up. I would protect them also in the same way that I've been protected. I know that kids like that bunch we nearly had a fight with think that we are over-protected, that we don't have as much freedom as they do. And it's true that my parents do protect me, and, in a sense, they always will protect me. They ask when I leave the house where I am going, when I am going to be back, whom I am going with. If they don't like where I am going. I don't go. I stay home.

But that's all. I am not in prison. I am free. I have my own life. They don't butt in, they help. I know that when they ask these questions or keep me from going certain places or doing certain things it's because they care for me — because they love me, and I'm grateful for that and I understand why.

A boy like those others isn't any more courageous than I would be in that situation. I mean if suddenly I were as poor as he is — all of a sudden in his situation — I would be terrified. But I would be able to work up to it and bear it as much as he can if I had the time to adjust to it. Then, I am not afraid to go out, to go wherever I like. I go out, I meet my friends, and we have a good time.

And we're not afraid of the girls, the way they think. We have a lot of fun with them. Nice times, nice relationships. Now I don't think that a boy who has sex experiences when he's very young is going to be hurt by it. But I think that he is really too young and he should really be waiting. Then it's not as if that's the only way to get kicks out of life. In my family and with my friends, we're always laughing, always horsing around, having fun. More than they do, really.

Then, I think they grow up faster, but by the time we're all grown, most of us will have learned to take care of ourselves better. Just through experience we'll have learned ways of backing out, of picking the smartest way, the safest way to handle things. Even now, they're only braver than us because they've got a knife or a chain in their pocket. We don't lead a sheltered life at all. We lead a very well-backgrounded life. A better life, with a wider span of knowledge. I mean not only at school, but in all of life. In the rest of the city outside of this little neighborhood, we learn what to do with different problems that come up. I mean not all problems are fight problems — those, they can take care of better.

For example, if anything ever came up with the police, like the time my friend had trouble at the luncheonette, we could handle ourselves much better than they can. I know exactly what a policeman can do and what he can't do. The police see that and they leave us alone. More than that, the rest of the world respects us.

Then, the truth is, that the two Puerto Rican boys in our group aren't like that, or the couple of colored boys in our school. Even though their parents have to struggle to keep up with the tuition, they are just like us about fighting and knowing what's important. One of the Puerto Rican boys has a father who is even worse than mine as far as being strict goes. He watches his son's grades, he watches his homework, he watches everything his son does. He has a Spanish name and he can hardly speak English and his wife can't speak at all, but he's a very smart man and he's decided that his boy is going to get in some college and that's all he thinks about. He is thinking ahead. Any time that boy gets a bad mark, he can't go out for a week.

Then, that boy in our gang who is a Puerto Rican is very Ivy League. Really, the way he dresses, and the way he acts, and everything. He is really a lot of fun to be with, and he is a very nice guy. He brought a Puerto Rican girl to the last dance we had and she was very nice, too. She got along well with the other girls, was talking to them and doing well. She was quiet and she had good diction and was tall and beautiful. That boy goes to a good school and so does she, and it showed.

I think that if I knew some Puerto Rican girl like her, who was so refined and spoke so well, I might want to date her. I haven't done that yet and I'm not sure what my family would say. I'm really not. I think they'd leave it up to me and say, "If you really like her . . ." or something like that. But I've never done it.

There is a minority of those people who have those ideas and their kids are going to do better. The important thing is to give them the opportunity to get an education. You can't expect the Negro to be a sophisticated person without that. Like those awful people down South. I really can't stand them. Their leaders, they're really dumb men. They're white, but they *know* that the Negro is no good, that he is an animal. I think that those white men are really afraid of Negroes. They're afraid they're going to get together and rise up against the whites.

That's the trouble with all these demonstrations. There isn't any real segregation problem here in New York. Just from the neighborhood around where I live, I see there is almost none. But when you have all these demonstrations and all this tension, I think that the Negroes and the Puerto Ricans are really ruining their own chances. Everybody is fed up with all the demonstrations. I don't think its a good way to go about it. When they first started out, I thought it was a good idea, but now I see it's doing nothing; it's just hualing more police out, that's all.

I think that Negroes and Puerto Ricans realize that they're not getting all they should, and they want it bad enough, but they don't know how to get it. It's taking too long. It should have happened long ago for the Negroes, except they started out being considered slaves and that's hard to shake off. Puerto Ricans, they're a hard-working people if they have a good education, but I don't see any opportunity for them to get it because they're born on filthy streets, in rat-infested tenements and then they go to bad schools. For example, if they were put in a hard school, the kind that I've gone to, in first grade, I think they might learn to work hard and be trained in the right way. But if you put that kind of boy in a school like mine, right now, he wouldn't do anything.

The kind of schools that Puerto Rican and colored boys my age go to are much too easy. The kids make their own time, do what they want. The teachers can't do anything with them. They can give them homework, but the children can't be kept after school. They can't get punishment assignments overnight and they can't be hit. The teachers have no way to control them. They try to frighten them by failing them, but the boys don't care if they fail because they're not looking forward to college.

I don't know what they're looking forward to. I don't know. I've tried to figure it out when they sit on the stoops all day long, and I don't know. All summer you see them. What are they looking forward to?

I think it will take a long time, an awful long time for these people to pick themselves up. It's taking too long for it to work. Their whole life is fight. They're interested in building up a reputation and in a way it's the same thing as when the Irish came over. They were exactly the same way. But they knew how to go about it better. These people just don't understand what's going on, they don't really know.

For example, take all the exictement in New York about bussing children to school. I think it's just a lot of noise. I couldn't be bothered with this. I mean you see a picture of a mother crying over a child and it looks like a very good argument. But there is absolutely nothing wrong when a kid walks out of his house and walks into the school bus and is driven home. It's true he goes into a different neighborhood, but he doesn't get out of the bus five blocks away from the school. He gets out right at the door. It's the same for the whites and for the Negroes who are fighting that. I don't see anything wrong with it. I don't see why they fight it. In my neighborhood kids go on buses to private schools from the time they're in kindergarten.

Another example of using the wrong tactics was the riot they had in Harlem and other places around the country. I suppose there were some people, maybe a good proportion of them, that were really rioting because of what they feel about segregation. But I would say that very many were really out to get some loot. I was told a story that a CORE leader was saying that white people were looting and taking things. Then the day after, in the papers, there was a picture of a colored man in a full-length mink coat, a pocketbook, eight watches, carrying a bowling ball. Right there out on the street. When I see that, I know they're not rioting because of racial tension. I think they just want to get some loot.

I don't believe that even the incident that touched it off was legitimate. I kept saying to myself, if a colored man was a policeman, and he was on a street where troublemakers were, and a white boy came up to him carrying a knife, he wouldn't just stand there, he wouldn't just wait to be run through. I just couldn't see that. Because a whip, like that boy that was shot, was going wild and I know that if I were that policeman, I would have shot. Colored or no colored. I believe that the policeman shot for his hand and when the boy kept coming the policeman kept shooting. That's my feeling about it.

I'm against all this violence, against people like Malcolm X because if he says violence is what is going to beat the white man, he is not going to get anywhere. Because whether they are rioting in Harlem or in Rochester or anyplace else, they are just destroying themselves, because it's ruining their chances.

I think there's almost no discrimination in New York. Maybe some of the unions discriminate, but almost anywhere else in New York there are equal rights. I think that the trouble is that there is a real hate for the white man. A real hidden hate.

For example, Negroes can live anywhere they like in New York. I would feel terrible if a bum, a white bum, came to live in our apartment house with his family. I mean I wouldn't want a drunk or anyone who's noisy or ill-mannered to live there. I wouldn't want him, no matter what his color was. But if there were a respectable colored man, with a respectable family, I'd take him for sure. I don't think I'd even mind if there were seventeen or eighteen colored families in the building.

Maybe some of the older families, the older people in the building, would cause some trouble. But it would be some insignificant something which everyone would get over after a while. It would work out after a while. It would just take a little time.

But if I had my own method and I had enough power, I would have every child who said he was discriminated against put into a school, a good private school, if I had enough money. I'd put him in a school, I'd give him a great education and give him a background and a good home. Then he couldn't say that he was discriminated against and I'd show the rest of the people that there's nothing wrong with him. The white people could see that he was well backgrounded and a sophisticated person. All I can say is that someone who is respectable and refined and sophisticated is welcome in my house.

The important thing is the way parents are toward their children. How the parents care for their children, for their children's recreation, schools, what the parents do to help their child is the only thing that matters. I think that colored children have almost no help from their parents. They're not freerer than we are, they're in a real prison. They have to be taught everything in school because at home they learn nothing. I mean they have to be taught words like "good," simple things.

As for the parents, all they are interested in is whether the teachers discriminate aginst their children, whether they could get anything on the teacher for hurting their pride. They don't value education, because they never had any education themselves and they don't know what it's like. They don't understand that people can have a better life that way.

On the other side, I think those people would like to have a better life. Any one of them, any of the Puerto Rican boys, the tough guys in the neighborhood, he'd like to live as comfortably as we do. To have so many privileges. For example, we can go swimming at the private pool and they can't. I don't know why they can't, except they don't know anyone there. We have connections.

Our parents belong to the club, or know people on the staff, so we can go there.

The other kids can swim in a public pool or go to the public-school gym, but they realize that we have more. The trouble is that what they do about it is all wrong. When we go to the pool, we always make sure that we keep our privilege. We keep to the rules, never make a racket, see that there are never too many of us in the corridors. We're careful to wash up before and not to run around the pool.

Well, about three days ago, about thirty of them came in a group with towels and bathing suits, right to the pool. We were in there, six of us, because we never go with more than six or eight at a time so that we don't take up too much room. Well, the members were using the pool when these kids ran in. They were stomping into the locker rooms and screaming and yelling, jumping off the diving board and throwing each other into the water. The life guard didn't know what to do. He looked around and he was bewildered. So Mr. Anderson, who runs that place, called the security guards and told them to get those boys out. If they had gone about it correctly, it might have been all right for them.

There's the same problem in church, at dances, or at clubs. Everybody is welcome and some Puerto Rican kids do come, but again, a lot of them do things the wrong way. For example, there's one priest that I like very much. He's a real nice guy and he feels sorry for them and tries to help them. But they don't want him. They won't pay attention to him and they tell him that. They say, "Get away from me."

He goes out into the street and he sees them. He goes over to talk to them, but if they don't respond, there is nothing he can do. It's not going to hurt him, but he feels sorry for them and can't help. Well, if they treat a priest like that, I don't think they're very nice.

I never see them at church, at Mass or at confession. Most of my friends were in the choir or altar boys when younger. Very few of the others ever were. I was in the choir for six years. Up until the time that my voice cracked. I loved the choir, I loved to hear the music. It's great.

I go to church every Sunday with my family and it's part of the good feeling of security I have about my family. I enjoy the music, but I am really not the spiritual type. There is one boy in our parish whom everybody knows. He's an altar boy, all his life, and now he is a master on the altar. He went into the seminary for four years. He's very holy, pious, very nice. I think he really gets more out of church than I do, but I don't wish that I was more like him. I don't find a great interest in that kind of life. I like the music and I feel secure, and that's about all.

Two of the priests are very nice men and we often go and sit and talk with them all evening. We're very frank with them, but, for example, we wouldn't have told anybody there about that night we almost had the big fight. They wouldn't really understand and we'd be sort of looked down upon for being in that kind of predicament. We'd be considered instigators or something like that.

I don't mean to say that it's only Puerto Rican kids or colored kids who ever do anything wrong. I mean what makes me the most disgusted, no matter what color a person is, is someone who is always making stupid moves. What really destroys me is when a person who is about eighteen years old thinks and acts like a twelve-year-old. The kid I'm talking about is not very bright and he sometimes comes along to the movies with us. Once we went to a movie and he was watching and whenever a funny line came up and everyone else tittered quietly, he would guffaw and get up in his seat and whoop and then plop down. That destroys me.

Another incident like that, which really got me, happened a few weeks ago when I took a girl to a school dance. I only took her because she was my last resort, because she is very talkative and very giddy and I don't like that much. Well, after the dance a few of us went to a restaurant around the corner. I had on a raincoat that zips way up and as I was putting on the raincoat, she thought she would be really cute. She pulled the zipper up very hard and caught my neck in it. I was really furious. By the time I got it off my neck was bleeding and I was ready to pick up the table and throw it at the wall. I don't know how to explain this, but it really got me angry and I had all I could do to control myself. It was the closest I have ever come to exploding besides a few times on the football field when you can really get wild, when someone keeps clipping you, or when you keep getting your lumps with elbows in the mouth or something. Once, in that kind of game, I really saw red and my quarterback had to grab me by the neck and sit on me until I calmed down.

Most of the time though, I don't get that angry. Just sort of disgusted with something. And I don't get into any fights or serious trouble, because I try to avoid it. Even if I saw a fight or saw someone getting hurt, I'd stay away. If a gang of kids were beating up one boy, and I didn't know him, I'd wait until after they left and if the kid was hurt I'd help him. But I wouldn't want to get caught myself. I would not go over there like a fool and get myself killed. You can't do anything with the police in that sort of situation because they'd say it's my word against the word of a whole gang of boys. And I'd have to be a witness and that kind of trouble. I might try to get some adult who was standing around to help. But they feel the same way and would say that they didn't see it. They'd try to stay out of it themselves. Even my father told me one thing. He said that if there is more than one of them, run. If there is one of you against one of them, and the other guy is the same size as you are, see what you can do, but don't ever try to take on more than you are.

I pretty much follow that advice. One time, though, some girls from our sister school were walking across the park and they were attacked by some rough colored girls. We just happened to walk through at the same time, after a parade we'd all been in, and we saw what was going on. Those colored girls were vicious. They were scratching and beating up the poor girls from the school, and our girls couldn't defend themselves. That time we really beat them off and escorted the girls to a taxi at the other end of the park.

All in all, though, very little of this sort of thing goes on in my own life. Pretty much, we go our own way, having a very good time, learning a lot, and preparing for life. Even when I think very hard, I wouldn't want to live anywhere else than where I live now. I love the block, the park, the neighbors. I am completely happy with my life. I've had a good life so far. Nothing dramatically wrong with it. Lots of laughs, lots of fun.

Fourth Grade *

Jonathan Kozol

The room in which I taught my Fourth Grade was not a room at all, but the corner of an auditorium. The first time I approached that corner, I noticed only a huge torn stage curtain, a couple of broken windows, a badly listing blackboard and about thirty-five bewildered-looking children, most of whom were Negro. White was overcome in black among them, but white and black together were overcome in chaos. They had desks and a teacher, but they did not really have a class. What they had was about one quarter of the auditorium. Three or four blackboards, two of them broken, made them seem a little bit set apart. Over at the other end of the auditorium there was another Fourth Grade class. Not much was happening at the other side at that minute so that for the moment the noise did not seem so bad. But it became a real nightmare of conflicting noises a little later on. Generally it was not until ten o'clock that the bad crossfire started. By ten-thirty it would have attained such a crescendo that the children in the back rows of my section often couldn't hear my questions and I could not hear their answers. There were no carpetings or sound-absorbers of any kind. The room, being large, and echoing, and wooden, added resonance to every sound. Sometimes the other teacher and I would stagger the lessons in which our classes would have to speak aloud, but this was a makeshift method and it also meant that our classes had to be induced to maintain an unnatural and otherwise unnecessary rule of silence during the rest of the time. We couldn't always do it anyway, and usually the only way out was to try to outshout each other so that both of us often left school hoarse or wheezing. While her class was reciting in unison you could not hear very much in mine. When she was talking alone I could be heard above her but the trouble then was that little bits of her talk got overheard by my class. Suddenly in the middle of our geography you could hear her saying:

"After you compare, you have got to bring down."

Or, "Please give that pencil back to Henrietta!"

Neither my class nor I could help but be distracted for a moment of sudden curiosity about exactly what was going on. Hours were lost in this way. Yet that was not the worst. More troublesome still was the fact that we did not ever *feel*

*Jonathan Kozol, *DEATH AT AN EARLY AGE; The Destruction of the Hearts and Minds of Negro Children in the Boston Public Schools.* Boston: Houghton-Mifflin Company, 1967. Chapter IV, pp. 29-40.

apart. We were tucked in the corner and anybody who wanted could peek in or walk in or walk past. I never minded an intruder or observer, but to notice and to stare at any casual passer-by grew to be an irresistible temptation for the class. On repeated occasions I had to say to the children: "The class is still going. Let them have their discussion. Let them walk by if they have to. You should still be paying attention over here."

Soon after I came into that auditorium, I discovered that it was not only our two Fourth Grades that were going to have their classes here. We were to share the space also with the glee club, with play rehearsals, special reading, special arithmetic, and also at certain times a Third or Fourth Grade phonics class. I began to make head-counts of numbers of pupils and I started jotting them down:

Seventy children from the two regular Fourth Grades before the invasion.

Then ninety one day with the glee club and remedial arithmetic.

One hundred and seven with the play rehearsal.

One day the sewing class came in with their sewing machines and then that seemed to become a regular practice in the hall. Once I counted one hundred and twenty people. All in the one room. All talking, singing, yelling, laughing, reciting – and all at the same time. Before the Christmas break it became apocalyptic. Not more than one half of the classroom lessons I had planned took place throughout that time.

"Mr. Kozol – I can't hear you."

"Mr. Kozol – what's going on out there?"

"Mr. Kozol – couldn't we sing with them?"

One day something happend to dramatize to me, even more powerfully than anything yet, just what a desperate situation we were really in. What happened was that a window whose frame had rotted was blown right out of its sashes by a strong gust of wind and began to fall into the auditorium, just above my children's heads. I had noticed that window several times before and I had seen that its frame was rotting, but there were so many other things equally rotted or broken in the school building that it didn't occur to me to say anything about it. The feeling I had was that the Principal and custodians and Reading Teacher and other people had been in that building for a long time before me and they must have seen the condition of the windows. If anything could be done, if there were any way to get it corrected, I assumed they would have done it by this time. Thus, by not complaining and by not pointing it out to anyone, in a sense I went along with the rest of them and accepted it as something inevitable. One of the most grim things about teaching in such a school and such a system is that you do not like to be an incessant barb and irritation to everybody else, so you come under a rather strong compulsion to keep quiet. But after you have been quiet for a while there is an equally strong temptation to begin to accept the conditions of your work or of the children's plight as natural. This, in a sense, is what had happened to me during that period and that, I suppose, is why I didn't say anything about the rotting window. Now one day it caved in.

First there was a cracking sound, then a burst of icy air. The next thing I knew, a child was saying: "Mr. Kozol — look at the window!" I turned and looked and saw that it was starting to fall in. It was maybe four or five feet tall and it came straight inward out of its sashes toward the heads of the children. I was standing, by coincidence, only about four or five feet off and was able to catch it with my hand. But the wind was so strong that it nearly blew right out of my hands. A couple of seconds of good luck — for it was a matter of chance that I was standing there — kept glass from the desks of six or seven children and very possibly preserved the original shape of half a dozen of their heads. The ones who had been under the glass were terrified but the thing that I noticed with most wonder was that they tried very hard to hide their fear in order to help me get over my own sense of embarrassment and guilt. I soon realized I was not going to be able to hold the thing up by myself and I was obliged to ask one of the stronger boys in the class to come over and give me a hand. Meanwhile, as the children beneath us shivered with the icy wind and as the two of us now shivered also since it was a day when the mercury was hovering all morning close to freezing, I asked one of the children in the front row to run down and fetch the janitor.

When he asked me what he should tell him, I said: "Tell him the house is falling in." The children laughed. It was the first time I had ever come out and said anything like that when the children could hear me. I am sure my reluctance to speak out like that more often must seem odd to many readers, for at this perspective it seems odd to me as well. Certainly there were plenty of things wrong within that school building and there was enough we could have joked about. The truth, however, is that I did not often talk like that, nor did many of the other teachers, and there was a practical reason for this. Unless you were ready to buck the system utterly, it would become far too difficult to teach in an atmosphere of that kind of honesty. It generally seemed a great deal easier to pretend as well as you could that everything was normal and okay. Some teachers carried out this posture with so much eagerness, in fact, that their defense of the school ended up as something like a hymn of praise and adoration. "You children should thank God and feel blessed with good luck for all you've got. There are so many little children in the world who have been given so much less." The books are junk, the paint peels, the cellar stinks, the teachers call you nigger, and the windows fall in on your heads. "Thank God that you don't live in Russia or Africa! Thank God for all the blessings that you've got!" Once, finally, the day after the window blew in, I said to a friend of mine in the evening after school: "I guess that the building I teach in is not in very good condition." But to state a condition of dilapidation and ugliness and physical danger in words as mild and indirect as those is almost worse than not saying anything at all. I had a hard time with that problem — the problem of being honest and of confronting openly the extent to which I was compromised by going along with things that were abhorrent and by accepting as moderately reasonable or unavoidably troublesome things which, if they were inflicted on children of my own, I would have condemned savagely.

A friend of mine to whom I have confided some of these things has not been able to keep from criticizing me for what he thinks of as a kind of quiet collusion. When I said to him, for example, that the Reading Teacher was trying to do the right thing and that she was a very forceful teacher, he replied to me that from what I had described to him she might have been a very forceful teacher but she was not a good teacher but a very dangerous one and that whether she was *trying* to do the right thing or not did not impress him since what she *did* do was the wrong thing. Other people I know have said the same thing to me about this and I am certain, looking back, that it is only the sheer accident of the unexpected events which took place in my school during the last weeks of the spring that prompted me suddenly to speak out and to take some forthright action. I am also convinced that it is that, and that alone, that has spared me the highly specialized and generally richly deserved contempt which is otherwise reserved by Negro people for their well-intending but inconsistent liberal friends.

After the window blew in on us that time, the janitor finally came up and hammered it shut with nails so that it would not fall in again but also so that it could not open. It was a month before anything was done about the large gap left by a missing pane. Children shivered a few feet away from it. The Principal walked by frequently and saw us. So did supervisors from the School Department. So of course did the various lady experts who traveled all day from room to room within our school. No one can say that dozens of people did not know that children were sitting within the range of freezing air. At last one day the janitor came up with a piece of cardboard or pasteboard and covered over about a quater of that lower window so that there was no more wind coming in but just that much less sunshine too. I remember wondering what a piece of glass could cost in Boston and I had the idea of going out and buying some and trying to put it in myself. That rectangle of cardboard over our nailed-shut window was not removed for a quarter of the year. When it was removed, it was only because a television station was going to come and visit in the building and the School Department wanted to make the room look more attractive. But it was winter when the window broke, and the repairs did not take place until the middle of the spring.

In case a reader imagines that my school may have been unusual and that some of the other schools in Roxbury must have been in better shape, I think it's worthwhile to point out that the exact opposite seems to have been the case. The conditions in my school were said by many people to be considerably better than those in several of the other ghetto schools. One of the worst, according to those who made comparisons, was the Endicott, also situated in the Negro neighborhood and, like my own school, heavily imbalanced. At Endicott, I learned, it had become so overcrowded that there were actually some classes in which the number of pupils exceeded the number of desks and in which the extra pupils had to sit in chairs behind the teacher. A child absent one day commonly came back the next day and found someone else sitting at his desk. These facts had been brought out in the newspapers, pretty well documented, and they were not denied by the School Department. Despite this, however, as in most cases like this, nothing had been done. When the parents of the Endicott children pressed the School Department to do something about it, a series of events transpired which told a large part of the story of segregation in a very few words.

The School Department offered, in order to resolve the problem, to buy a deserted forty-year-old Hebrew school and then allot about seven thousand dollars to furnish it with desks and chairs. Aside from the indignity of getting everybody else's castoffs (the Negroes already lived in former Jewish tenements and bought in former Jewish stores), there also was the telling fact that to buy and staff this old Hebrew school with about a dozen teachers was going to cost quite a lot of money and that to send the children down the street a couple of miles to a white school which had space would have saved quite a lot. The Hebrew school was going to cost over $180,000. To staff it, supply it with books and so forth would cost about $100,000 more. To send the children into available seats in nearby white classrooms (no new teachers needed) would have cost $40,000 to $60,000 for the year. The School Department, it seemed, was willing to spend something in the area of an extra $240,000 in order to put the Negro children into another segregated school. It was hard for me to believe, even after all I had seen and heard, that it could really be worth a quarter of a million dollars to anyone to keep the Negro children separate. As it happened, the School Committee dragged its heels so long and debated the issue in so many directions that most of the school year passed before anything of a final nature was decided. Meanwhile the real children in the real Endicott classrooms had lost another real year from their real lives.

In my own school, there was another bad situation in a Fourth Grade class across the stair-landing. Here in a room in which one window was nailed to the window sill and in which words could not be read clearly on the blackboard because that old blackboard was so scratchy and so worn, there was a gentle soul on the apparent verge of mental breakdown and of whom it was said that he had had a mental collapse not long before. He had been dismissed, I was told, from a previous position in the Boston system after it had grown evident that he could not effectively handle the problems posed by an ordinary crowded class. Instead of being retired or else given the type of specialized work in which he might have been effective, the man had simply been shunted along into another over-crowded ghetto school. The assignment was unjust both to him and to the children. The classroom to which he had been assigned was filled with chaos, screams and shouting all day long. The man gave his class mixed-up instructions. He was the sort of mild, nervous person who gives instructions in a tone that makes it clear in advance that he does n t really expect to be either believed or obeyed. He screamed often but his screams contained generally not force but fear. Bright children got confused; all children grew exhausted. There was very little calm or order. Going in there on an errand during the middle of the morning, it was not always immediately possible to find him. You would not be able to make out where he was in the midst of the movements of the shouting, jumping class. On rare occasions, the children, having no one else to blame for this except their teacher, would rise up in an angry instant and strike back. I remember a day in the middle of January, in quite cold weather, when the teacher went out onto the metal fire escape for a moment for some purpose – perhaps just to regain his composure and try to calm himself down – and one of the children jumped up and slammed the door. It locked behind him. "Let me in!" the man started screaming. It was unjust to him but he must have seemed like Rumpelstiltskin, and the children, not ever having had a chance at revenge before, must have been filled with sudden joy. "Let me in! How dare you," etc. At last they relented. Someone opened up the door and let the man back in.

After I went in there the first time in November, I began to find my attention being drawn repeatedly by two of the children. One of them was a bright and attractive and impatient Negro girl who showed her hatred for school and teacher by sitting all day with a slow and smoldering look of cynical resentment in her eyes. Not only was she bright but she also worked extremely hard, and she seemed to me remarkably sophisticated, even though she was still very much a little child. I thought that she would easily have been the sure candidate for Girls' Latin School or for one of the other local girls' schools of distinction had she not been Negro and not been a victim of this segregated school. For two years now she had had substitute teachers, and this year a permanent teacher in a state of perpetual breakdown. Her eyes, beautiful and sarcastic, told that she understood exactly what was going on. Enough shrewdness and sense of dignity belonged to her that she made no mistake about where to place the blame. She was one of thousands who gave the lie, merely by her silent eloquence, to the utterances of the Boston School Committee. She was a child who, in her insight and calm anger, gave the lie to every myth of a slow and sleepy Negro timidly creeping up and creeping along. Five years from now, if my guess was correct, she would be fourteen and she would be out on picket lines. She would stand there and she would protest because there alone, after so much wasting of her years, would be the one place where her pride and hope would still have a chance. But how could a child like her, with all of her awareness and all of her intelligence, ever in her lifetime find a way to forgive society and the public school system for what it had done to her?

The other child whom I noticed in that Fourth Grade room was in an obvious way less fortunate. In this case it was the situation of a boy who was retarded. For this child, whom I call Edward, there was no chance at all of surviving inwardly within this miserable classroom, still less of figuring out where the blame ought to be applied. The combination of low intelligence with a state of emotional confusion resulted, in him, in behavior which, while never violent, was unmistakably peculiar. No one could have missed it — unless he wanted to, or needed to. The boy walked upstairs on the stairway backward, singing. Many teachers managed not to notice. He walked with his coat pulled up and zippered over his face and inside he roared with laughter, until a teacher grabbed him and slammed him at the wall. Nobody said, "Something is wrong." He hopped like a frog and made frog-noises. Occasionally a teacher would not be able to help himself and would come right out and say, "Jesus, that kid's odd." But I never did hear anyone say that maybe also, in regard to the disposition of this one child at least, something in the system of the school itself was wrong or odd. This was his situation, repeated hundreds of times in other public schools of Boston:

The boy was designated a "special student," categorized in this way because of his measured I.Q. and hence, by the expectation of most teachers, not teachable within a normal crowded room. On the other hand, owing to the overcrowding of the school and the lack of special teachers, there was no room for him in our one special class. Again, because of the school system's unwillingness to bus Negro children into other neighborhoods, he could not attend class in any other school which might have room. The consequence of all of this, as it came down through the channels of the system, was that he was to remain a full year mostly unseen and virtually forgotten, with nothing to do except to vegetate, cause trouble, daydream or just silently decay. He was unwell. His sickness was obvious, and it was impossible to miss it. He laughed to near crying over unimaginable details. If you didn't look closely it seemed often that he was laughing over nothing at all. Sometimes he smiled wonderfully with a look of sheer ectasy. Usually it was over something tiny: a little dot on his finger or an imaginary bug upon the floor. The boy had a large olive head and very glassy rolling eyes. One day I brought him a book about a little French boy who was followed to school by a red balloon. He sat and swung his head back and forth over it and smiled. More often he was likely to sulk, or whimper or cry. He cried in reading because he could not learn to read. He cried in writing because he could not be taught to write. He cried because he couldn't pronounce words of many syllables. He didn't know his tables. He didn't know how to subtract. He didn't know how to divide. He was in this Fourth Grade class, as I kept on thinking, by an administrative error so huge that it seemed at times as if it must have been an administrative joke. The joke of HIM was so obvious it was hard not to find it funny. The children in the class found it funny. They laughed at him all day. Sometimes he laughed with them since it's quite possible, when we have few choices, to look upon even our own misery as some kind of desperate joke. Or else he started to shout. His teacher once turned to me and said very honestly and openly: "It's just impossible to teach him." And the truth, of course, in this case, is that teacher *didn't* teach him; nor had he really been taught since the day he came into this school.

In November I started doing special work in reading with a number of the slowest readers out of all of the Fourth Grades. It was not easy to pick them, for few children at our school read near grade-level. Only six or seven in my own class were Fourth Grade readers. Many were at least a year, frequently two years, behind. Those who had had so many substitutes in the previous two years tended to be in the worst shape. In selecting this special group of children, it seemed to me that Edward deserved the extra help as much as anyone. He wanted it too — he made that apparent. For he came along with excitement and with a great and optimistic smile and he began by being attentive to me and appeared happy for a while. The smiling stopped soon, however, because he could not follow even the extremely moderate pace that we were keeping. The other children, backward as they had seemed, were far ahead of him. He soon began to cry. At this point the Reading Teacher came rushing on the scene. Her reaction was not unusual, or unexpected. Rather than getting angry in any way at all at either the school or the city or the system for this one child's sake, her anger was all for him and her outrage and her capacity for onslaught all came down upon his head. "I will not have it!" she said of him and of his misery and then, virtually seething with her decision-making power, she instructed me that I was not to teach him any longer. Not taught by me and not by his regular teacher. I asked her, in that case, by whom he would be taught from now on, and the answer in effect was nobody. The real decision, spoken or unspoken, was that he would not be taught at all. In this, as in many of the other things I have described, I was reluctant at that time to argue forcefully. Instead, I acquiesced in her authority and I quietly did as I was told. For the duration of the fall and for the major portion of the winter, the little boy with the olive smile would ask me, it seemed, almost every morning: "Mr. Kozol — can I come to reading with you?" And almost every morning I pretended that his exclusion was only temporary and I lied to him and told him: "I'm sorry, Edward. Just not for today."

After a while he got the point that it was permanent.

Additional Reading

Amos, William E. and Jean D. Grambs (eds). *Counseling the Disadvantaged Youth.* Englewood Cliffs, N. J.: Prentice-Hall, 1968.

Coleman, James S. *Adolescents and the Schools.* New York: Basic Books, 1965.

Friedenberg, Edgar Z. *The Vanishing Adolescent.* New York: Dell, 1962.

Frost, Joe L. and Glenn R. Hawkes (eds). *The Disadvantaged Child.* Boston: Houghton Mifflin Co., 1966.

Goldstein, Bernard. *Low Income Youth in Urban Areas.* New York: Holt, Rinehart and Winston, 1967.

Holt, John. *How Children Fail.* New York: Dell Delta Book, 1964.

Martin, John M. and Joseph P. Fitzpatrick. *Delinquent Behavior: A Redefinition of the Problem.* New York: Random House, 1964.

Roberts, Joan I. (ed). *School Children in the Urban Slum.* New York: The Free Press, 1967.

Rosenthal, Robert, and Lenore Jacobson, *Pygmalion in the Classroom.* New York: Holt, Rinehart and Winston, 1968.

chapter 3

Teachers

Teachers in urban schools face a wide variety of problems and unfortunately not all of them within the classroom. The range includes the type and quality of leadership in the school, the nature of the curriculum to which the teacher may be limited, the question of professional and nonprofessional assistance available in the classroom, and the teacher's relationship with her students.

Estelle Fuchs describes through the words of beginning teachers and through her own analysis the important phenomenon of culture shock which seriously affects the performance of middleclass teachers as they first move into schools serving lower class and nonwhite youngsters. Elliott Shapiro, former principal and now district superintendent in New York City, is not a classroom teacher. However, as Nat Hentoff's description suggests, Mr. Shapiro is clearly an educator who supports his teachers in a way which helps them to meet some of the problems and difficulties identified by Professor Fuchs. G. Alexander Moore's systematic, anthropological observations of a second-grade class provide a useful approach to finding out what really goes on between teachers and pupils in a classroom setting. Charles Isaacs, from the Ocean Hill-Brownsville experimental district in New York City, describes forcefully a community operated school from the point of view of a committed teacher. One of the most significant hurdles facing lower class nonwhite youngsters in America is that of acquiring standard English and using it effectively. J. L. Dillard outlines one program which seems to be meeting with some success in solving this problem.

Culture Shock*

Estelle Fuchs

The first few weeks in a school represent a dangerous period for the beginner. Fatigue, discipline problems, and self-doubt appear typical. Early in this critical period the new teacher exhibits symptoms of what anthropologists term "culture shock."

* * * * * *

October 5   Mrs. Bender

There are two ways of looking at the most important thing that happened this week in school: a positive and a negative. As a positive way, Bobby, my "friend," has been taken from my class. He was transferred to a 5-4 class.

From the beginning of the term I have had discipline problems with him. I didn't call his mother because she was in the hospital having a baby. I don't know who the father is; I don't believe she does either. Anyway, I haven't been able to contact her. I did, however, speak to the guidance counselor, Mrs. Rogers, about him and she's been watching him for a while. She's started a file on him but I haven't seen it yet.

Tuesday was an impossible day for me. I just didn't know what I was going to do with him. *I came home. I was hysterical. I cried all afternoon, all evening and all night. I really felt that this was the end. I was not going back and what was the sense of knocking myself out? It wasn't worth it. Here I was trying to help people. They don't want to accept you and this is exactly what I felt, very useless.* /my emphasis – E. F./ I felt that I was not a teacher; I was a policeman. What did I need this aggravation for?

Wednesday, everything was fine. The class was marvelous. There was no problem.

Thursday, again, because of Bobby, everything went wrong. He had stolen . . . well I didn't actually see him and couldn't accuse him . . . but paper clips were missing from my desk and while we were going up the stairs at lunch time Bobby was throwing paper clips at the other children. I was afraid that one of these clips would end up in someone's eye. But, too, it was just one of those things. Everything that he did really got under my skin. I'd gotten to the point

*Estelle Fuchs, Teachers Talk: A View From Within Inner City Schools. New York: Hunter College, 1967 (unpublished) Chapter II, "Culture Shock," pp. 15-25.

where I just wanted to take him and throw him down the flight of stairs we were on. He was just impossible!

On that same day, Mrs. Rogers, the guidance counselor passed by my room to observe Bobby. He was in his seat so she just really couldn't understand what my fussing was all about. It just so happened that when she came in, he was in his seat taking a diagnostic test that I had prepared in math. She questioned me as to what was wrong and why I was so upset. I explained exactly what he was doing and told her that I just couldn't take it any more. "It's either him or me. I won't continue this way any more." I said, "becuase I'm becoming a manic depressive. Monday, I go home; I'm fine. The next day I'm just very, very upset. I can't deal with my feelings any more." Well she sent me out of the room and said that I should take a rest. She said she felt that I was very upset. She knew it! I'm sure she could see it!

I went down to the office to rexograph some stencils I had prepared and the principal walked in. All he had to do was say something nice to me! And that's exactly what he did. He said, "Well, Mrs. Bender, how is it going?"

I just started to cry. I could not control my feelings. I couldn't control anything. He asked what the problem was and all I had to say was, "Bobby."

"Is it just Bobby?" he said.

"Yes, it's just Bobby."

He said, ' Well, if this is truly the problem, Bobby will be taken out of your class tomorrow. There is no need for you to feel so upset about it." Then he sort of scolded me saying, "Why didn't you come to me before and tell me about this? Don't let things go so far. You are a human being; you have feelings. This isn't the way to react."

Now I was so upset that I just wanted to be left alone. I didn't want him to come near me. I didn't even want to go back to the classroom. I just wanted to go home.

I did go back to the classroom, however, and handed out the stencils I had run off and we did a music lesson. But my heart wasn't really in it because I felt that I was never going to come back. What's the sense?

Later I discussed this with my parents and my husband and with my contemporaries in the school. We all decided . . . well, I decided actually that the best thing would be for Bobby to get out of my class. Friday, yesterday, when I walked into the room the guidance counselor informed me that Bobby would be taken out of my class as of that day. And, yesterday the class was a class. I was a teacher! I wasn't a babysitter; I wasn't a disciplinarian. I was a teacher. I had prepared lessons; I had done my lessons; I had completed what I planned. This is the first time that this had ever happened and I felt that this was the most important thing that happened to me in the school — never mind the week! — in the school so far.

In a negative way another important thing happened to me in school this week. There is a girl in my class (her name is Jean), a tall Negro girl who is constantly talking. I'm constantly reprimanding her for talking in class and in the hallways. Well, coming up from the assembly this week, Jean was hiding behind another girl, another Negro girl, and she was talking. I happened to catch her and I said to her, "Jean, I can see you." Well, Jean broke out in a rage. She started to cry and I couldn't imagine what was wrong. I thought perhaps she wasn't feeling well. She walked into the classroom. She was still crying with her head down on the desk. I went over to her and said, "Jean, what's wrong? Tell me and I'll help you if I can."

She wouldn't answer me but a few minutes later Bobby delivered a note to me from Jean. The note said, "Mrs. Bender, do you think my face is too black? Just let me know."

I became hysterical. I couldn't imagine what this was all about. So I asked her to stay with me during lunch and explain what she was talking about.

She did stay but she just couldn't answer me. I kept asking her questions. I told her I was her friend; I was her teacher; I was not there to hurt her, I was there to teach her. I don't know if it penetrated or not. She just stood there looking at me. I just couldn't make her out. She just stared at me with her eyes opened wide and she looked away from me. It was just like nothing, absolutely nothing.

Then, on Thursday, I also discussed the matter with her. I had a special conference with her and I wanted to know why she continued to disturb the class and talk. Well, in the course of our conversation, she said, "Well, why do you keep only the Negro kids in and let the Puerto Ricans go home? You don't like us, do you?"

Again, I was very upset because this was, of course, a lie and I told her so. I told her, "Jean, you know the people who stay and you name them for me." She named about seven Negro children.

I said, "But, Jean, you're not telling everything. There are more people that I keep in. You know that as well as I do. So go ahead and name everyone."

She proceeded to name the Puerto Rican children.

I asked her, "Jean, why did you say this to me if you know that I'm not being partial to one group? I don't understand how you reason."

Well, she didn't answer me but from then on everything seemed to go smoothly with her. She's my pal now, and she's really motivated in some way. I really don't know why or how. Perhaps it's because I've been giving her special jobs and this is what she needs and probably wants. I kept her jobs to a minimum, however, because there are good children in the class who deserve to have jobs and why should they see that a bad person gets jobs and they don't? What's the sense of being good? This is what I am afraid of and we'll see what happens later.

DISCUSSION

With few exceptions, beginning teachers during their first days and weeks in their classrooms, exhibit symptoms of severe emotional and physical stress.

Mrs. Bender's display of hysteria, weeping, state of near collapse, depression, self-doubt, and hostility and aggression toward some youngsters in her class is not atypical.

Most of us are aware of the tensions and strains accompanying unfamiliar routines or activities. However, the symptoms expressed by beginning teachers, and described so vividly by Mrs. Bender, go far beyond the ordinary fatigue associated with a new mode of employment. They are surprisingly similar to the phenomenon described by anthropologists as "culture shock."

It is important to know that the new teacher is not moving into a different culture, however. She is still in our own society. Nonetheless, the new locale, the unfamiliarity of the people, both staff and children, the sense of containment, the new responsibilities and the strange routines and problems, seem to precipitate a syndrome which has been experienced by many others throughout history when thrust into the unfamiliar life-ways of a foreign culture. Immigrants, tourists, students of other cultures are among those who have experienced this phenomenon.

The symptoms of culture shock have been studied by anthropologists. One of the symptoms is a "ludicrous tendency to raise one's voice to a shout when one finds a foreigner unable to understand simple English." How many new teachers exhibit this tendency to shout and scold at their youngsters! Other reactions include numb fatigue, anger against the strangers confronting one, or a frenzied retreat into the familiar. There is often, in addition, a feeling of helplessness and a desire for company of one's own kind.[1]

Why should this happen to individuals who move into strange situations? The shock and forced readjustment which occur are a result of the strain of heightened attention to strange cues and signs in an unfamiliar environment. The reaction is compounded by frustration, exasperation and irritation.

Some disturbances always occur for the individual thrust into the strangely upsetting world of the unfamiliar, although the severity of culture shock may vary. Some people are more tolerant of new experiences, and less anxious when faced with new, unusual, and baffling situations. The reasons for this arise from a multitude of factors which include temperament, earlier exposure to similar experiences, greater familiarity with a variety of situations or life ways, etc. The value of earlier exposure in overcoming or preventing the more acute manifestations of culture shock has been recognized by those who make an effort to e.nploy teachers in schools where they have had experience as student teachers. (It is important to recognize that such prior experience helps overcome the acute symptoms of culture shock — it does not mean the teacher is competent and without need of professional assistance. Her case, generally, does not represent an emergency situation, but culture shock can be experienced more than once.)

[1] Conrad M. Arensberg and Authur H. Niehoff, *Introducting Social Change: A Manual for Americans Overseas,* Chicago: Aldine Publishing Company, pp. 188-189.

For the new teacher, the first few days and weeks spent in the school are critical, for her attitude toward the children and her occupation can be set positively or negatively at this time. Contempt for the children is one unfortunate possibility. Others include serious self-doubt and even leaving the occupation of teaching completely, or at least leaving the inner city school where her services are needed.

Most people survive the period of culture shock. They do this by continual exposure to the unfamiliar until it no longer seems strange, unpredictable, and threatening. This requires a concerted effort on the part of the beginner. Retreat into brooding does not help, as this reassuring principal recognized. Survival in this period requires a real effort to get to know the situation. Although problems may continue to exist, it is the initial days and weeks which are the most critical for the beginner.

Given the existence of the phenomenon of culture shock, how can the principal help see his teachers through this crucial period toward a constructive functioning on her part? It would seem that certain things might help. One, too many new responsibilities ought not to be imposed upon the new teacher too early. Provision for physical relief in the form of time, or preferably a master teacher in the room to engage the children in constructive experiences together with the teacher are of value. To separate the teacher from her class too often may have the negative result of her not gaining enough familiarity with the children.

The pleasant principal who gives offers of general help is not providing an adequate solution. The teacher herself often does not know what she needs, until a crisis develops. This is not a period in which to anticipate creative teaching. All supplies, guides to lessons, and even visiting teachers who take over lessons will help tide the teacher over this period. Professional conferences, to jointly plan activities, interpret child behavior and learning, to clarify the clerical duties, will help her over this initial period of isolation and desperation, and help her to see her problem with perspective.

Just as the teacher is experiencing a critical time, so are the children in her class. Many of the youngsters, for a variety of reasons including earlier experience, will behave according to the school norms despite the crisis through which their teacher is going. Indeed, as described earlier, beginning teachers report their amazement at the fact that on the first day of school the children knew just what to do. Some children, however, are likely to exhibit the same symptoms she does. Certainly, at this time, the beginner ought not to be expected to cope with the seriously disturbed child. On the other hand, children who are having difficulty adjusting to the new class and teacher, or who are responding overtly to teacher behavior, frightening and confusing to them, are all too often victimized. The danger exists, for them, that they will become the scapegoats in a situation over which they have no control.

Here the principal is faced with a dilemma. His teachers expect his support, and expect him to punish or banish the child they view as the cause of their hysteria. The principal, if he recognizes that the teacher's difficulty is only in part a reaction to the individual child, is faced with the problem of what to do. Unfortunately, little exists in the school system in the way of non-punitive assistance to tide a youngster such as Bobby over his or his teacher's initial periods of difficulty. To sit in the office, to have the parent come to hear the child attacked verbally, to be treated as "disturbed" and in need of guidance, to become assoicated with a "record" that follows him through the school years can early establish the child in the role of troublemaker.

Helping the teacher through his or her initial culture shock must also include safeguards against the victimization of children. In this particular case, the principal's sympathy, the support of husband and family, and friends, and the removal of the child especially irritating to the teacher, helped Mrs. Bender over the critical period of danger. It would be interesting to know what became of Bobby.

Jean acted with hysteria and tears to the school situation just as her teacher had. Unlike her classmate, Bobby — who interestingly enough delivered to Mrs. Bender the note Jean had written — Jean made a determined and deliberate effort to investigate for herself what Mrs. Bender's behavior really meant.

Reacting quite differently to Jean than to Bobby, Mrs. Bender demonstrated rather clearly that her punishment of Negro youngsters in the class was not a function of conscious prejudice on her part. Apparently she succeeded so well that Jean, accepting the teacher's explanations, proceeded to have less difficulty in class after that. Together with the problem of prejudice, Jean, after viewing what had happened to Bobby, was unsure as to whether she, as an individual, was being rejected as well. After her discussion with the teacher, this did not seem to be a serious threat anymore. Yet, the teacher persists in ascribing the value judgments of good or bad on Jean's behavior, which is not seriously aberrant at that.

Teachers and supervisors working in inner city schools with large Negro populations must be cognizant of the fact that teacher behavior is viewed in the light of the long and profoundly disturbed history of race relations in this country. Suspicion of the motives of school personnel, accusations of prejudice, etc., are not simply the reflection of agitation which may or may not exist in any given area. Studies of Negro youngsters have demonstrated awareness of race as early as age three. Much of the literature argues that this awareness is associated with a poor self-concept which reflects the dominance of whites in American life over the subordinate role played by Negroes.[2] Recent study has questioned that poor self-concepts are true of all Negro youngsters.[3] Undoubtedly, a wide variety of reaction and personal integration of self-concept and attitudes toward whites does exist.

[2]See, for example, D. Ausubel and Pearl Ausubel, "Ego Development Among Segregated Negro Children," in A. Harry Passow, *Education in Depressed Areas,* New York: Bureau of Publications, Teachers College, Columbia University, 1963, pp. 109-141;

Mrs. Bender's hysteria and obvious distaste for Bobby provoked Jean into a hysterical reaction as well. But, Jean's forthright "laying the cards on the table," so to speak, forced Mrs. Bender to a considerate, respectful discussion with Jean to clarify the issues. That Jean could now see Mrs. Bender's behavior as not emanating from her own blackness helped improve the climate for learning. The fact that the teacher indicated her respect for the child by inviting her to a discussion to clarify the problem and to better communicate with one another was very valuable for it is only when effort is expended to understand the meaning of cues in the new environment that the more negative effects of culture shock can be avoided. Whole new fascinating insights that are non-threatening open up to the teacher, or the student of cultures, who reach the point that Mrs. Bender did in indicating a genuine willingness to listen and learn from one of the young people with whom she would be working.

Mrs. Bender, in describing her week, saw her experience with Bobby as being positive, her experience with Jean as negative. It would seem that the reverse judgment more accurately describes the situation.

Kenneth B. Clark and Mamie P. Clark, "Racial Identification and Preference in Negro Children," in Eleanor E. Macoby, et al., *Readings in Social Psychology,* New York: Holt, Rinehart and Winston, Inc., 1958, pp. 602-611; and Abram Kardiner and Lionel Overysey, *The Mark of Oppression: Explorations in the Personality of the American Negro,* Cleveland: The World Publishing Company, 1957.

[3] David W. Johnson, *Changes in Self and Racial Attitudes of Negro Children Derived from Participation in a Freedom School,* New York: Institute of Urban Studies, Teachers College, Columbia University, 1964, p. 35.

Elliott Shapiro*

Nat Hentoff

In the corridor I saw Mrs. Lanckton, back again as a volunteer teacher. I asked her what she was specializing in during this school year. "It's supposed to be reading," she said, "but mostly it's just loving. Many of the children feel they're not at all important, that they won't amount to anything. It's no wonder some of them lose interest in reading. For a time, then, to get them to care about reading, they really need someone to read *to* them, to enjoy the pictures with them, to talk with them about a lot of things. About New York and home and loving and mothers and fathers. It's self-confidence they need; then the ABC's will come easier."

Mrs. Lanckton, I also discovered, had raised enough money to send John to camp for nine weeks in the summer that had just passed. "He enjoyed it a great deal," she said. "Of course, he didn't tell me that right away. My first day back, he was so glad to see me he pretended he didn't know who I was. When I came into a room, he stormed out of it. But we're talking again. And there is marked improvement. Do you know the worst thing that's happened to him in school so far? When he had a fight with some kids in the yard, he was deprived for a time of the right to stay in his regular classroom. He could only just wander around the corridors. My, he was upset. But a year ago, who would have thought John would have so wanted to stay in a classroom?"

I dropped in to see Miss Carmen Jones. The assistant principal was in her office, looking glumly at a sheaf of achievement scores. "I'm always dismayed," she said, "that some of our children do so poorly on tests. I go into classes and see children who are so bright and knowledgeable, who express themselves so freely. But often none of those qualities are reflected in their test scores. I don't know why. If I did, I'd do something about it. Sure, the scores show that we're doing a little better, but the scores are not good enough for the time and effort we put in. Part of it, I'm convinced, is that, even though we no longer have the group intelligence tests, there's a middle-class bias in the language used for the achievement tests. Much of the terminology is simply outside our children's experience. Look." She showed me a page of questions in a third-grade vocabulary test. "Trout. These kids don't know about trout. Their mothers buy

*Nat Hentoff, Our Children Are Dying. New York: Viking Press, 1966. Chapter 13, pp. 122-134.

porgies. And their fathers certainly don't go fishing. Well, we're going to have to give the children more practice in the types of tests they have to take."

I asked her view of teachers like Mr. Greenfield who feel that the child first has to feel important before he can learn. "Of course," she said, "I agree that the child must develop a strong ego. But I'm one of those old-fashioned people who believe the child needs the fundamentals in addition to a strong ego. We have to work on both. I'm old-fashioned about John too. I have a hard time with him because my background leads me to expect children to defer to adults, to those in authority. But, on the other hand, if you believe the salvation of one child is worth any sacrifice, then perhaps the way Dr. Shapiro has treated John is justified. Who knows what John will become?"

Miss Jones was looking again at the test scores. "Some days," she said to me wearily, "I feel I'd get greater satisfaction if I were out digging ditches. At least at the end of the day, you can see you've made a hole."

The conversation with Miss Jones reminded me of a talk I'd had during the summer with a woman who has long been active in organizations committed to greater integration in the New York City public school system and to radical improvement in the education of all slum children. She has been a frequent visitor to P.S. 119 and is an admirer of Dr. Shapiro. "But there's still something wrong there," she had told me. "Those kids are not scoring as high as they should in the tests. It may be that all the understanding they get in that shcool, while it does help them develop a better self-image, doesn't help them to achieve. Shapiro and his teachers are certainly compassionate, but the children's parents are *ambitious* for their kids. Shapiro is like from another world. He has the kind of values all of us ought to have. But when they leave the school, those kids aren't going into his kind of world. They're going into a world that's increasingly competitive, and increasingly cybernated as well. Maybe it damages a kid to push him, but I keep wondering whether Shapiro isn't damaging them in another way. Are his kids going to have enough competitive drive to do more than survive?"

Later in the day, while we were walking again to the parking meter, I told Shapiro what the woman had said. "I agree with her," he began, "at least on the point that our children do not achieve enough. We're far behind. But as for the style of our school, just because they are going to have to be in a cybernated world, it's imperative that children remain human beings. In that respect, it's vital, for example, for children of all kinds of backgrounds to be in small enough classes so that they can have close and pleasurable relationships with adults. All of us are becoming more and more like I.B.M. machines in an increasingly organized and rationalized society, and all children ought to have the experience of real human contact, so they'll remember later on that human contact is both possible and pleasurable. And our children, of course, need that most of all.

"Getting back to achievement, you have to remember that our children are among the poorest of the poor. But they are achieving more, as a group, than children used to achieve here in the past. And again, part of the measure of their achievement is lost, because in the fourth grade we send out our best achievers to I.G.C. classes. The children, moreover, are also achieving the courage of their convictions. The very fact thaat Mr. Marcus' fifth-graders were able to write critically to publishers and to superintendents about the inadequacies of social studies textbooks is an indication they may have the spirit to contend with what lies ahead. It's most important to nurture that kind of spirit. Our children are Negro, and as young Negro adults, they'll have more than their proper share of responsibility for making the human race live like human beings."

Shapiro was silent for a minute or two. "However, there is disturbing validity in the criticism about underachievement, and it pertains to every school that is seriously understaffed." I asked Shapiro about an observation by one of the parents that at P.S. 119, it was the middle group — rather than the best and worst of achievers — which was often overlooked. He nodded. "Around 1955," he said, "I became aware of the fact that no child in the school at the time was going to make it to college. It seemed to me that we therefore had to put a sizable amount of the resources we had into working with those children who seemed to be the most likely achievers. And since those resources were so slight, we had very little left over. Now, barring not too catastrophic circumstances in junior high school, in high school, in their lives, and in the community, twenty per cent of our children have a good chance to reach college. That's a great improvement, but the degree of our deprivation can be measured by the fact that sixty per cent of *all* children in the country are now reaching college.

"What of the others here? While we were focusing a great deal of energy and resources on the better achievers, we were also trying to make the entire school a place more favorable for, as it were, human contact — a freer place in which to teach and in which to be a child. Gradually, we were able thereby to develop a relatively stable staff, so that the middle range of children also would have a sequence of teachers who were relatively more experienced than those the children used to have here. And there has been some degree of improvement in the achievement of the middle children. But the fact remains that, after we get past the best achievers, there is a precipitous drop. We have a very long way to go. And we need a great deal of help."

We had stopped in front of the new school. Three stories high, its clean reddish-brown bricks and extensive window space made it look particularly cheerful by contrast with the gloomy battlements of P.S. 119. "Percival Goodman was the architect," Shapiro said. "He wouldn't take the job unless he was assured that the parents, teachers, and the principal would be involved in the planning. And we were. He and I also explored a relatively new school building in the next block. We walked all over it, including the roof. Its custodian was both astonished and pleased to see us. It was the first time in his experience that anyone had examined the drawbacks of one new building before going ahead to build another.

"We didn't get everything we wanted from headquarters at Livingston Street. Almost all the new elementary schools have a capacity of twelve hundred children — forty classrooms with thirty kids in each. We asked for seventy classrooms with twenty children in each. The compromise was fifty-five classrooms. Theoretically, fourteen hundred children are to be distributed among them, but I won't permit the number to go above eleven hundred.

"Goodman worked a long time on the designs, and in some ways, the school is really well planned. For example, very few, if any, of the new schools have an inside play area that can be used during inclement weather. The children have to stand in the halls or sit in the auditoriums or lunchrooms. Putting that much constraint on children during what should be their free periods leads to a lot of hostility when they go back to the classroom. But we have an inside play area. Also, there's a great deal more soundproofing in this school than has been put into any other so far, and as a result, we can encourage livelier activities without too much concern that the noise will bother neighboring classrooms. And a special unit for disturbed children has been set up — two classrooms with an office. Those have been especially soundproofed. But we may have to give that unit up. If P.S. 92 does become a More Effective School, we'll have small enough classes so that we won't need a particular unit for children with problems. Another asset is a somewhat larger library than any other elementary school has had up to this point. It's still not as big as I'd like, but that was another compromise."

A few days later, I found Shapiro involved in studying and advising a new project in teacher-training for slum schools. Early in 1965, the Coordinating Council on Education for the Disadvantaged had been formed as a clearing-house for information on education of children who have been discriminated against. It also helps develop new programs and tries to act as a liaison between various elements in the community committed to basic improvements in this area of education. Its support comes primarily from the labor movement and civil rights groups; and its chairman is Benjamin F. McLaurin, an official of the Brotherhood of Sleeping Car Porters and a member of the New York City Board of Higher Education.

The Council had now devised a plan to train sizable numbers of new teachers, particularly members of minority groups and particularly men, as specialists in the education of poverty-stricken children. The recruits, largely consisting of liberal arts graduates with the desire but not the financial resources to become teachers, would be interns assigned to schools requiring special services. Since the interns would be paid from Federal and possibly foundation funds, those schools could have smaller adult-to-pupil ratios without additional cost to the city. Under the supervision of a regular teacher, the interns would work with small groups of children in both remedial instruction and on new material. Corollary institutes, seminars, and workshops, staffed by faculty members from cooperating colleges, would also be provided the interns after school hours. In a year or a little more, the interns would be able to earn a master's degree and then enter the school system as regular teachers.

The initial goal was to be two hundred and sixty-five interns to be recruited by minority-group teachers in the school system, civil-rights groups, colleges, and other organizations.

"The possibilities are very exciting," Shapiro said as he gave me the news. "Just informally, I asked thirty-five Negro teachers about potential recruits, and each knew at least one person who would like to become a teacher if there were financial backing for his training. You know, for example there are any number of Negro men who were graduated from college in the early 1950's — some from law schools as well — who are working as mail clerks and in similar jobs. We can raise enough funds so that if the project goes through, we'll simultaneously be giving more children the experience of a small world in which adults protect them and we'll be bringing teachers into the system who can more easily identify with the children. Not only teachers. Some of the interns might be trained as guidance counselors and as catalysts to get people in poor neighborhoods to organize themselves for social action.

"The training will be in the direction of developing an organic relationship between the interns and the life of the school and the community — much more so than in any other proposed teacher-internship program I know about. That's why I'm happy the United Federation of Teachers is involved in this. The interns and the cooperating teachers need to feel free to criticize, to experiment, to become part of the life of the community without fear of retaliation.

"We've also received evidences of support from the United Parents' Assoiations, the Board of Education, and the Board of Higher Education, the latter being in charge of the city universities and colleges from which we'll get our specialists. The interns will be encouraged to participate in parents' association meetings, and they'll sit in on conferences with neighborhood people, welfare investigators, church leaders, and other elements in the community. They'll get to be able to analyze housing problems, for instance, and once they know what can be done, they'll also know the degree to which they can most effectively participate — and in what ways. I've already drawn up a list of possible courses for the interns."

Shapiro handed me a paper. At the top of his list was the notation: "Most, if not all, of the courses should be of a workshop or practicum type, immediately related to the classroom experiences of the interns." Among the suggested courses were:

> The relationship of different educational philosophies to classroom management, activities and experiences.

> Methods and principles of teaching as developed from the classroom experiences of the interns.

> Methods and principles of teaching reading and mathematics through analyzing the classroom experiences of interns.

Methods and principles for presenting the history of Africa and the contributions of the American Negro to American History.

Analysis of the deficiencies of social studies textbooks in order to develop a desirable social studies curriculum.

Dynamics of a changing society as observed in classroom activities and experiences.

The psychology of expressive behavior of children and teachers as observed in the classroom experiences of the interns.

The psychology of normal and of abnormal behavior of children and teachers as observed in the class.

The psychology of the motivation of human behavior.

The psychology of individual differences.

Seminar in educational research.

Methods and materials for studying Latin-American cultures.

Spanish for teachers from Puerto Rico.

Critique of research in language arts, curriculum, and teaching.

Principles and methods of developing original, creative dramatizations that would reflect the problems of the community.

The role in the school life of teachers' organizations and participation in them.

"I don't know when this project will be able to start," said Shapiro as he took back the paper. "There are obstacles. There is always resistance to change in education, especially when the ideas for change come from outside what might be considered the establishments. There's not just one; there are several educational establishments. And they prefer concepts they've thought up themselves."

"In the meantime," Shapiro stood up, "there are the immediate problems. This fall we set up one third-grade class of only nineteen. We selected children who seemed to have the greatest disparity between their ability and their achievement so far in reading. It has been indicated to me from above that we can't afford the luxury of a class with an adult-to-pupil ratio of one-to-nineteen. Well, I've remained adamant on the subject."

I followed him into the corridor. Shapiro paused at a window and looked at a group of older boys playing basketball in the yard. They seemed to be fifteen or sixteen, and they appeared to be playing hooky from wherever they were supposed to be.

I asked Shapiro about the growing belief among some educators involved in preschool training for slum children that, if a child is not sufficiently stimulated to learn in elementary school, irreparable damage has been done in terms of his capacity to achieve later. "No," he said. "I don't believe it. It does make a real difference if you catch them earlier, and it's easier to reach them early. Also, there probably is a net loss if the child is caught quite late. And if the attempt isn't made until late, much more resources are needed. But I don't believe they're beyond help. Look at those boys. I know them. They can hardly read, but they certainly do have hostility; and if they could become involved, let us say, in action against slum landlords and in similar projects to change the community, they'd be motivated to learn to read in order to be more effective in what they were trying to do."

As we walked to the gym, I asked Shapiro if there was still doubt that P.S. 119 would be torn down, as promised, to provide a play area for the new school. "I'm now convinced it will be," he said. "But what," I asked "of the considerable investment in repairs that was suddenly put into P.S. 119?" He grinned. "That is simply another illustration of the surrealism of the school system."

Inside the gym, amid the roar and rush of children, a small boy, crying, came up to Shapiro. The principal leaned over, listened intently, and said, "I'll get the ball back for you. You stay here." He moved swiftly across the floor, talked to two sixth-graders playing basketball, and came back to the boy. "They'll be finished soon. You stay here."

Two girls from a kindergarten class came up to Shapiro. The principal leaned over again, listened, and as one of the girls took his hand, he moved quickly into the lunchroom. "Do you maybe have two oranges?" he asked an aide. She did, and he gave each girl an orange. They skipped away. "Their teacher," Shapiro explained, peering around the gym, "had promised everyone an orange, but those two had forgotten their coats. When they came back, the teacher was gone. Now where's that boy?" Shapiro couldn't find the little boy who had first stopped him when he'd come into the gym. The principal looked disturbed. 'That was a retarded child. Two bigger kids had taken away his ball, and I told him I'd get it back as soon as they finished a few points. I didn't want them to be so angry they'd beat him up later. But I made a mistake. I should have stayed until they were through. The girls would have waited. Well, the boy's gone. Now he thinks I betrayed him."

A neatly dressed boy of about nine, holding a small briefcase, rushed up to Shapiro. He was crying loudly. Shapiro hugged him and took him over to a teacher. "He couldn't find his older sister," Shapiro said to me. "She takes him home. He was crying because he was afraid he wouldn't know how to get home. He's been here three years, and he lives near by. Is he retarded? Or is it some other problem? It's hard to tell."

A boy whizzed over to Shapiro, whispered to him excitedly, and whizzed away. "He saw a boy break a window near the door. It was apparently done quite deliberately. This one says he'll point out the boy who did it when they line up in the morning. I took him seriously, not because I want to encourage snitching, but because he feels so strongly that it was wrong to break the window, and I have to go along with him. If he remembers to come over to me tomorrow morning, I'll have to follow through."

On the far side of the gym, John was shooting at a basket. He saw Shapiro and waved. The principal waved back. "He's having a good day," said Shapiro. "There's another complication this year. The older youngsters on the block where John lives have been caught up in black nationalism. He hangs out with them, but at school he's with an integrated group of people he's come to trust somewhat. So there's a conflict. And when he gets particularly frustrated here, the racial epithets come flying out. But the epithets are bi-racial. He'll call me a white something or other, and he'll call a teacher a black something or other. It's hard for him."

A very little child, perhaps five, was alone in the center of the floor. He was crying. Shapiro went over, picked him up, touched his head to his, listened through the sobs, and brought him to a teacher. "He'd lost his class," said Shapiro when he came back.

We left the gym, and as we came toward his office, I remembered the conversation I'd had the previous spring with several teachers fantasizing Shapiro in the role of Superindendent of Schools. "What *would* you do?" I asked. He obviously enjoyed the chance to speculate.

I'd go to all the poorest neighborhoods and stir up the parents. I'd have a few offices — not just one — and most would be in the poor communities. I'd travel to them on a regular schedule, so that the parents would know when I'd be there if they wanted to see me. My main office would be in Harlem or in Bedford-Stuyvesant. I'd also approach as many groups throughout the city as possible to get as much community support for the funds we need. The middle class. The business community. I'd make it very clear to them they haven't been helping nearly enough. And I'd constantly urge the Board of Education to demand larger budgets. Constantly.

"Also," Shaprio continued, "I'd set up a permanent office in Washington, because much of the funding from now on has to be Federally based. In that office we'd develop specialists in formulating programs and in knowing how to get them through all the various agencies in that governmental maze. Then we'd have to relate their specialized knowledge to the political strength of New York City. In other words, we'd have to devise ways to keep the populace alert as to who has been helping education, and hopefully their votes would signify their continuing concern. That's the beginning."

"It would certainly be a lively administration," I said.

"To say the least," Shapiro smiled. The bench in the outer office was nearly full of waiting children.

A Second Grade Class*

G. Alexander Moore, Jr.

THE BACKGROUND

The class is one that the principal himself warned visitors, with a kind of negative pride, to be one of the "wild" classes. He was not at all reluctant that visitors should witness the problems his school faced. The class is in ill repute throughout the school; several teachers commented on it, one calling it "a zoo." It ranks ninth and lowest of the second grade classes. There are twenty-four students on roll, fifteen boys and nine girls. They are all in the reading readiness stage. They are either non-English-speaking or are considered "seriously disturbed" by the administration. Remembering the large turnover of pupils in the school — only 15 per cent remained from last year — it should not be surprising to find many pupils entering this school still speaking only Spanish. However, the visitor does not readily imagine why a second grade class should still be on the kindergarten level and, like the pupils, the observer enters the classroom "somewhat disturbed."

This observation was on a spring day, starting at 9:30 in the morning and continuing till 11:15, or lunch time. On this day there are only eighteen of the twenty-four students present. Six of these struck the observer as being American Negroes; the remaining students were Hispanos.

Mrs. Auslander, the teacher, is a tall woman in her late forties or early fifties. Her hair is mixed gray and white and her face is deeply lined. One's first impression of her is that of a nervous and harrassed woman.

The classroom itself is in the full sense of the word nondescript.

THE MORNING SESSION

It is 9:30 and Mrs. Auslander is telling the children to hold their hands up in order that she may inspect them to see if they are clean. Completing this, she tells the children to sing their morning song. "This is the way we wash our hands," the children start singing, and make appropriate motions as they continue through the various verses. Looking around, one notes that the boys

*G. Alexander Moore, Jr., *Realities Of The Urban Classroom*, Garden City, New York: Doubleday Anchor Book, 1967. pp. 52-67.

have long trousers, not short pants, and the girls are wearing cotton dresses. In general the children appear somewhat unkempt in comparison to other second grade classes noted in the hall. This is particularly true of the boys.

The Morning News

The song is over and the teacher, attempting to drill them on the days of the week, asks them, "What day is today? What day was yesterday? What day will tomorrow be?" As the children call out the names of the various days, she stops to correct them: "Give your answers in sentences!"

Meanwhile several children are noisily running around the room hitting one another. Others sit in a stupor, apparently quite unaware of thier surroundings. In the space of the first ten minutes, the teacher has used physical force and actually hurts the children in an attempt to control them. Yet she has not achieved control of the class, nor does she at any time during the morning. She frequently addresses her noisy, restless class, saying, "When I have everyone's attention and your hands are folded, then I will listen to what you're trying to say." Since this never happens, she never really listens to any of the children during the morning, yet many of them do seem to want to say something to her.

She suddenly turns upon a child who was quietly looking at a book, and says, "Why are you playing with your book?"

Some children in another part of the room then begin to write; the teacher calls out, "We're talking. We're not writing now." In the meantime a few children do give her the proper names of the days; however, most of the class is not paying any attention.

"Take out your notebooks," she calls. "We are going to write our morning news." She turns to the board and prints the number of the school, the class number, and the date.[2] Under this she writes the words "Our News." Underneath this she begins to write sentences: "Today is Friday . . . . There are nine days left in May. . . . It is sunny and warm and clear . . . . We saw a film about flowers." This last is a reference to a film that the class had just seen minutes before in the second grade weekly assembly which started off this Friday. These sentences are a long time in appearing on the board for she tries to elicit them from the children by such questions as "How many days are left in May?" or "What kind of weather are we having?" The children are not paying any particular attention and though a few replies are called forth, she is left to do most of the work. In any case, the exercise is going on the board for the children to copy down in their notebooks; she tells them to do this sentence-by-sentence.

Leaving the sentences on the board and giving the children more time to copy them, Mrs. Auslander goes back to the observer and starts a conversation.

---

[2] In this school system this is a standard heading which teachers must teach children to use for written work.

"This is a discipline class. It is not an ordinary class. I have emotionally disturbed children and mentally retarded children and I can't get perfect attention. I don't try to. I can't ride them all the time. I hope you understand that it is this type of class and will not be too upset by what you see in this classroom." The observer reassured her, saying that we wanted to see the problems presented by this kind of class, and she seemed completely at ease. Indeed she never appeared to feel a threat from any visitors.

At 10:05, Mrs. Auslander walks around the room to see if the children are copying the work from the board in their notebooks. Frequently she approaches a child and asks, "Where is your book?" If the child does not answer, she repeats the question until he or she does. In one case, she repeated it a good six times, each time raising her voice more until she was shouting.

Some children are not copying the work because they do not have pencils, so she tries to persuade other children to lend them one. "George, will you lend a pencil to Lucille?" she asks. George has a small pencil case from which he removes a pencil to lend to Lucille. "What a nice boy you are," she commends George.

While she was looking for a pencil for Lucille, Mrs. Auslander remarked to the observer what a problem she has because the children forget or lose pencils. The observer offered a pencil for Lucille, but Mrs. Auslander protested, saying without lowering her speaking voice, "You'll never get it back." After George has lent his pencil to Lucille, Mrs. Auslander comments aloud to the observer, "You know, George *could* be a very *good* boy."

She returns to the board and attempts to elicit a response to the sentence under discussion. "Does anybody know how many days are left in May?" She sends a child to the front of the room to count the number of days on the May calendar. She tries to engage the rest of the children in counting along with him but only a few children join in.

Suddenly the observer realizes that several children have been out of the room on pass all this time. One boy is returning with his pass and six children have raised their hands to ask for permission to go to the bathroom. They shout, "Teacher, can we leave the room? Can we leave the room?" Whenever anyone wants Mrs. Auslander's attention, she is addressed as "Teacher." Not one student has called her by name yet.

To the students' requests she answers, "Nobody may leave." Nonetheless, in a moment she gives the pass to one of the children, who quickly leaves the room. When he returns, the same commotion begins anew and she hands the pass to another child. The pass is constantly in use.

Another sentence has been left on the board and the children have been told to copy it. Mrs. Auslander then shows the observer some of her children's work. She shoves a handful of papers forward and says they belong to a boy who is almost ten years old. A glance shows that the child has not even been able to begin to copy the work from the board. In a loud voice she comments, "This is the best this child can do." All those sitting in the back of the room must have overheard her, for it is obvious that several children are listening. She shows a second notebook and comments, "Now this girl, she's slow, but she writes very nicely."

There is a momentary lull in the noise. But soon the sounds of voices, shuffling feet, moving chairs, and scuffling children fill the room with a din. A boy comes back with the pass and the noise is diverted to him as others also want to leave the room. The teacher declares, "A girl goes after a boy. You know that after a boy goes, a girl goes." Mrs. Auslander is now in the back of the class. She tells the children to look at their clowns, which are clown posters made by the pupils. The balloons the clowns hold are of litmus paper and change color according to the weather. "Today the balloons are blue. This means that it is a fair and sunny day." Having answered her own question, she returns to the blackboard to write the sentence she was trying to elicit from the children: "It is sunny and warm and clear."

"Now copy that," she calls, and returns to the observer to comment, "I bought pencils for all these children when I first came here and gave each one a small pencil case with pencils in it. But all these children lost their pencils and the only way I have now of solving the pencil problem is to get them to lend pencils to each other because obviously I can't be providing pencils for them all the time."

She spies a child chewing gum. "Empty your mouth and keep it closed when it's empty." She stops and stands in front of a boy who is quietly working at his desk and tells him, "Take your jacket off. Take your jacket off. Take it off." It is a suit jacket.

The boy protests: "I don't want to take if off because I'm afraid something will happen to it."

"The other children trust you. Why should't you trust them?" she retorts, and insists once again that he remove his jacket. "And hang it up. Or would you like to visit Mr. Selby?" The last remark was said with a threatening sound. (Mr. Selby is the name we have given to the principal.) The boy reluctantly gets up, goes over to the closet, takes his jacket off, hangs it up, and stomps back to his desk.

It is 10:19. Mrs. Auslander is telling Carol, a Negro girl, "Get up and stand in the corner and face the wall. Put your hands on your head." The girl obeys, standing in a corner at the back of the room, and immediately begins to cry. In a moment, she takes her hands off her head and stops crying.

A boy who has been given the pass flourishes it. As he leaves the room, he pauses at the door and salutes the class. Once he is gone, the teacher goes to the door and, taking out her key, locks the door from the inside. Some older boys are passing in the hall. They stop at the door, look into the classroom, and make faces through the window.

Mrs. Auslander is standing alongside the boy that she had earlier forced to remove his jacket. She addresses him: "Would you like to stay in Mr. Selby's office all day?" Carol is sucking her thumb in the corner. Disorder reigns.

The teacher pulls Vera, a Hispano girl, over to the observer and introduces her. She explains, "Vera is a C.R.M.D. child."[3] Mrs. Auslander waves the page Vera is working on in front of the observer, who silently notes that the work is very poor. Vera likes the idea of showing her work to the observer and no sooner is she at her seat than she picks up her entire notebook and returns with it. The idea catches on. Other children follow so that the observer soon is surrounded by six or seven children, all anxious to display their work.

Vera came first. One or two of the other children in this impromptu line become eager and attempt to push ahead of her and shove their notebooks in front of her. Vera, who is husky, pushes them back out of the way. Several small fights begin this way with Vera winning. One is lasting more than a few seconds, and the observer puts her hand on the shoulder of Vera's rival and tells her quietly, "I will look at your work but Vera is first." The children wait quietly without pushing. But now Vera is the problem, for as the observer turns the pages of her notebook, Vera turns them back to the first page. The observer explains, "I will have to look at the notebooks of the other children." Vera steps aside docilely to let the others come forward. The observer finds some of the copying work done quite well and some that is incoherent or illegible.

Allen, a Negro boy with crossed eyes, is standing in front of the observer. The observer asks him, "May I look at your book?" He nods eagerly. On the first page there is a note written by the teacher. "Allen has exposed himself in school today. He has many kinds of problems. Take this note home to your mother and have her sign it." A signature below this shows his mother has read it.

A second entry is her reply. "I beat Allen at home for having done this but Allen says he didn't do it but that another boy has done it to him." On the second page there is another note from Mrs. Auslander in ink, as her first had been. "Allen did expose himself but I do not want to make an issue of it." All these notes are in the ordinary pages of Allen's class notebook, an article he carries around with him and uses daily. The observer passes quickly on to other pages for fear of embarrassing Allen, who must know what the notes are about. She tries to find a particularly nice comment as she closes his book and hands it back to him.

A group of children still surround her and begin to ask questions. She asks their names and such things as "How long have you been in this school?" All of the children who speak to her do so in English, thus showing some knowledge of it. Mrs. Auslander quickly breaks up the exchange, sending them back to their seats.

To all outward appearances, Mrs. Auslander is spending all of her time pushing the children around, frequently hurting them as she does this. At the

---

[3]C.R.M.D. is an abbreviation for Children with Retarded Mental Development.

moment she is pinching Allen on the arm; he grimaces in pain. Then she shoves him into the corner and he begins to cry. Moments later similar events befall a boy named Edward.

Suddenly Mrs. Auslander makes an attempt at teaching the concept of time. "What time is it?" she calls out. A child begins to pack up his books and arranges his briefcase, perhaps taking her cue. But she turns on him sharply: "What time do you go home? Put your books down. It's not time to go home."

She notices that Carol has left the corner and joined a group that is back lingering near the observer. "So you want me to smack you. Get back in the corner and put your hands on your head." Carol does so and starts sucking her thumb again. A girl near the observer remarked to her, "Carol is our baby because she sucks her thumb." From the front of the class Mrs. Auslander cries shrilly, "Listen, are you going to get into your seats or are you going to stay there?" The children return to their seats.

The observer turns her head to survey the room. Things seem to be getting worse. Fighting occurs frequently among the children. A child will run around the room and hit another child who will then give chase or retaliate later. Edward, who has remained only briefly in the corner to which he was sent, has been feuding with George, the boy who lent a pencil to Lucille.

The teacher pulls a child by the hair. It is short hair on a Negro boy's scalp, and he yells from the pain.

At 10:50, she makes her second concerted effort to get the class quiet by silently doing exercises, expecting them to join in. Earlier, at 10:00, she had done it for a moment with little effect. Standing in the front of the room, she has both hands on her hips. The exercises are simple ones involving placing and removing the hands on the hips while raising one leg and then the other. A few children take them up, but most remain seated with a few children still running around the room. She meets this challenge by going directly to a child's desk and standing in front of it, glaring at the child and continuing the exercise until he gets up and joins in. She says not a word. This technique finally succeeds in getting all the children up and exercising quietly for a few minutes. But as soon as the exercies period ends and the children sit down again, noise begins to fill the air.

At 10:55 Mrs. Auslander releases Carol from her place in the corner, by walking over and asking, "Are you going to do you work, Carol? I'm going to give you one more chance. If you don't do your work, you'll spend the rest of the day standing." Thus Carol went back to her seat for the second time between 10:19 and 10:55, the period she was officially disciplined, save for a few moments of grace during which she had resumed her seat. Although she was supposed to have stood with her hands on her head, she did not do so. Her hands went down to her sides whenever the teacher was not looking.

Angel, a Hispano boy, is becoming particularly obstreperous. He runs around the room and pushes some of the children, an act he has engaged in several times before. Two or three times earlier in the morning the teacher had threatened him with being sent to Mr. Selby's office. At one point she had told the observer, "This boy does not like or trust anybody. He is a problem child." At 11:00 A.M. she makes good her threat, marching out of the room saying, "I'm going to get John." As soon as she is out of the door, the noise in the room drops. Attention seems to be centered on the door. Several of the children "ooh" and "ah." One child says, "Here he comes." Mrs. Auslander enters, accompanied by a tall, slender Negro boy from an older grade. They approach Angel, the small Hispano boy, who is in his seat, clutching his desk for dear life and bawling loudly. The teacher tries to pry him loose but without success. She turns to her companion. "John, would you take him, please."

Angel is wailing louder all the time and babbles, "Leave me alone. Leave me alone." He clings to his desk but John succeeds in prying him loose and drags him screaming from the room. His screams can be heard echoing down the hall.[4]

Mrs. Auslander explains to the observer, "When I use one for an example, the rest behave. It's the only way."

The observer inquires, matter-of-factly, "Where does John take the children when he takes them out?"

"He takes them to Mr. Selby."

If that is so, the observer wonders why there has been so much screaming in the process.

It is 11:00 A.M. and another child is being put in the corner and told, "Put your hands on your head." Mrs. Auslander turns to go through some words on the board. These are part of the vocabulary appearing in the Dick and Jane Series of readers. The list numbers from fifteen to twenty words. She reads each word aloud and the children repeat it in unison. Their task is to copy the words down into their notebooks at the same time. A few do. Her reprimands are constant: "Will you please do your work?" Or again, "Why are you not writing?" To a third, "Do you want to go to Mr. Selby?"

Presently Angel reappears at the door with John on one side of him and a beefy, tough-looking Negro child on the other. They take him over to the teacher and have him apologize to her. He goes to his desk to sit, and he's quiet for at least ten or fifteen minutes.

Two or three of the boys have, of their own accord, gone back to the observer to show her their work. While she glances through their notebooks, she asks them, "Where do the big boys take the children when they take them out of the room?" "To see Mr. Selby," they say.

A cry goes up as the teacher pulls Allen by the ear over to the wastepaper basket where he must spit out his gum. She shouts at several other children, "You want me to get John? Let me see you act up once more and you'll be in

---

[4] An observer in another classroom heard the commotion which the teacher in that class tried to shut out by closing the door while she commented, "Tears, tears, and more tears."

trouble." She hustles another boy off to the corner to stand with his hands on his head. Ann, who was already in another corner, is now sucking her thumb.

Lining Up

At 11:50 the children are in line for lunch, which they must eat on an early shift. During the line-up two of the children are continually fighting one another. One of the children has been "teacher's pet" all morning. Several times he seconded her commands to children and mimicked some of her behavior. An example of this would be when he pulled a boy's hair and told him to behave. Now two or three children are hitting him and he begins to cry.

In the midst of this bedlam, a Negro girl approaches the observer and asks her to tie her hood. She turns her face up and the observer ties a bow under her chin. While she is doing this, the teacher comes over and says, "It is ridiculous for this child to be wearing a hood on a warm day. She might get sick if she wears it." Silently the observer ties the bow and the child lines up with the others. Out in the hall, the class is not as noisy. The teacher leads them down the stairs to the cafeteria. At each landing, the class halts before descending the next flight. The noise has been sufficient to bring a man teacher out of his room to see what is going on. He re-enters and closes his door with a bang. The children have started out ahead of the teacher and, as they go downstairs, she asks to pass between the two lines in order to get to the head of the class. The children separate and make a passageway for her along the double line. As she goes down the staircase, several children raise their feet as if to kick her.

THE AFTERNOON SESSION

During the afternoon another person came to observe Mrs. Auslander's class. She came after the lunch period was over and the children were back in their room.

As the new observer came in the door, Mrs. Auslander greeted her, saying, "You see that child over there? She clings all the time. That's all she does, cling." She was referring to a Hispano girl who has a piece of cloth which she is rubbing up and down a steampipe at the side of the room. The new observer next notices a boy sitting in the front of the room, sucking his thumb. The teacher audibly continues her discussion of the class: "This is a class of low intelligence. They have taken all the worst children in this grade and formed this class. I'm a new teacher! What do you think of the fact that I was given a class like this? All of these children are terrible problems."

The observer sees the teacher has a lesson on the board but notes that there is a great deal of activity among the children. One boy is crawling on the floor looking for a nickel. Allen, the Negro youngster with crossed eyes, is sitting in the front of the room, but maintaining constant activity from his seat. Many of the children are hitting one another; a child will get up from his seat, go over to another child for no apparent reason and slap him in the face, or perhaps push him or strike his body before rushing back to his seat. These are all initial impressions made after the first few minutes in the classroom.

One boy, Angel, runs over to Allen, throws him on the floor, and jumps up on his back with both feet. Allen quite naturally screams and yells. The teacher screams too: "Get away from there!" She continues to scream and we learn the names of the two brawlers.

Many children are calling out and shouting to one another across the room. As the observer looks around the room, she sees many children hitting each other on the head with pencils.

Handwriting

The teacher withal is attempting her lesson. She has written the letter G on the board and now prints the word *goat.* Chalk in hand, she turns from the word directly to a child: "Where is your book? Get to work! Why don't you write?" Her face is severe and threatening. Chalk still in hand, she sends a boy to stand in the corner, where he remains for some time before she releases him.

A crash is heard. A child has hit another student and thrown his books on the floor. The teacher ignores this incident, as she does most of its kind. The child directly in front of the observer is striking the child next to him with his pencil, so much so that the observer fears for his eyes. But the teacher takes no notice; she is telling the boy in the corner to put his hands on his head. Allen, who is in the front of the room, is constantly dancing away from the teacher in a boxing step whenever she approaches as if to dodge her. He seems to be engaging in a mock boxing dance but she is not striking him. However, children are, for he seems to be a target for the rest of the class. Yet, he does nothing to resist or protest the constant barrage of attacks he is under; he just dances away from the teacher. The observer spies Edward hitting another boy over the head with a book. At one point or another as many as ten of the eighteen pupils are out of their seats. Some of the children are chasing each other. At times the teacher darts forward to quiet students. One method is to pull a child up by his ear. She does this twice, once to a Negro boy and once to a Hispano boy. Each cries out, and then obeys her momentarily. The ear-pulling is accompanied by the threat, "All right, if you won't be quiet, I will go get John."

Presently Mrs. Auslander leaves the room. Shortly she is back with John. She stations him at the front of the room where he stands quietly and says, "If you children get bad, you must go to Mr. Selby."

Science

With John watching from the front, the teacher turns her attention to teaching, saying, "The class is going to have a science lesson. I want to show you a good way to pour water." She presents them the idea of a funnel. Her demonstration actually awakes some interest in the children. But, to her annoyance, they are soon shouting answers to her.

Her face and stance grim and tense with annoyance, the teacher takes a piece of paper and dips it into water, asking the children, "Why does water go up in the paper?" The children are listening but have no answer. She answers, "The reason that water goes up is that there are tiny holes in the paper." A number of children are out of their seats to gather around the teacher as she conducts this experiment.

She is saying, "We are going to learn some of the facts about water." John, at this point, is trying to make the children return to their seats. Sometimes he grabs a child and pushes him down into his seat. The boy in the corner begins to move away from there. The teacher calls out sharply, "Get back into that corner quickly." She darts forward and pulls him back by his ear.

Leaving the corner, the teacher passes by the observer and says, "You see what I have to put up with. These children's parents have given me permission to beat them because they do not know what to do with them in order to get them to listen. You see that child there? There is no one at home to talk to her." While she is saying this, Edward, a Hispano youngster (who had been in the corner in the morning), is constantly striking George, a Negro youngster (who had lent his pencil to Lucille).

A child in the front of the room raises his hand to ask to leave the room, but is ignored. Edward is now going around hitting other children; however, each time he hits George, Robert arises and hits him, defending George. The teacher explains to the observer, "Edward really thinks he is helping me. That's why he is hitting other children." Another frequent target for Edward's barrage is Allen.

The teacher points out a boy, Frankie, and says in a normal speaking voice, "His father killed his mother. The boy stays with an aunt and thirteen children. The home background of most of these children is simply terrible. They are all emotionally disturbed. They are really problems. They don't understand normal psychology. They only know brute force."

At this point the observer got up, excused herself, and left hastily. She had been in the room one hour exactly.

A J.H.S. 271 Teacher Tells It Like He Sees It*

Charles S. Isaacs

Landlord, landlord
My roof has sprung a leak.
Don't you 'member I told you
about it
Way last week?

Landlord, landlord
These steps is broken down.
When you come up yourself
It's a wonder you don't fall down.

Ten bucks you say I owe you?
Ten bucks you say is due?
Well, that's Ten Bucks more'n
I'll pay you
Till you fix this house up new.

What? You gonna get eviction orders?
You gonna cut off my heat?
You gonna take my furniture and
Throw it in the street?

Um-huh! You talking high and
mighty.
Talk on — till you get through.
You ain't gonna be able to say a
word
If I land my fist on you.

Police! Police!
Come and get this man!
He's trying to ruin the government
And overturn the land!

Copper's Whistle!
Patrol bell!
Arrest.

Charles S. Isaacs, "A J.H.S. 271 Teacher Tells It Like He Sees It," *The New York Times Magazine,* November 24, 1968.

Precinct station.
Iron cell.
Headlines in press:
   Man Threatens Landlord
   Tenant Held; No Bail
   Judge Gives Negro 30 Days in
      County Jail

1. Who is the man in the poem?
2. Why is he angry? Should he be?
3. What does he do to the landlord?
     Was he justified in doing so?
4. What happens to him? Does he deserve the penalty?
5. Would it happen if he were white? Why? Why not?
6. Does this poem remind you of things that happen here in Ocean Hill-Brownsville? What?
7. Why do you think Mr. Mayer has used this poem in our class?

— A social-studies lesson
at J.H.S. 271

The above poem is "Ballad of the Landlord," by the late Afro-American poet Langston Hughes, and it has dual relevance to the Ocean Hill-Brownsville story. Replace the landlord with the educational establishment, the tenant with the black parent, and the leaky roof with a history of inferior education — then write a sequel to the poem. The sequel will be about an educational system crumbling from its own inner decay, a bureaucracy which is afraid to enter the ghetto without police protection and a community which will settle for no less than the freedom to rebuild for itself.

The tenant decides to raze the old structure and build a new one, with a new construction company of his own choice. That is where my colleagues and I come into the story.

When Jonathan Kozol, author of "Death at an Early Age," taught a lesson similar to the one quoted to his Boston public-school students, he was fired; no J.H.S. 271 teacher will be dismissed for teaching that lesson. Whether we label this change "innovation," "academic freedom" or "dangerous," it illustrates the new outlook to education which the Ocean Hill-Brownsville experiment in community involvement has brought about, the type of teacher it has attracted, and the threat which produced a massive effort to destroy it before it began. Despite the concessions granted the striking teachers' union over last weekend, the sense of innovation lingers in the air.

Actually, although innovation is a major purpose of decentralization, we have had a basically traditional program at J.H.S. 271; we have few formal changes that other schools could not copy if they were so inclined. There are many reasons for this, perhaps the most prominent of which is the pressure to get more children into decent high schools. Last year, only nine out of

491 graduates went on to the "better" schools. The parents of my eighth-grade students have this very much on their minds, and many of them want community-controlled schools just so their children will be able to enter the better high schools and colleges. In discussions with these parents, it is difficult to discuss the new math, or doing away with old-fashioned grammar lessons; they want their children to learn the 3 R's. In this respect, these black and Puerto Rican parents are no different from white parents; they don't want their children to be used as guinea pigs.

The experiment has had an educational effect on many of the parents and will, in time, bring about a change in the community's basic conservatism. At one meeting, a father stood up to ask a question. He said that when he "was a boy," he wouldn't talk back to a teacher because he would get "whupped" both at home and in school if he did; he wanted to know why we didn't encourage more "whupping." He was answered by a young black college student who explained that the awe and fear of authority figures felt by children in a bygone era is counter-productive today.

The reply received considerably more applause than the question, but, sitting on the speakers' panel, I was wondering how that parent would react if his child came home and told him what he learned in "Charlie's class" that day. I had told my students thay they were allowed to address me by my first name, and I had done this precisely to break down the wall of fear that usually exists between student and teacher. (It is a monument to the past that so many children have found it impossible to take advantage of this familiarity.)

Other frustrations to real innovation have been police in the schools, the uncertainty of not knowing whether school will be open or closed tomorrow, and the general tension which these have created. But there have been two more basic obstacles.

The first of these has been the presence of reporters, a presence which transforms any situation into something different from what it would otherwise be. The daily mass media understand an orderly hallway, suits and ties, but not pyschodrama, or *dashikis*. As one teacher explained: "Of course we have to make the children go up the 'Up' staircase, and down the 'Down' staircase; there might be a television camera at the end of the stairs." To experiment means to accept the risk of possible failure, and no one wants to take the risk of falling flat on his face in 60 million living rooms.

An even more fundamental obstacle is built into the very nature of the project. Our experiment will be evaluated in terms of the established conventional criteria: reading scores, discipline, standardized achievement tests, etc., some of which measure what they are intended to measure, *for middle-class children*. We have a problem when these criteria fail to measure the extent to which a child has been educated, when they simply test rote memorization, stifling of initiative and training in sitting through standardized examinations. Unleashed creativity, or a critical outlook, for example, would probably lower a child's scores on these exams, rather than raise them.

If the conventional criteria measure the wrong things, their effect is harmful to our students, yet they will determine to a great extent whether or not we will ever be free to develop our own yardsticks. In effect, we must miseducate the children before we will be allowed to educate them.

If we succeed where others have failed, the explanation will not lie in minor reforms of a decadent educational system. If the children learn now, it will be because they want to more than ever before. It will be because they do feel the sense of community which is developing, and because their parents now participate actively in their education. They know that their teachers have faith in them, and, most important of all, they are learning to have faith in themselves. Appeals to manhood and to pride in blackness are far better motivational and disciplinary tools in J.H.S. 271 than threats of suspension or detention.

In order to encourage these positive factors, the faculty is trying to become truly close to the students and their families. One *Saturday,* we arranged for free buses and took 600 children on a trip to Bear Mountain. No red tape, no waiting period, and, of course, no pay for the teachers; they were having too good a time themselves even to consider it.

A large group of teachers attend all open community meetings, and the teacher-community solidarity at these gatherings strengthens all of us; at one meeting, the only speaker to receive a standing ovation was Fran Aurello, a white teacher. We have been arranging informal get-togethers with the parents at school and in their homes, and every teacher is pledged to get acquainted with the parents of *all* his students. All this takes time, but the possibilities for the future, as well as our successors, in this short period of time are lost on none of us.

Our assistant principals have offered an interesting comparison between the "old" supervisory personnel and those who will replace them. In September, when I began teaching, we had five assistant principals, including one Negro, who were imposed on us by the central Board of Education, and two who were hired by the local governing board. Since I had not known at first that any of our staff was of the former group, my initial experiences with them shook my faith in the experiment more than a little. One spent an entire staff meeting instructing the teachers that our major function was to discipline, regiment and routinize the children. Another admonished the staff to wear rubber-soled shoes, as she did, so we could "sneak up on the children in the halls." Still another barged into the middle of an orderly class to exclaim: "Close those windows! If a child falls out, *we'll* really be in a fix." If this was experimentation, I thought, how much worse could things have been before?

It was not long before I found out that these people were not part of the experiment, did not want to participate in the experiment, and were, in fact, sabotaging the experiment by forcing students and teachers simply to refuse to implement such repressive policies. Finally, unable to influence their staff in any way, they were kind enough to transfer voluntarily out of the district as a group.

That left us with John Mandracchia, an experienced administrator who transferred into the district last February, and Albert Vann, an acting (uncertified) assistant principal who doubles as president of the African — American Teachers Association. Mandracchia is that rare individual who managed to survive in the so-called "merit" system despite substantial merit. He is white, 40 years old and lives in the suburbs; yet he has no trouble in relating to black people or young people, including pupils, and seems to understand the problems of the cities. Few teachers wake up at 4:45 each morning, as he does, and stay late every afternoon. He once slept in school overnight because he did not have time for his daily four hours of driving.

Mandracchia is an exception to the rule that a lifetime of being white, combined with a career within the New York City school system, will prevent anyone from becoming a competent supervisor in a black school. Still, when I asked him what he thought our major administrative innovation was, he said: "For the first time, black kids have the opportunity to identify with black leadership in their schools."

Al Vann is one of those black leaders. Ten years in the system have taught him to hate it, and his battle against it seems to have brought wrath down upon him. One newspaper reported that he arrived at school at 9 one morning and organized and led a parent-teacher march through the community beginning at 9:02. Anyone who could have organized that march in two minutes certainly should throw a scare into the system.

It is perhaps because of fear, mixed with a generous portion of racism, that the press, the U.F.T. and the Board of Education credit Vann with having instigated many unfriendly actions, some of which never even took place. These allegations have led him, and three other teachers, into the Board of Education's "due process" mechanism for transfer and dismissal. Vann is a forceful, popular figure who is capable of instilling awe, respect, terror, or pride in any of the children as the situation demands. He sees his future, that of his organization, the A.T.A., as well as that of his people, bound up in the struggle for community control.

While most of our teachers are part of this struggle, some are apprehensive about the A.T.A.'s role in it. Just as a narrow, "careerist" view of self-interest corrupted the U.F.T. and forced it to oppose quality education in order to protect its membership, it is feared that the A.T.A. might simply replace the unresponsive white bureaucracy with a similar black one, in order to further the career goals of *its* constituency. Here, Vann faces the dilemma which all black leaders must eventually come to grips with: Is he to advance himself within the existing system, and lose touch with the "grass-roots" black community, or will he remain a part of that community, at whatever cost to his own career?

Les Campbell, another "black militant" facing accusations before the Board of Education, teaches Afro-American history. In a sense, both he and the course (twice a week for all students) are innovations. Both are objected to by the central system, and descriptions of both are usually distorted.

When I first met Campbell, I hardly knew what to expect; physically, vocally and intellectually, he seemed far larger than the norm, and, supposedly, he had no use for whites. Two months of conversation and observation have discredited the latter speculation and confirmed the former. Campbell wants to see the institutions that determine the lives of black people controlled by those people, not by white colonial masters, but he recognizes the role that can be played by white allies in the struggle.

His suspicion of the "white liberal" arises out of a history of double cross and meaningless rhetoric, and seems to be shared by his true constituency, the black community. I expected more distrust than I actually found. I was almost disappointed.

When the U.F.T. press releases proclaimed that "hate whitey" was being taught in Campbell's classes, I had to find out for myself. I walked into a class five minutes after it began, and took a seat in the back of the room. Campbell was showing a series of slides on the origins of African civilization. They portrayed the recent anthropological discoveries suggesting man's origin in the Olduvai Gorge in central Africa, depicted the builders of ancient Egyptian culture, including their Negroid features, and led the class into a discussion of the social institutions of some of the early, highly developed African civilizations.

The course will trace the African people from this point through the European invasion, forced emigration to the New World, slavery and slave revolt, to the present day, none of which is covered in conventional history texts or courses. According to Campbell, it is designed to answer the questions: "Who am I? Where have I been? Who and where am I today?" If the white man turns out to be the villain in this story, such is the testimony of history. If things are different today, if the children will have reason to expect anything different in the future, they must be educated by their own, and by the black faculty's everyday interaction with the white faculty. This is no insignificant part of our job.

The white teachers (70 per cent of the faculty) are an interesting, diverse group of individuals. In addition to being younger and better educated, we have less experience in working for the system, and more in working against it, than any other faculty in the city. Forty per cent of us are Jewish (some Orthodox), 30 per cent will need draft deferments in order to continue teaching, 25 per cent have never taught before; all are licensed by the central board, and nearly all are "committed" to social changes. Many sections of the country are represented, as are most major colleges and universities. Alan Kellock, a teacher of Afro-American history, is writing a doctoral dissertation for the University of Wisconsin in that field Sandy Nystrom is a former white organizer for the Mississippi Freedom Democratic Party; Stu Russell is a returned Peace Corps volunteer; Steve Bloomfield is an organizer of the Brooklyn Heights Peace and Freedom Party.

My own background is simply this: grammar school in Brooklyn, bar mitzvah, suburban high school, Long Island University, marriage, law school at the University of Chicago. My father owns a parking lot; my mother is a working housewife. While they spend most of their time explaining me to their friends and neighbors, they actually enjoy suburban life. In another day, my 23d birthday would not have found me teaching in the ghetto. This generation, though, has grown up at a unique time in history. I am not alone in being a contradiction to my upbringing.

While many of us have done our best to disestablish the Establishment, no single ideology unites us, no plan of action is taken without heated debate. We do not even agree on a single analysis of the situation in which we are engaged. The school has set the stage for an interesting day-to-day drama involving the complex relationship between this group and the more united black faculty.

One observer of the opening of school noted a "checkerboard" seating pattern in the teachers' cafeteria, black teachers together at some tables, white teachers at others; this pattern, for instance, has since broken down somewhat into one of agreement on — and interest in — whatever issue is being fought out in any particular part of the room. We are integrated now, but not by pretending that black is the same as white; it is, rather, integration born out of respect for individual and group differences, and pride in, as well as recognition of, one's own heritage. We form a mixture, not a solution — a *smorgasbord,* not a melting pot.

The moment of truth, in this respect, came for many white teachers when we decided to organize the faculty and elect a steering committee. The black teachers demanded equal representation on the committee even though they were a numerical minority; there would be a black caucus to whom the black representatives would be responsible, and a white caucus to elect the white representatives. Some (not all) white teachers objected to this plan, maintaining that it would institutionalize race differences, and instead proposed at-large elections, based on traditional "color-blind" integration.

A long debate ensued, with Campbell calling the "at-large" plan "a step backward in the fight for black self-determination," while himself being charged with "segregationism" and "separatism." When someone suggested a vote on which plan to accept, his proposal had broad support.

At this point, Steve Mayer, a white teacher, pointed out that, in a vote on the question, the white majority would be deciding whether or not the blacks were to have self-determination. Most of us recognized this as the colonial situation we all were determined to avoid, and the vote no longer was necessary. The two caucuses met separately, elected their representatives, and the steering committee was formed. The two-caucus system has lessened racial tensions on the committee rather than having exacerbated them, and its work has been made more effective by removing the fiction on which it would otherwise have rested.

Despite whatever tension has existed among the faculty — and I think this tension has been constructive — we have been united on a few major issues and goals: We are for community control of schools, we want to educate the children, and we want the power structure (U.F.T., Board of Education, politicians, Selective Service) to leave our experiment alone so that we can make it work.

It was in this context that the transferred U.F.T. teachers were put back into the school, along with a force of 2,000 to 3,000 armed police bodyguards. It was absurd to think that an agreement between the U.F.T. and the Board of Education, with community representation excluded, could have made either the community or the faculty accept those teachers back with open arms. It was more absurd to think the intimidating presence of the police would help. There had to be harassment on both sides, and there was. The harassment was petty, though, and, to the best of my knowledge, it never escalated to threats on people's lives, no matter what the newspaper stories supposedly leaked from a still-unreleased report by impartial observers may have said.

Examples sound absurd when repeated. One of the U.F.T. teachers, for instance, walked into the middle of a math class I was teaching, marched to the center of the room, and began picking papers up off the floor. I asked: "What are you doing here? You're disrupting my class." In reply, he told me that he was not disrupting the class, but I was. Then, with the students (13 to 15 years old) looking at him — their eyes filled, some with amazement, some with hatred, some with confusion — I walked toward the door, opened it for him and told him to leave. He went to the door, but rather than leave, he started rummaging in the wastebasket, for no apparent reason. Finally, he straightened up, turned to the class, belched loudly and walked out. Barely containing myself, I slammed the door shut.

Presumably he had wanted to disrupt the class and provoke either me or a student into taking a swing at him. If so, he succeeded in his first objective, and almost succeeded in the second.

After he had left the room, the students, miles from algebra by this time, released the accumulated tension by applauding and, after quieting down, they asked questions: "Why can't the kids take care of them?" "Why did they have to come back? Everything was going so good!" These questions may not display a high degree of political sophistication, but they certainly raise doubts as to whether teachers like the one who disrupted my class can ever be effective in one of our classrooms.

Sometimes, the U.F.T. teachers did not even have to take overt action to arouse our ire. The air of arrogance with which they carried themselves was described by one non-union teacher this way: "It's as though they're saying, 'We're back. We won. You lost. Ha! Ha! Ha!'" When the mathematics staff gathered for a departmental meeting, we found three U.F.T. people smugly waiting in the room, their arms folded. We caucused for a few minutes, then walked out to meet some place else, leaving them alone with two of our "old" assistant principals. At the time, this seemed the only way to prevent a real incident from occurring, so high were feelings running during those days. If this was harassment, I plead guilty.

All of the abuse was verbal. We told them what we thought of them, and they reciprocated. Perhaps the U.F.T. leadership has forgotten the distinction explained in the old "sticks and stones" rhyme. The entire issue of harassment was best summed up by the Rev. C. Herbert Oliver, the chairman of the governing board, when he said, "I wish people wouldn't interpret an exclamation of 'Drop dead!' as a threat on their lives."

All discussions of harassment evolve into allegations of anti-Semitism. The U.F.T.'s skillful use of this issue has intensified the fears of the liberal Jewish community and turned potential supporters against us. I have spent up to 18 hours a day in the Ocean Hill-Brownsville community, and I have never experienced any racial or religious slur against me there, nor has anyone with whom I have spoken, nor have I seen any "hate" literature besides that which is distributed by the U.F.T.

On the contrary, the community and the governing board have demonstrated again and again that these fears are unfounded. On the day before Rosh ha-Shanah, the governing board distributed to all the children in our schools a leaflet explaining the holiday, what it means to the Jewish people, and why all the city schools are closed on that day. As far as I know, no other school district has taken the trouble to do this.

The issue of black anti-Semitism is a major element in the black-Jewish confrontation which threatens to devastate New York City. Yet, here in Ocean Hill-Brownsville, in the eye of the storm, the problem seems not to exist. I read in the U.F.T. literature and in the Jewish press about "black racism," but I have never experienced it in Ocean Hill, and, to my knowledge, neither has anyone else on the faculty. While the storm rages around Ocean Hill-Brownsville, it is not *about* Ocean Hill-Brownsville. But one fact of life does stand out: This issue of anti-Semitism, true or false, preys on the fears of the one ethnic group that, united behind it, could destroy us; if this happens, I expect a real problem of black anti-Semitism, and the cycle of self-fulfilling prophecy will be complete.

Unfortunately, there seems to be no effective way to discredit the U.F.T. charges. Rumors abound in the Jewish community of armed hordes of "black Nazis." Recently, I spoke in Forest Hills to a group of Jewish parents who were understandably concerned about this issue. The meeting was organized by a veteran of concentration camps who hoped that I could relate my personal experiences to the parents, and lead a discussion of facts, rather than of wild accusations. He meant well, but the mission was pretty hopeless. These parents simply could not — or would not — believe that the charges of anti-Semitism had no basis in fact. Sometimes, they went to great lengths of logical distortion in order to continue believing what they had been told. One woman said: "You only tell us what you've seen. Shouldn't you tell us about what you haven't seen?"

This is not, however, to say that I have not been threatened. Each time my name or picture appears on television or in the newspapers, I receive a flurry of anonymous letters and, sometimes, telephone calls, all trying to put into question my job, my health, my sanity or my continued existence. I have been called everything from "scab" to "Commie bastard" to "nigger-lover lout." One letter said: "I hope you can live with yourself. Have you been intimidated yet?" Another put a "black curse" on me; another placed the hopes of the Jewish people in not producing any more like myself. All this is sad and childish, but it does not indicate that there is an organized campaign in the white, Jewish community against me.

Black people hate the "Uncle Tom" more than any white man, and this is probably how the white racists feel about me. Depending on their particular problems, they feel that I am a traitor to my race, my religion, my neighborhood, my family, or any combination of these. It was interesting that, during our confrontations with large contingents of police and U.F.T. pickets, the black parents spent most of their energy haranguing and lecturing the Negro cops, while the white U.F.T. pickets harassed the white "scabs" far more than the black ones.

A year ago, I never thought that I would be crossing picket lines today. I have always supported unions, and I led a nine-day student strike at Long Island University's Brooklyn Center while I was student-body president there. Since I did not believe in the teachers' strike, I had decided not to let the pickets disturb me. Nevertheless, they did. The few pickets on the line that first day spouted more hate in two minutes than I had heard in my lifetime, and it shook me up. I knew that this could not continue long without, at the very least, making my teaching less effective.

The next day, as I approached the picket line, the U.F.T. teachers began their catcalls. I walked to the middle of the line, turned my back, folded my arms, and simply stood there while they poured out their verbal venom. I heard a surprising number of references to my personal past, and I wanted to turn and ask where they got all this information, but I didn't. After 5 or 10 minutes (it seemed much longer), their catharsis ended, the chanting and raving stopped — and I walked on.

It could be that my little nonviolent confrontation with the pickets made them realize how foolish they really were; they have not bothered me since. But I still don't enjoy crossing picket lines, and, after a couple of weeks, I found another route to the school.

The police, while they were at school in large numbers, were less easy to avoid. They stationed themselves on the streets, on the roofs, in the school and in our meetings. During the first three weeks of school, our attendance was lower than we expected, and a team of teachers canvassed the parents to find out what was keeping the children home. The answer they most frequently received was: "I don't want to send my kids into an armed camp," and no one could blame the parents for being apprehensive. The children had to squeeze through police barricades in order to reach the front door, and parents were not permitted to accompany them; more than one parent was beaten for insisting that she be allowed to bring her child into school. Even teachers were asked for identification; since none of us had any, we sometimes had to circle the block to find an entrance where there was less resistance.

The police were drawn from all over the city, from Yankee Stadium to Staten Island, they were working overtime, and they did not seem happy to be there. There was also a great deal of confusion at critical moments. At one demonstration, while we were retreating from one line of police advancing in front of us, we turned and found out we were also supposed to be retreating from those behind us. The result was blood and chaos. One quiet morning, I myself was arrested because of a similar mixup. One officer said to move on; another said to stay; whatever I did, I had to end up in jail.

I spent that entire day in the stationhouse, the paddy wagon and the courthouse, and this afforded me an opportunity to find out how the police themselves felt about what they were doing. One cop I spoke to was, more than anything else, angry. It was his 14th consecutive day of work, he was miles from his precinct, and he knew there were too many police on the scene. He didn't understand why he had to keep parents out of their schools and take abuse from those who hated him for being there. Nevertheless, he would be back the next day and the day after that; he wanted that pension.

And this is where we came in. The cop, the teacher, the landlord – all want to collect the rent while the roof leaks, the house decays, and the tenant boils.

Landlord, landlord
My roof has sprung a leak
Don't you 'member I told
      you about it
Way last week?

The English Teacher and the Language of the Newly Integrated Student *

J. L. Dillard

One of the more heartening signs of social progress in our time has been the successful integration of Negro children into previously all-white classrooms. This has been a hard-won battle, and many a liberal teacher will be dismayed to have a specialist in another field suggest that the newly unified classroom should be broken up even for a few moments by the use of differing teaching techniques for some groups of students. But results of recent studies suggest that the language problem for the Negro child of a certain socio-economic background is indeed different.[1]

The study of the language problem is new — not the language problem itself. There is every reason to believe that the field slave and sharecropper in the South had their opportunities limited, and that a language difference was one factor in that limitation; but no one worried about analyzing their language or about teaching them standard English. It was only when they migrated in great numbers to the large cities of the nation that they came to the attention of leading educators, of congressmen, and of political figures. Only then did the difference between their dialect and standard become a problem for which it was felt necessary to find a solution — not just a problem which could be ignored. What was basically a rural language problem, of the plantation and of the sharecropper's farm, has recently become a full-fledged urban language problem.

The apparently common origin of these dialects — postulated by William A. Stewart to be traceable to a slave pidgin — is reflected in their common grammars. Of course, there are differences, especially in pronunciation and in vocabulary. A Washington ghetto Negro girl is unlikely to know *soul sister,* 'fellow Negro (female)'; whereas a New Yorker would have it in her everyday vocabulary. Washington Negroes say *serve the newspaper;* New Yorkers, white or Negro, *deliver the newspaper.*

*J.L. Dillard, "The English Teacher and the Language of the Newly Integrated Student," *The Record,* November 1967, Vol. 69, No. 2, pp.115-120.

[1] Virginia F. Allen, "Teaching Standard English as a Second Dialect," *Teachers College Record,* Vol. 68, No. 5 (Feb. 1967), pp. 355-370, deals with the problems of non-standard speakers and suggests a TESL approach. She does not, however, deal with dialects as greatly divergent from standard English as that under discussion here.

MAPPING THE NEGRO DIALECT

Perhaps largely by coincidence, at just about the time that the problems, including the language problems, of the inner city Negro became prominent to educators as to the rest of the nation, the steps preparatory to the study of the problem were being taken by a small group of Caribbeanists, who perceived clear relationships between the "Creole" or "Calypso" language and the dialect of certain Negroes in the United States and who raised once again the issue of Afro-American language relationships which Melville J. Herskovits had raised in the anthropological literature in the 1930's and 1940's. William Labov of Columbia, a more traditional dialect geographer but a noted innovator in linguistics, came independently to have the idea that Negro dialect had not been adequately described. In part, this constituted a challenge to the traditional position of American dialect geographers, who had recognized the existence of varieties like Gullah and Louisiana French Creole but had tended to treat them as dialects which *had developed* in isolation, not as survivals which might be found in lesser degree in other Negro dialects. Actually, the linkage had been made in Bloomfield's *Language* (1933, pp. 474-5). Defenses of a long tradition of study of the Negro dialect without any special revelation are now being met by the rebuttal that the speech of Negro children was what should have been studied.[2] The theoretical issue thereby raised is a considerable one: is it a general linguistic condition, or perhaps a special characteristic of this dialect, that archaic forms are preserved longer in the speech of children than elsewhere? Obviously, a linguistic study which focuses on the language of children will be much more relevant to the educational world than the older studies which utilized adult informants.

The creolist has long insisted that the English-based Creoles differed from the standard language in syntactic properties (more basic matters from the point of view of the linguist), rather than in local idiosyncrasies of pronunciation and vocabulary. Transformational-generative linguists, like Marvin Loflin, who have worked independently on the dialect have found one of the major defining characteristics of Afro-American (and Creole) dialects, according to Herskovits and others: dominance of aspect over tense in the verb system. Thus, in this particular dialect, *She sick* contrasts with *She be sick;* the difference signalled is not one of past or present action but of length of duration. Speakers of standard English, including English teachers, do not have this category in their grammatical system; thinking that anything besides *She is sick* is "bad", they tend to conclude that there is a haphazard distribution of these forms. They hear *She sick* and *She be sick,* and do not apply the simple linguistic test of co-occurrent adverbs in test frames *(She sick today; She be sick for a long time).*

---

[2]W.A. Stewart, "Urban Negro Speech: Sociolinguistic Factors Affecting English Teaching" in *Social Dialects and Language Learning,* NCTE, 1964, p. 16.

The test with the co-occurrent adverb is, of course, a mildly artificial device utilized by the linguist and does not mean that the adverbs must accompany the verb forms; English teachers who fail to understand this point offer the occurrence of "unaccompanied" *She sick* and *She be sick* in rebuttal to public statements by linguists who have worked exhaustively on the dialect.

THE CORE OF THE LANGUAGE

The verb system utilized by these children turns out to be a quite complex one, with forms as "bizarre" from the viewpoint of the standard speakers as I *been see it,* which is an anterior form somthing like a preterite. The linguist is not especially surprised, since he knows that comparable forms occur, for example, in "Wes Kos" (the pidgin English of a part of West Africa), and in Sranan (the English creole of Surinam). As the Negro adolescent finds it necessary to adjust to middle class American society, he gives up something of his earlier verb paradigm — either forgetting it completely or, more likely, using it only for special speaking styles and for special audiences. His acquisition of a second language, standard English, is handicapped by a lack of awareness of the dialect difference. As a matter of fact, there is not even a name for the dialect from which the Negro speaker starts. Further complicating the problem is the matter of group loyalty. The requirement is satisfied, at certain social levels, by the imposition of ethnic slang upon the often quite standard grammar of certain Negro groups. This gives rise to the picturesque vocabulary which is often written up as the "language" of the Negro or of the ghetto. As in other fields, the public finds the superficialities of language much more attractive than the elusive solid core.

The typical speaker of the Negro dialect who makes part of the long trip toward standard English retains some of the less strikingly different forms. The "zero copula" as in *She busy* is often retained, since it can pass (almost in the racial sense) for *She's busy* with a "lightly articulated" — *s.* Many a speaker who would no longer say *I been see that already* will say *I been seeing that a long time;* the latter can pass for *I have been seeing that* with a "lightly articulated" auxiliary. On the other hand, certain Negroes who remain low on the social scale actually retain *basilect*[3] in a relatively pure form.

TEACHING A SECOND LANGUAGE

But the emphasis, for the educator, is clearly on the child. Since the child's linguistic system may be radically different from that of standard English, it makes a great deal of sense to treat the teaching problem as a second language teaching problem, using the technique which have been developed for teaching

---

[3] In the sense in which Stewart uses the term. *Ibid.,* p. 15.

English as a quasi foreign language during the past few months, and it has worked unexpectedly well. Contrary to certain expectations, the drills, in the hands of a competent teacher, have been very well received by the student. Eight grade students at a high school in the District of Columbia are even making their own drills on a volunteer basis, so popular has this approach to English teaching been. One materials developer reports that only in the rare case of students with a greater mastery of standard English (perhaps acquired in the home and not at school) is there boredom with this method of teaching.

One of the most promising aspects of the research concerns the degree of age-grading in the non-standard dialect. (This age-grading is fairly well documented by Loban, but linguists would disagree with some of the taxonomy of his work.)[4] It is known already that a great deal of such age-grading does occur in the Washington dialect, and a prime target of future research will be the detailing of its exact characteristics. Consider, for example, the sex reference of pronouns – again, one of those things which the average speaker of standard English, including the English teacher, is likely to take for a language absolute. It would surprise most educators to learn that many of the world's languages do not distinguish formally between the third person singular masculine *(he)* and the third person singular *(she)*. Among these are the Creole languages of the Caribbean, the pidgins of the west coast of Africa, and certain West African languages. It is, then, not surprising to ULS linguists that forms like *he a nice little girl,* and *I don't know her name* (referring to a man) are encountered in the Washington non-standard dialect among children in the five to six-year-old group. It is also not surprising that the age-grading eliminates this "small-fry" grammatical form (more popular terminology would say that gender, differentiation is "introduced") very quickly. Speakers of standard English are likely to be hard on the person who can be considered to have trouble with gender forms. Other forms, which bear no such personal or pseudo-psychological stigmata, disappear more slowly. The undifferentiated form of the pronoun as possessive *(he book, she brother)* apparently disappears between the ages of nine and fourteen.

AGE-GRADING

If the learning of something like standard English were the only aim of education (remember that what the adult Negro typically uses is an attempt to approximate standard English), a hands-off attitude toward age-grading might be in order. But, clearly, the child's educational problems are most critical at just that age when his dialect is most different from standard English. The six-year-old who is trying to learn to read standard English tests – usually taught by a teacher who has no idea how different the student's language is – when his

---

[4]Walter Loban, *Problems in Oral English,* NCTE Report.

dialect is Negro non-standard faces much more of a problem than does the middle-class white child who need only master the print-to-sound decoding system of what is essentially his own dialect. Even granting the somewhat unlikely premise that the Negro child acquires standard English perfectly somewhere in his teens, one could not proceed to any logical conclusion that he would then be ready to start learning to read. The school system expects him already to have mastered quite complex reading skills in the dialect which only the most advanced have acquired by their late teens. In this context, statements like that of Kendall in *White Teacher in a Black School* about being "shocked by the illiteracy of the students" appear culturally naive. The wonder is rather that the student, without guidance based upon an accurate knowledge of what the dialect is, has been able to progress at all. Imagine trying to learn to read Spanish without ever being told that Spanish is not the same language as English!

The pedagogical implications of an age-grading study should be far-reaching. Only after such a study should one really feel justified in writing grade-by-grade pedagogical materials. It will also be necessary to conduct some research into language acquisition matters in the Negro non-standard speaking community, if only to forestall criticism that the age-grading forms are really language acquisition forms. The pronoun-gender "problem", for example, is one which is eliminated very early from the language acquisition problem of the white, standard-speaking child. It is contrary to the basic knowledge which we have about language communities to conclude that the Negro children are simply slower at language acquisition. On the other hand, the assumption of archaic dialect features (some of them resembling Gullah and the Creoles of the Caribbean to some extent) is a possible first step in separating dialect forms from language acquisition forms.

TOWARDS WIDER KNOWLEDGE

In addition to the pedagogical utility of such discoveries, this kind of research seems to be revealing a great deal about certain areas of liberal knowledge, such as the history of the English language in the United States. Long ago McDavid suggested that it was unwise to look for factors other than the total language environment of the Negro for explanation of the differences between the English of the Negro and of the white in the United States.[5] Unfortunately, such statements tended to be interpreted in terms of African survivals, rather than in consideration of slave *lingua franca* forms which are rather well attested to have been current among the plantation field hand population. In a way, a bit of romanticism may have been lost along with the new emphasis; but there has been a great compensating gain in accuracy and clarity.

[5] Raven I. and Virginia McDavid, "The Relationship of the Speech of American Negroe to the Speech of Whites," *American Speech,* XXVI, pp. 3-17.

It would be well to put such matters into an accurate light; there is no more reason to read into everything said by Negroes a survival of a creolized form derived from a pidgin which was in turn derived from the *lingua franca*. Clear archaisms like *hit* for *it,* even though they are widely found in the Negro community, should probably be attributed to survivals from earlier stages of English; that such forms are used in Appalachia is a relatively important contribution to this conclusion. The lack of distinction between pairs of words such as *ten* and *tin* is also widespread enough among white English dialects to make it unlikely as a "Negroism." But there remains the very strong possibility that the speech of American whites – and especially of Southerners (perhaps, ironically enough, even some of those Southerners who are most bitterly racist) – has been influenced by the speech of the Negro to a greater degree than historians of the language have been willing to admit. The folklore has long maintained that the Negro influence was great in the South, and a lot of ink has been spilled to prove that it is wrong. Unfortunately, the purely scientific linguists have in effect given up the study because statements that some Negroes speak differently from whites can be taken to mean that physiological differences are responsible. But we have apparently reached the point where these absurdities need no longer stand in the way of serious research. When such research is completed, the picture of what went on in the history of American English may be changed a great deal. It may also be a shift in attitude would be beneficial to many English teachers.

Fortunately, experiments made in cooperation with the District of Columbia school system tend to indicate that special drills for such studies need not be lengthy to be effective. A drill unit of five to ten minutes, using pattern practice procedures from English as a Foreign Language methods, has proved to be most effective. Experimental practices like the non-graded[6] school provide a beautiful setting for this kind of improved language teaching. Computerized and programmed techniques are also being suggested, but they may be viewed with alarm by less prosperous school systems. There is, however, help on the way for the oldest of teaching "machines" – the human teacher.

[6]The non-graded approach was suggested to me by Mrs. Marie Barry of the U.S. Office of Education, to whom gratitude is hereby expressed.

Additional Reading

Eddy, Elizabeth M. *Walk the White Line: A Profile of Urban Education.* Garden City, New York: Doubleday Anchor, 1967.

Koerner, James D. *The Miseducation of American Teachers.* Baltimore, Maryland: Pelican Books, 1965.

Kohl, Herbert. *36 Children.* New York: Signet Books, 1968.

McGeoch, Bloomgarden, Randolph and Ruth Furedi. *Learning to Teach in Urban Schools.* New York: Teachers College Press, 1965.

Schrag, Peter. *Voices in the Classroom.* Boston: Beacon Press, 1965.

Strom, Robert D. (ed). *The Inner-City Classroom: Teacher Behaviors.* Columbus, Ohio: Charles E. Merrill Books, 1966.

Usdan, Michael and Frederick Bertolaet (eds). *Teachers for the Disadvantaged.* The Report of the School-University Teacher-Education Project. Chicago: Follett Publishing Co., 1966.

Wisniewski, Richard. *New Teachers in Urban Schools: An Inside View.* New York: Random House, 1968.

Zeigler, Harmon. *The Political Life of American Teachers.* Englewood Cliffs, N.J.: Prentice-Hall, 1967.

chapter 4

School Systems

It has become evident in recent years that school organization may have a direct and serious effect on teacher performance. The relationships between teachers and principals, between principals and citywide boards, and between local community boards and committees are all important for classroom teachers. School organization also dictates what kinds of students are to be found in an individual school. Desegregation, for example, requires certain very specific kinds of structures. The recent struggles of the urban poor to gain power and make decisions which affect their lives would certainly be advanced by changes in urban school systems.

Robert Havighurst in "Metropolitan Development and the Educational System" argues that the only effective way to organize urban education is on a metropolitan basis including both the central city and suburban communities in one educational system. The Bundy Plan for decentralization, although unlikely to be adopted in total, has become the basis for a considerable educational and political debate in New York City. A serious controversy has been raging among educators for a number of years concerning priorities in attacking the range of urban education problems. One position supported by Schwartz, Pettigrew, and Smith argues that desegregation, in addition to being the ultimate goal, should receive the top priority now. Another position represented here by Joseph Alsop's answer to the Schwartz, Pettigrew, and Smith piece, argues that desegregation is politically and socially impossible and so there must be an attempt to create quality segregated education in the schools as they are presently organized. A more radical suggestion made recently for solving certain problems of urban education is contained in Christopher Jencks' "Private Schools for Black Children." It is interesting to note that Jenck's program is at least as much political as it is educational since he clearly does not argue that private black schools would solve all educational difficulties.

Metropolitan Development and the Educational System*

Robert J. Havighurst

According to census reports, in 1960 more than half the population of the United States was living in metropolitan areas. That year these areas accounted for sixty-one per cent of the population. If these areas, which are growing faster than the remainder of the country, continue to grow at their present rate, by 1980 they will account for between seventy and seventy-five per cent of the total population. Chains of urban-industrial communities will stretch along the principal axes of communication — from Boston to New York, from New York to Philadelphia to Baltimore to Washington, from Chicago to Detroit to Toledo to Cleveland to Pittsburgh, from Los Angeles to San Diego.

In the past, urban evolution has on the whole been advantageous. But it has had some disadvantages that are now forcing massive and costly urban renewal programs aimed at making metropolitan areas more fit for human living and more conducive to human values.

Metropolitan growth presents two major concerns. First, it has led to increased segregation on the basis of income and race. This segregation is a threat to democratic unity and educational opportunity, for slums or gray areas of the central cities breed political and social divisiveness and discontent. Second, space is not used properly. The location of industry, business, and dwellings have made the daily journey to work longer and more difficult than is really necessary for a large part of the population. The distance from residential areas to centers of leisure and cultural activity — theaters, museums, concert halls — is too great. Open space for recreation and for the enjoyment of nature has not been distributed so as to be available to the majority of the people.

Metropolitan developments have produced or intensified many social problems, most of which have had repercussions in education. The net effect has been to make the educational system less efficient and less effective in achieving its democratic goals. We shall call the complex of a central city and its surrounding suburbs a megalopolis and analyze some of its problems.

One major problem is increased socioeconomic and racial segregation of the population. As the total population of a megalopolis grows, the slum belt around the central business district becomes thicker. This is a result not only of the

*Robert J. Havighurst, "Metropolitan Development and the Educational System," *School Review,* 69 (1961), pp. 251-269. University of Chicago Press.

growth in total population but also of the concentration of lower-class people in areas of poorest housing, which are usually in the oldest parts of the city. Those who can afford to do so move away from the inner city as their economic circumstances improve. In general, working-class people whose income permits it move out of the slum district and take up residence farther from the center of the city, while people in middle-class districts of the central city move out to middle-class suburbs. Thus the ever growing total population divides itself into a lower-class conglomerate at the center, with successively higher socioeconomic groups at greater distances and the upper-middle class and the upper class largely in the suburbs.

Data from the Detroit area illustrate this generalization, which applies to most, if not all, of the other great cities. In the Detroit Area Study of the University of Michigan, information was collected on the incomes of families in Detroit and its suburbs (Detroit Area Study, 1960). According to a report on this research, which covered family income from 1951 to 1959, the median income per family in the Detroit metropolitan area was related to the distance the family lived from the central business district. For families living within six miles of the central business district, the median income rose three per cent between 1951 and 1959, while the cost of living rose twelve per cent; thus during this period the median family in this area lost real income. Families living farther out, between the six-mile radius and the city limits, gained five per cent in median real income. Meanwhile, families in the Detroit suburban area gained thirty-seven per cent in median real income. Thus, during these years the people in the central part of the city grew poorer, while the people in the suburbs grew richer. In other words, the central part of the city became more solidly lower class in composition, while the suburbs became more middle class.

This process can be seen in detail by looking at what happened between 1955 and 1960 in Leibnitz School, an elementary school in another northern industrial city. The district served by the school was located about seven miles from the center of the city and close to transportation lines. Parents of some of the pupils had attended the same school.

In 1955, enrolment totaled 1,250 pupils, most of them from lower middle-class and upper middle-class families of German, Dutch, and Swedish origin. Then came a period of rapid change. The owners of some of the three-story apartment buildings cut them up into smaller units and rented to southern white and Negro families. By 1960 enrolment at Leibnitz had climbed to twenty-four hundred, and the school had two shifts. One group of pupils came for four and a half hours in the morning, and another group came for four and a half hours in the afternoon to a new shift of teachers. To accommodate the hundreds of pupils who arrive at noon and mill around waiting for their shift to begin, the campus of the school, once beautifully landscaped, was covered with gravel.

Transiency is calculated at about seventy per cent. From September, 1960, to June, 1961, nineteen hundred pupils transferred in or out of the school. During times of heavy turnover, the children who are waiting to transfer sit in the auditorium, some of them with their parents and some unaccompanied. Two clerks work at desks on the stage. The clerk at one side of the stage processes transfers and records for incoming children, while the clerk at the opposite side processes papers for outgoing children. The records of pupils transferred out during the past several years show that most of these children have gone to schools farther from the center of the city or to schools in the suburbs.

There is not only increased economic stratification in the schools, but there is also increased racial and ethnic segregation. In northern cities Negro ghettos have come into being, and the schools reflect this fact. In New York City the superintendent of schools in his report for 1958 showed a net loss of fifteen thousand white pupils a year for the preceding five years (Sixteenth Annual Report of the Superintendent of Schools, 1959). These pupils had moved out of New York City to the suburbs. In 1958 Negroes formed twenty per cent of the school enrolment, and Puerto Ricans fifteen per cent. In one of New York City's five boroughs, Negroes and Puerto Ricans outnumbered other pupils in the public schools. In 1958, of 704 public schools, 455 had enrolments in which ninety per cent or more of the pupils were Negroes, Puerto Ricans, or other whites (Morrison, 1958). Thus about two-thirds of the schools were segregated in the sense that less than ten per cent of the pupils did not belong to the majority group of the school.

While this process goes on in the central city, the suburbs themselves become stratified into communities that are predominantly upper-middle class or lower-middle class, or upper-lower class. The city dweller who aspires to a house in the suburbs will find that the amount of money he can pay for a house determines the type of suburb he will live in. If he is employed as a manual worker in an auto assembly plant or an electronics factory fifteen miles out of the city, he is likely to make a payment on a two-bedroom bungalow in a real estate development that has hundreds of similar houses, all variants of one basic design, all on small lots with a plot of grass in front, a garage and a clothesline in the rear. He will live in a working-class suburb. If he is a lawyer with an office in the city, he will buy a ranch-type house on a large lot in an area where all the other houses are of similar type and cost, in a new section of a well-established upper-middle-class suburb with a reputation for good schools and a good country club.

One result of the segregation of lower-class boys and girls into elementary and secondary schools where they are exposed only to other young people of similar socioeconomic status is to deny them the stimulation of associating with middle-class youth in the school and the classroom. If lower-class boys and girls are in classes where a third or more of the pupils are from a middle-class family, they will be stimulated to keep up with the middle class children in schoolwork, and they will also be in a position to form friendships and thus learn some of the social behavior and social values of middle-class children. But when lower-class youth are segregated in slum schools, they may lose these advantages.

A study made by Patricia Sexton in Detroit shows how the socioeconomic characteristics of schools are related to important educational factors (Sexton, 1961). She obtained the average incomes of the families living in the various school districts and then grouped the 243 schools by income rank. The schools in a given income group tended to be located at about the same distance from the central business district. The schools that had children from highest-income families were farthest from the center of the city. The schools in the lower-income areas had poorer records of achievement, intelligence, and behavior, and a higher dropout rate. The schools in the higher-income areas had more pupils who were chosen in elementary and junior high school to take part in programs for gifted children and more students from senior high school who were going to college. Also the schools closer to the center of the city had a higher proportion of families with mothers working and with mothers receiving aid for dependent children. The assistance indicated that there was no father in the home.

Another problem in megalopolis is the weakening of civic and social relations between the various socioeconomic groups. While it has always been a principle of American democracy that all kinds of people should participate in the same schools and churches and political organizations, the growing segregation in megalopolis lessens the opportunity for this kind of interrelationship. Middle-class boys and girls grow up in antiseptic suburbs. Slum children grow up with no contact with middle-class children, with whom they might learn the art of co-operative citizenship.

Poverty in the central city is another problem. The central city suffers from a progressive economic downgrading of its population but must maintain increasingly expensive urban services — expressways, subways, schools, hospitals, many of which serve the entire population of megalopolis.

With the polarization of megalopolis into lower-class urban areas and middle-class suburbs comes a chronic state of cold war between the two sets of interests, with no authority in a position to bring about co-operation for the common welfare.

Problems of megalopolitan housekeeping become critical. Certain essential services are not readily available to some areas. New suburbs may have difficulty in getting fire protection, a water supply, and sewage disposal. The various police departments in a metropolitan area may not co-operate, and law enforcement may become lax. Transportation and traffic problems arise, and people have increasing difficulty in getting to places of work and recreation. The daily journey to work becomes more and more time-consuming, eating up the time gained by shorter working hours. Distances and difficulties of transport cut down freedom of movement.

Suburban slums arise in the unincorporated areas outside the central city.

People living in these areas may have primitive sanitary facilities, insufficient water, inadequate fire protection, inadequate schools and other cultural facilities. Absence of a strong county or metropolitan government permits this kind of haphazard development.

Finally, there is the problem of the rustication of suburban dwellers. Middle-class suburban dwellers become almost parochial in their outlook and attitudes. Because of transportation difficulties they lose contact with the vigorous and variegated culture of the central city. Their children grow up in isolation from many of the educational influences of a great city.

Because of the many problems associated with metropolitan growth and megalopolitan complexity, it might be supposed that people would cease fleeing from the central city to the suburbs and instead remake slum areas into middle-class residential areas. This course is being urged, and urban renewal plans are under way to make the central city attractive for middle-class living. However, these efforts at urban renewal are meeting with difficulty, and the schools are at the heart of the difficulty.

People who have a choice as to where they will live in a metropolitan area look first at the schools if they have children. They generally want schools that have good standards of schoolwork and behavior. They also like schools that have new buildings and wide play spaces. Some who are prejudiced against non-whites, or fearful that the presence of non-whites will cause the neighborhood and the school to deteriorate, look for schools that are all white and likely to remain so. Others look for schools that have a mixture of races and economic levels, because they believe that such schools can teach their children democracy.

As more and more people, including working-class people, can choose among various places to live, they become more aware of and interested in school policies and school performance. Among other things, they try to sense the spirit, or ethos, of the school. Does it stimulate children to do well academically? Does it encourage children to want to finish high school and go to college? Does it have a program that is useful and interesting for children from all kinds of families? Does it provide a social life they like for their children?

There is a crude quantitative index, called the *status ratio*, which is useful for studying the ethos of a school. The status ratio is simply the ratio of the number of pupils from middle-class families to the number of pupils from working-class families. The ratio is $[2(U + UM) + LM] \div [UL + 2LL]$. The number of pupils from the upper class and the upper-middle class is weighted twice as heavily as the number of pupils from the lower-middle class, and the number of pupils from the lower-lower class is weighted twice as heavily as the number of pupils from the upper-lower class.

The reason for weighting the number of pupils from the upper-middle class and the lower-lower class more heavily in the formula is that pupils from the upper-middle class are about twice as likely to go to college and to exhibit other forms of academic interest and achievement as youth from the lower-middle class are, while youth from the lower-lower class are only about half as likely as pupils from the upper-lower class to show these characteristics.

The *race index* is also an important indicator of the desire of middle-class families to send their children to a particular school. The race index is a ratio that shows the proportions of white and Negro children in a school. Middle-class parents are likely to favor an index of 1.5 or higher, or a proportion of sixty per cent or more of whites. Negro middle-class parents might accept a lower ratio, but they generally favor a mixed or integrated school over a segregated one. Some white middle-class parents favor complete segregation, but most middle-class whites in northern cities would accept a school for their children that was stabilized at a race index of 1.5 and a status ratio of .6 or higher.

The most powerful factor in determining whether a family that can choose among places to live will stay in the central city or move to a suburb is the nature of the school to which its children will go. If the status ratio is close to a critical point, middle-class parents become anxious and start to think of moving away. This critical point depends on the attitudes and the experience of a particular parent and therefore is a subjective thing. The critical point also depends on the race index, the tradition of the school, the type of curriculum, and the quality of the teachers. However, among middle-class parents there is substantial agreement on the critical point — enough agreement to cause them to stream out of a school district as if by common agreement when the status ratio reaches a certain point.

This is what happened in the Leibnitz School. In 1955 this school had a status ratio of about 1. Then as apartments were subdivided and rented to working-class families with large numbers of children, the ratio dropped. The crowding of the school, the introduction of a double-shift program, and the appearance of Negro children all combined to cause some people to move out of the district. As a result the status ratio dropped past the critical point, which by 1960 was $7 \div 117$ or .06.

Secondary schools are more vulnerable than primary schools to desertion by middle-class parents when the status ratio reaches the critical point. In a community where the residents represent a cross section of the American population in socioeconomic status the high school has a status ratio of about 1.0. The ratio is higher than that of an elementary school in the same type of community because a number of boys and girls from families of the lower class drop out of high school. In an upper-middle-class suburb the status ratio is very high. But in the central city the slums continually encroach upon high schools in formerly middle-class areas and reduce the status ratio. When the critical point is reached, there is a rapid flight of middle-class families that have children of high-school age.

In spite of these difficulties and problems that stand in the way of the improvement of life in metropolitan areas, the coming decade will see various programs aimed at achieving the following goals:

Maximum freedom of choice for the people. All kinds of people should have as much choice as possible on such matters as where to live, where and how to spend free time, where to work, with whom to associate, where to educate their children.

Maximum opportunity for people to better themselves through employment, education, recreation, and use of libraries, museums, theaters.

Maximum use of the city as an educative experience for all kinds of people. People of all ages should be in a position to learn through experience with the whole city — its rich variety of ethnic groups and its wide range of work and cultural opportunities.

There are two alternative approaches to the realization of these goals. One is adaptation to the trends of megalopolitan evolution; the other is a bold effort to reverse the trends and design and build a new megalopolis for the future. Both approaches require co-operation by the schools, and both involve much change in school programs and school organization. The twin functions of the school — to mirror the present community and to aid the community in achieving its goals — are both called into action.

The policy of adaptation to existing metropolitan trends assumes that the future structure of megalopolis will follow present trends. The belt of the lower-class residential area around the center of the city will expand and grow thicker. The flight of middle-class families to the suburbs will continue. Suburbs will increase in number, size, and variety. Low-cost public housing will gradually make a physical improvement in the gray areas and result in physical renewal of slums. Expressways will give automobile owners quicker and more comfortable access to all parts of megalopolis. The present trend toward residential segregation by socioeconomic status will continue, together with at least as much racial segregation as now exists. Only a few small countertrends will be seen, such as the growth of working-class suburbs and the construction of expensive apartment houses near the center of the city for well-to-do people with few school-age children.

The major educational adaptations will consist of attempts to provide educational stimulation and opportunity for children in slum areas and programs for the identification and the separation of the abler children in special classes and groups in the school.

A multitrack system will be introduced to separate children into groups formed on the basis of learning ability and social status. In schools in slum areas or areas threatened by encroaching slums, the system will have the effect of maintaining at least one subgroup that has a fairly strong academic motivation. The children of higher social status tend to be placed in the superior group, an arrangement that makes the school more tolerable for their parents. Whatever the value of homogeneous grouping in helping children achieve according to their intelligence, and the alleged benefits are repeatedly questioned by research studies, there is no doubt that most teachers and parents favor a multitrack system in a school where the status ratio has fallen below the critical point. The multitrack organization gives middle-class parents and working-class parents who seriously want their children to get the most out of school some assurance that they will be given special help and special consideration.

Enrichment programs will be set up for working-class children who achieve fairly well. These programs will supplement the multitrack program. The more promising children will be placed in smaller classes and given special counseling and guidance, and their parents will be encouraged to take more interest in their education. The children will be given access to museums, libraries, theaters, and concerts. One widely known example of such an approach is the Higher Horizons Program of Junior High School 43 and the George Washington High School in New York City. This program has stimulated a considerable number of boys and girls to graduate from high school and to enter college who would not have done so if they had not received special attention. Financial assistance for college attendance is a necessary part of such a program.

Enrichment programs will be set up for culturally deprived children at the kindergarten-primary level. Several large cities are already trying programs that give special assistance in the primary grades of slum schools on the theory that many of these children lack stimulation from parents to read and to achieve well in school. If these boys and girls are not given special attention, they may fail to master the task of reading. For the first few years in school, they will stumble along. In time they will become confirmed non-learners and during adolescence, social misfits. These children can get a better start in school and thus a better start in life. The school can give these boys and girls the better start they need by assigning specially trained teachers to small classes, by using social workers or visiting teachers to bring home and school into contact, and by giving the children the enrichment that middle-class children are likely to get in their homes.

Work-study programs will be introduced for youth who are failing in school. Under present conditions about fifteen per cent of all boys and girls fail to grow up successfully through the avenue the school provides. At about seventh grade they react to school with apathy or hostility and aggression. In slum areas this group is likely to make up twenty-five or thirty per cent of the young people. These boys and girls are alienated from the value of the school and other middle-class institutions. It is these boys and girls who make teaching difficult in seventh, eighth, and ninth grades, and who make junior high school and the early years of senior high school difficult for academically motivated youth in schools where the status ratio is below the critical point. For alienated youth, especially for the boys, a good deal of experimentation with work-study programs is now going on. The aim is to give the young people who take part a chance to grow up satisfactorily through the avenue of work. Most such programs commence with young people at the age of sixteen, when they may drop out of school if they wish. The programs appear to be having some success. Possibly better results will be achieved in programs that provide work experience as a part of the school program as early as age fourteen, or eighth grade.

Some people, including some educators, are not satisfied with accepting the present trends of metropolitan development and adapting the schools to them. They believe that the civic ills of metropolitan growth require fundamental urban renewal. These critics ask that a rational megalopolis be designed. They call for plans that will lead to new growth from the center of the city to the suburbs, with parks, shopping centers, libraries, churches, and schools organized to serve people near where they live, and with industry, the central business district, and the centers of residence linked by fast, comfortable transportation, public and private. Billions of dollars are already being spent on bold new shopping plazas, garden villages, high-rise apartment buildings, and expressways.

Urban renewal has the physical goal of restoring areas of comfortable middle-class living in the central city and establishing areas of comfortable, slum-free, lower-class living. Beyond this, urban renewal has the social goal of making the whole of megalopolis a good place for all kinds of people to live in. Leaders of urban renewal often say that their goal is to increase the range and the amount of choice people have among good ways to live.

Among specialists in city planning there is much discussion of the typical physical plan that will make megalopolis a good place to live. It is generally agreed that residential areas should be decentralized, that each area should be self-contained with respect to shopping facilities, schools, libraries, and churches. One type of arrangement is the galaxy, in which constituent communities are spaced more or less evenly over the territory, with a network of highways and transportation lines leading to areas of specialized activity, such as industrial sites, airports, freight docks, and financial centers. Another type of arrangement is the many-pointed star or wagon wheel, with residential areas radiating from a central business district, industry located in certain sectors of the star, and transportation routes leading out from the center, crisscrossing other transportation routes that circle the area at various distances from the center.

There seems to be agreement among city planners on two matters: first, megalopolis should consist of residential areas that meet nearly all the ordinary needs of family and cultural life: second, many residential areas should contain a cross section of the social structure, with people of the upper class, the middle class, and the working class living in the same area. In particular, it is felt that many residential areas near the central business district should be populated by middle-class as well as working-class people.

Several large cities have embarked on major programs of slum clearance with the aim of restoring cross-sectional communities in the central city. Chicago has such areas to the south, the southwest, and the northwest of the central business district. St. Louis has the Mill Creek Valley District, southwest of the city center. New York City has several such areas, including one north of Columbia University. In these and other places slum buildings have been cleared, and land has been made available to private builders for apartment buildings and single-family residences to be sold or rented to people who can afford to pay substantial prices and rents.

The future of these developments is uncertain, however, and further urban renewal is likely to be delayed until these experiments are evaluated. One major question is whether middle-class people with children will move into these renewal areas. Their decision will depend on their attitudes toward the schools. They may want new, modern school buildings, and in many places they will get them because the old buildings are obsolete. More important, they are likely to want assurance that the status ratio of the schools will be above the critical point. This assurance may be present for elementary schools, which serve relatively small areas, but not for secondary schools, which may serve both a renewal area and a large neighboring working-class area. The secondary school is likely to be the crucial element of the school system. The secondary school may well make or break programs for urban renewal.

Urban renewal of a fundamental nature will require major developments in school policy. The megalopolis of the future will probably have a single area-wide governing and taxing unit, with constituent local communities of fifty to a hundred thousand in population, each with its own local government. School policies and programs will be determined partly by an area-wide educational authority and partly by local community school boards. The following propositions concerning educational policy would seem to fit a rational plan for megalopolitan development.

1. A single area-wide educational authority with its own tax authority should be supplemented by local community school boards with authority to levy supplementary taxes for educational purposes.
2. A metropolitan area educational council or commission should work with the metropolitan area planning council on plans for establishment of new suburban school districts and area-wide educational institutions, such as a university, a teachers college, and technical institutions.
3. The area-wide educational authority should have responsibility for such educational functions as purchasing, teacher certification, pensions, the planning and the construction of school buildings.
4. The school board of the local community should administer its own school system up through the secondary school and probably through the junior college. It should provide a school program suited to community needs and should levy supplementary taxes if the area-wide tax support is inadequate.

Any metropolitan area that commits itself to a fundamental program of urban renewal needs to provide for a transitional period of perhaps twenty years. During this period the local communities would gradually become organized and separated from other communities by green belts, parks, and open spaces; and they would be linked by a system of highways and transportation routes.

Certain educational policies would need to be adopted for the transitional period. The policies should be aimed at stopping the flight of middle-class people from the central city. The goal should be self-contained communities of fifty to a hundred thousand in population, communities made up of a social cross section of the entire area. Some policies would be temporary, while others would become permanent policy for the megalopolis of the future. The principal transitional policies might well call for:

1. A set of regional high schools generously selective on the basis of intelligence and school achievement so as to be open to the top third of the high-school age group. Admission to these high schools should be controlled so that no school would have less than sixty per cent white students and every school would have a status ratio higher than .6. By the end of the transitional period these schools would probably become comprehensive high schools serving local communities and open to all high school students.
2. A set of work-study centers at the junior high school level for boys and girls who have demonstrated that they cannot profit from the regular academic high-school program. These centers should be located in junior and senior high schools but run on a separate schedule. They should enroll ten to twenty per cent of the school population at age thirteen or fourteen to sixteen, but enrolment should drop as the elementary schools improve their kindergarten-primary programs.
3. A set of general high schools with strong commercial and vocational training programs for young people who are not attending other types of schools. By the end of the transitional period they would probably merge with the selective schools into comprehensive high schools serving local communities.
4. Special attention at the kindergarten-primary level to children from culturally and emotionally inadequate homes so as to give these children as good a start in school as possible, thus reducing the number who would later go to the work-study centers.
5. A set of regional junior colleges so located that there would eventually be one in each local residential community.
6. An adult education program on an area-wide basis, a program that uses junior colleges and branches of the public library, a program that exploits the educative potential of the metropolitan area and seeks to make adult education available to all kinds of people.

Some of the adaptations now being made in great cities to the problems of metropolitan development can be fitted into a rational plan for urban renewal. There is no need for educators to take sides in a controversy between the two alternatives posed here — that of making the best of existing trends and that of working toward fundamental urban renewal. However, the choice of fundamental urban renewal requires more exercise of rational foresight, more thought about goals of megalopolitan development and about ways of reaching these goals. Educators can impede urban renewal by holding stubbornly to practices that were good before World War II but have now lost much of their value.

REFERENCES

Detroit Area Study. *Family Income in Greater Detroit: 1951-1959.* Ann Arbor: Survey Research Center, University of Michigan, 1960.

Morrison, J. Cayce. *The Puerto Rican Study.* New York: Board of Education of the City of New York, 1958.

Sexton, Patricia. *Education and Income.* New York: Viking, 1961.

Sixtieth Annual Report of the Superintendent of Schools. New York: Board of Education of the City of New York, 1959.

Excerpts from School Panel's Letter to Mayor, Proposals, and Giardino's Dissent *

Following are excerpts from the letter sent to Mayor Lindsay by the special panel on school decentralization, the text of a dissent by Alfred A. Giardino, president of the Board of Education, and a summary of the panel's recommendations:

LETTER TO LINDSAY

Dear Mayor Lindsay:

We enclose herewith the report of your Panel on the Decentralization of the New York City Schools. Back in May, pursuant to an act of the 1967 Legislature, you asked us to study the question and provide you with a plan for decentralization, and this report contains our conclusions and recommendations. We find that major change is needed.

The first premise of this report is that the test of a school is what it does for the children in it. Decentralization is not attractive to us merely as an end in itself; if we believed that a tightly centralized school system could work well in New York today, we would favor it. Nor is decentralization to be judged, in our view, primarily by what it does or does not do for the state of mind, still less the "power," of various interested parties.

We have met men and women in every interested group whose spoken or unspoken center of concern was with their own power — teacher power, parent power, supervisory power, community power, board power. We believe in the instrumental value of all these forms of power — but in the final value of none. We think each of them has to be judged, in the end, by what it does for the education of public school pupils.

Neglect of this principle, in our judgment, is responsible for much of what is wrong in the New York City schools today. We find that the school system is heavily encumbered with constraints and limitations which are the result of efforts by one group to assert a negative and self-serving power against someone else. Historically these efforts have had ample justification, each in its time. To fend off the spoils system, to protect teachers from autocratic superiors, to ensure professional standards, or for dozens of other reasons, interest groups

The New York Times, November 9, 1967, p. 50.

have naturally fought for protective rules. But as they operate today these constraints bid fair to strangle the system in its own checks and balances, so that New Yorkers will find themselves, in the next decade as in the last, paying more and more for less and less effective public education.

Responsibility Not Assessed

We underline our conviction that this is not a case in which it is appropriate to level charges of individual guilt, or to assess responsibility more against one group than another. We have been deeply impressed by the honesty, the intelligence, and the essential goodwill of leaders of all elements. We heard angry denunciations of militant parent and community groups, but when we met with them we found them reasonable, open, and usually clear in their understanding that it is the education of the child, not the power of the community as such, that is the true end of their efforts.

We have met with union leaders and we find them very different from the villains portrayed by some self-righteous observers; they are determined to advance the interests of their members, but they are also well aware that the school system of New York cannot support those members by proper salaries if it loses the confidence of the people. We find the union's commitment to more effective education – and to closer community involvement – to be real and strong.

We have also heard much criticism of the central staff and the Board of Education which we are unable to accept. . . .

Yet the crisis is grave indeed. A system already grown rigid in its negative powers has been called upon to meet the unexpected challenge of an extraordinary immigration of impoverished citizens whose children have special needs for the very best our schools can offer, and the system has not effectively met this challenge. The new needs of large numbers of Negro and Puerto Rican students from low-income families may be the most dramatic, but they are certainly not the only group which now needs better schools.

No plan of government can be successful if it aims only at the particular needs of particular groups. It is all the children in all the schools who must be our concern. Half the school population still consists of white pupils, and in addition there are many from middle-class families from other social and ethnic backgrounds. Along with the poorer Negro and Puerto Rican students, these other pupils also suffer from the weaknesses in the present system of public school government.

The premise upon which we were appointed was that effective decentralization could help. Our studies have solidly confirmed the validity of this premise. We recognize that the Board of Education has already taken steps in this direction, but we are convinced that far more must be done and done quickly. A properly designed and executed reorganization can liberate new constructive energies and rebuild confidence in all parts of our educational system, among parents, teachers, administrators, and supervisors — and then in the minds of the children in the schools.

Decentralization is no substitute for other deeply needed changes — and in particular it is no substitute for the massive infusion of funds which the school system now needs — for new buildings, for better teaching, and for a higher level of performance in almost every field.

Shift in Authority

The essence of the plan which we propose is that the present centralized system should be reformed by a clear grant of new authority to Community School Boards, partly chosen by parents and partly chosen by the Mayor and a central educational agency. We believe these school boards should have the power to appoint and remove community superintendents. Together the community board and the community superintendent should have a new and wider authority over curriculum, budget, personnel, and educational policy in the schools of the district. While we believe in decentralization, we are opposed to fragmentation.

We seek to keep the advantages without the disadvantages of the size and variety of the city's school system. We would envision a quite new role for the city's central education agency. Not only should it have important powers of service, support, and review, but it should also have citywide responsibilities for specialized education. Above all it should be free to carry out over-all policy and planning functions which at present it cannot handle effectively because of the press of daily concerns with the details of operating schools for a million children.

We have designed this plan of decentralization so that community boards may have as much authority as is consistent with citywide necessities. We have sought to be responsive to the deep and legitimate desire of many communities in the city for a more direct role in the education of their children. . . .

We believe that, with exceptions where leadership has been exceptional, the schools of New York have been dangerously separated from many of New York's communities. We do not think that the pupils in such schools can be aroused and led upward — or even kept in good order — if their parents are not offered the reality of responsible participation. It is of no use to say that others in the past have accepted a distant discipline and learned well from accepting unfamiliar authority. The proposition is open to doubt, on its own merits, and it simply does not apply at all to the state of mind in the urban ghetto today. The liberating force for the urban education of the Negro and the Puerto Rican must be a new respect, a new engagement, a new responsibility.

New York is not all ghetto, and the ghetto student has not been our only concern. The demography of the public school system is changing daily and dramatically; no district today is just like another, and almost none is the same for two years running. . . .

Safeguards Stressed

Because of the extraordinary importance of respecting the rights of all, in this unprecedented demographic complexity, we have devised a number of safeguards in preparing this plan. Some have to do with methods for choosing Community School Boards that will not permit a monopoly of power to any one group.

And there is one other element of flexibility which deserves special mention here. While we find strong pressure for decentralization from a clear majority of the city's communities, we also find some who are content with things as they are. We have therefore recommended that the proposed Community School Boards should have the right to use just as many services from the central agency as they choose. In effect, under our plan, districts which do not want to decentralize will be free not to do so.

These proposals will not bring instant educational improvements to New York. Many of the cruel inadequacies of the present system must continue for years, even if we are dead right, and everyone agrees, and action is taken at once. Our own proposed timetable requires nearly two years for the initial establishment of the new community boards; consequent changes will take longer; and we must repeat that reorganization without new resources will be empty. Indeed, the reorganization itself will cost money, and we believe it will be money well spent.

One other warning is in order: The educational system of New York cannot remake the city — or any part of it — alone. We have found many teachers and supervisors who properly resist the suggestion that somehow everything in the slums is their fault. . . .

Finally, we would express our sense of comradeship with Alfred Giardino. . . . From the beginning it has been understood that he was with us as a representative of the Board of Education and that the board would wish to make its own comments after our report is submitted. As his separate statement shows, the board shares our purposes but has doubts about some of our recommendations.

We ourselves remain confident of the main lines of change we propose, but we also know that the problem is one of great complexity, and we make no claim to have explored every element of it. . . .

But what we must warn against, with all the force we can, is the kind of debate which might seek to prevent by obfuscation. . . . The people of New York together can make their schools a new force for good if they will. But none of them can succeed alone. The reconnection of the concerned — to the problem and one another — is the heart of our proposals. We ask that those who read them resist the temptation of fear and respond to the challenge of hope.

Sincerely,

Frances Keppel

Antonia Pantoja

Mitchell Sviridoff
Bennetta B. Washington
McGeorge Bundy,
Chairman

GIARDINO STATEMENT

It was my privilege to serve as a member of the panel. When the invitation was extended by the Mayor to Mr. Garrison, then President of the Board of Education, all parties agreed and understood that the president would reflect the views of the full board.

Our Board of Education is committed to the principle of local involvement and decentralization of function in order to foster parent and community participation and greater flexibility of school operations. Its record of action in this sphere, within the confining constraints of the present law, is referred to in the panel's report. And more can be done. We favor progress in these areas.

On the basis of the board's experience, we cannot agree with a number of the specific recommendations proposed by a majority of the panel to effectuate our common goals. Serious problems must arise in recasting in one quick stroke, the largest educational system in the world. We must be reasonably sure that a plan will be successful and do not feel sufficient assurance in the plan submitted. Rather than a rigidly timed and mandated set of procedures we prefer a more deliberative process of movement and evaluation. Moreover, we believe there are constructive legislative alternatives that can achieve many of the same goals without as many dangers.

The Board of Education intends to issue a fuller statement of its views shortly.

SUMMARY OF RECOMMENDATIONS

In order to:

· Increase community awareness and participation in the development of educational policy closely related to the diverse needs and aspirations of the city's population,

· Open new channels and incentives to educational innovation and excellence,

· Achieve greater flexibility in the administration of the schools,

· Afford the children, parents, teachers, other educators, and the city at large a single school system that combines the advantages of big-city education with the opportunities of the finest small-city and suburban educational systems, and

· Strengthen the individual school as an urban institution that enhances a sense of community and encourages close coordination and cooperation with other governmental and private efforts to advance the well-being of children and all others,

All with the central purpose of advancing the educational achievement and opportunities of the children in the public schools of New York City,

The Mayor's Advisory Panel on Decentralization of the New York City schools recommends:

1. The New York City public schools should be reorganized into a Community School System, consisting of a federation of largely autonomous school districts and a central education agency.

2. From 30 to more than 60 Community School Districts should be created, ranging in size from about 12,000 to 40,0000 pupils — large enough to offer a full range of educational services and yet small enough to promote administrative flexibility and proximity to community needs and diversity.

3. The Community School Districts should have authority for all regular elementary and secondary education within their boundaries and responsibility for adhering to state education standards.

4. A central education agency, together with a Superintendent of Schools and his staff, should have operating responsibility for special educational functions and citywide educational policies. It should also provide certain centralized services to the Community School Districts and others on the districts' request.

5. The State Commissioner of Education and the city's central educational agency shall retain their responsibilities for the maintenance of educational standards in all public schools in the city.

6. The Community School Districts should be governed by boards of education selected in part by parents and in part by the Mayor from lists of candidates maintained by the central education agency, and membership on the boards should be open to parents and nonparent residents of a district.

7. The central education agency should consist of one or the other of the following governing bodies:
   —A commission of three full-time members appointed by the Mayor, or — A Board of Education that includes a majority of members nominated by the Community School Districts. The Mayor should select these members from a list submitted by an assembly of chairmen of Community School Boards. The others should be chosen by the Mayor from nominations by a screening panel somewhat broader than the current panel.

8. Community School Districts should receive a total annual allocation of operating funds, determined by an objective and equitable formula, which they should be permitted to use with the widest possible discretion within educational standards and goals and union contract obligations.

9. Community School Districts should have broad personnel powers, including the hiring of a community superintendent on a contract basis.

10. All existing tenure rights of teachers and supervisory personnel should be preserved as the reorganized system goes into effect. Thereafter tenure of new personnel employed in a particular district should be awarded by the district.

11. The process of qualification for appointment and promotion in the system should be so revised that Community School Districts will be free to hire teachers and other professional staff from the widest possible sources so long as hiring is competitive and applicants meet state qualifications.

12. Community School Boards should establish procedures and channels for the closest possible consultation with parents, community residents, teachers, and supervisory personnel at the individual-school level and with associations of parents, teachers, and supervisors.

13. The central education agency should have authority and responsibility for advancing racial integration by all practicable means. The State Commissioner of Education should have authority, himself or through delegation to the central education agency under guidelines, to overrule measures that support segregation or other practices inimical to an open society.

14. The Community School System should go into effect for the school year beginning September, 1969, assuming passage of legislation in the 1968 Legislature.

15. The main responsibility for supervising and monitoring the transition from the existing system to the Community School System should rest with the State Commissioner of Education. The principal planning and operational functions should be assigned to a Temporary Commission on Transition that should work closely with the current Board of Education, the Superintendent of Schools, and his staff.

16. The transition period should include extensive programs of discussion and orientation on operations and responsibilities under the Community School System and on educational goals generally. School Board members should be afforded opportunities for training and provided with technical assistance on budgeting, curriculum, and other school matters.

Fake Panaceas for Ghetto Education

A Reply to Joseph Alsop *

Robert Schwartz, Thomas Pettigrew and Marshall Smith

America has educationally failed fourteen generations of Negro Americans, and has paid a high price for this failure. Currently, the nation is failing to educate the fifteenth generation, and the price in human tragedy promises to be even greater. *The New Republic* readers recently (July 22) received the benefit of Joseph Alsop's thinking on this subject. Stripped of its rhetoric, Alsop's argument reduces to six central propositions:

1. Negro children are not being adequately educated in America's schools.
2. Effective action must be initiated at once to correct this situation
3. Ending *de facto* segregation as a "virtuous incantation" which cannot be a solution for many reasons. First, desegregation is not going to happen, "at any rate for a long time to come." Second, major federal studies which suggest the efficacy of interracial education in a variety of settings are either "extremely deficient" as in the case of the US Office of Education's monumental "Coleman Report," or "shocking," as in the case of the US Commission on Civil Rights' report on *Racial Isolation in the Public Schools.* Third, when Negroes are "unprepared" for desegregation, school quality goes "to Hell in a hack." Consequently, "unprepared desegregation" drives white parents to the suburbs, creates more school segregation, and causes our central cities to become increasingly Negro.
4. "Brilliant Negro achievements is *[sic]* the answer." Only when Negro American achievements, as in athletics and the army, are conspicuous can white Americans accept desegregation.
5. And brilliant Negro achievements will come only with quality ghetto education. Racially separate schools can do the job if only educators would take the newspaperman's advice and follow "a series of steps of the most ABC simplicity." These steps are demonstrated by the "complete victory" of New York City's "More Effective Schools" (MES) program.
6. As to costs, only "a monster" would deny funds to such a reasonably reliable "cancer cure" as MES.

*Robert Schwartz, Thomas Pettigrew, Marshall Smith, "Fake Panaceas for Ghetto Education," *The New Republic*, September 23, 1967, Vol. 157, No. 13, pp. 16-19.

Few would contest Alsop's first two propositions: a majority of Negro children *are* being cheated out of their American birthright to a full public education; and massive corrective action *is* desperately required. But from this point on he loses the thread.

The desegregation of the nation's public schools is indeed a slow process as long as the necessary structural changes, such as metropolitan consolidation, are not achieved. Although Alsop pays lip service to interracial education as "the ideal solution," his article resists these structural changes by obscuring them. For example, he asserts educational consolidation in metropolitan Washington would require a constitutional amendment. This is absurd, for effective consolidation by no means necessitates a single metropolitan school district as initial efforts in Boston, Hartford, and Rochester demonstrate. Admittedly, metropolitan consolidation is politically difficult to achieve, but the federal government could encourage it in education as it has effectively done in other realms through multi-district funding incentives. In any event, Alsop worries that any pursuit of desegregation will deter his version of "the practical solution." Instead, we worry that Alsop is supplying the self-fulfilling rationale for racially segregated schools "for years to come."

No studies are definitive, nor do the Coleman and Civil Rights Commission reports claim to be final. But no fair-minded observer can pass off the second largest study of American education as "extremely deficient" without a full explanation. Nor could such an observer attack the Commission monograph with libelous charges without detailed elaboration. Apparently, Alsop is peeved that the MES program was not included in the report on *Racial Isolation in the Public Schools.* Had he the courtesy to call down the street to the Commission staff, he would have learned the reasons: the first long-term evaluation of MES appeared too late for inclusion in the Commission report; and, as we shall note below, neither the mode of the operation nor the test data of MES are basically different from compensatory programs which are described in the study.

Most serious of all is Alsop's implication that the report of the United States Commission on Civil Rights is racist, that it maintains if you "put Negro with Negro, you get stupidity." If Alsop eventually reads the report, he will encounter the following rejoinder from Commissioner Frankie M. Freeman:

> The question is not whether in theory or in the abstract Negro schools can be as good as white schools. In a society free from prejudice in which Negroes were full and equal participants, the answer would clearly be 'Yes.' But we are forced, rather, to ask the harder question, whether in our present society, where Negroes are a minority which has been discriminated against, Negro children can prepare themselves to participate effectively in society if they grow up and go to school in isolation from the majority group. We must also ask whether we can cure the disease of prejudice and prepare all children for life in a multiracial world if white children grow up and go to school in isolation from Negroes.

Alsop would also discover the Commission finding that white children in mixed, predominantly white schools perform as well as those in all-white schools. He will learn, too, that only about one in 25 white suburbanites gives racial problems in central city schools as his reason for moving. Our largest cities are becoming increasingly Negro not because whites move to the suburbs at rates similar to those of other industrial nations, but because Negroes are not free to move with them.

Fortunately, neither Washington nor New York are prototypes of American cities. Urban areas with smaller ghettos can often desegregate without suburban cooperation — as Providence, Berkeley, White Plains, and Evanston illustrate. Cities with large ghettos, of course, pose the major difficulties. But metropolitan and public-private cooperation could do the job. Negroes comprise approximately the same percentage of metropolitan areas as they do in the entire nation — roughly 11 percent. And the six cities Alsop compares with Washington all have large Roman Catholic school systems that currently absorb large percentages of their schoolaged whites. "The ideal solution" of desegregation *can* be accomplished but not by abandoning the goal and cursing reports which demonstrate its necessity.

Alsop's "brilliant Negro achievement" theory is an insult to the millions of Negro Americans who *have* achieved. Many achieving Negroes have painfully learned, however, that racial discrimination is still a part of their American experience. And this recipe for improved race relations blithely consigns yet another generation to ghetto schools while the brilliant achievers "inspire the next generation." As daily headlines make clear, America's racial problems will not wait that long. Desegregation is not something Negroes "earn" but is their right. Furthermore, Alsop's own examples of American institutions with remarkably reduced racial discrimination — "the hard-bitten army and harder-bitten professional sports teams" — forcefully demonstrate the efficacy of desegregation.

Alsop's belief in the possibility of quality segregated education seems to rest almost entirely on his impression of the achievements of New York City's More Effective Schools, an experimental program which was initiated in ten elementary schools in 1964-65 and expanded to eleven more in 1965-66. The idea originated with the city's teachers union, the United Federation of Teachers, and the UFT has made the further expansion of MES one of the key items in its current negotiations with the Board of Education. In Alsop's opinion the MES program, by starting in early childhood, providing small classes, employing backup teachers, and offering "all the obvious extras," has achieved a breakthrough: it is "literally the first to produce clear test results showing that ghetto children can be given a fully adequate education in ghetto schools."

The independent evaluations performed by New York's Center for Urban Education corroborate Alsop's favorable description of the climate and morale in the More Effective Schools. While the Center's most recent evaluation is careful to point out that there is considerable variation in quality among the 21 schools, most of the Center's observers agreed they would willingly send their children to the particular schools they visited. Given the apathy and despair that typically characterize ghetto schools, the optimism, sense of commitment and parental support that seem to prevail at most of the program's schools are in themselves significant achievements.

But what kind of academic success have these schools had? In Alsop's view, the test scores indicate "all [MES] children have shown a very great average improvement, and those children who have begun in pre-kindergarten and continued on from there are actually performing, on average, *at grade level or above.*" (Italics his.) What exactly is Alsop asserting? What does it mean to say that *all* children have shown a very great *average* improvement? How is this improvement to be defined, and what data does he have to support this high-sounding claim? His second assertion at least has the virtue of clarity: it should be quite easy to ascertain whether the children who enrolled in MES pre-kindergartens in 1964 are now performing at grade level. But since no citywide tests are administered until the second grade, it cannot possibly be supported or refuted.

The youngest MES children for whom we have three years of test scores are those who have just completed the fourth grade. When these children were first tested in October 1964, their median reading score was only .3 of a year below the city norm. At the end of the first year the gap had widened, but the hope was expressed in the Board of Education's preliminary evaluation that after another year or two of MES the gap would be closed. The sad fact is, however, that the April 1967 fourth grade scores reveal that in only two of the More Effective Schools is the average child reading at grade level. On further inquiry, one discovers that these two "above-average" schools are not ghetto schools at all, but are 70 percent white schools located in a predominantly middle-class section of the Bronx!

Stated flatly, the reading scores show that from the fourth grade on, no majority non-white school in the MES program is reading at grade level. Moreover, when we compare the slope of reading retardation in More Effective Schools with that in control schools (so designated by the Board of Education on the basis of comparable ethnic composition), we find little difference. At each grade level both sets of schools fall further and further behind the city and national norms. The second grade classes at the control schools are on average four months behind city norms, whereas the fifth grade classes are a year and four months behind. The MES second grade classes are one month behind the norm, while their fifth grade classes are a year and a month behind. Alsop is free to hail these scores as representing "a complete victory over that terrible educational lag that is the curse of America's Negro minority." He may well wish to publish them in "Mao-style Big Character posters," but we hope we may be pardoned for not joining in the celebration. It gives us no pleasure to have to state that the MES reading scores simply provide additional evidence to support one of the basic findings of the Civil Rights Commission Report: compensatory programs in predominantly non-white schools have so far had little sustained success in raising the achievement levels of their students.

FALSE EXPECTATIONS

The saddest consequence of Alsop's headlong foray into the educational arena is that by creating false expectations he may have done irreparable damage to a program that is worth encouraging. Anyone who has worked in schools knows that there are no instant miracles. For a program as ambitious as the More Effective Schools, a three-year trial period simply isn't sufficient. At the very least, the program should be continued until the first pre-kindergarten classes have completed their eight years. Unless MES is continued, we will never know whether it could have made a difference for those children caught early enough.

As the evidence now stands, however, the verdict is at best a mixed one. Here are the concluding sentences from the summary of the Center for Urban Education's most recent MES evaluation, conducted by Dr. David Fox of City University:

> In short, this evaluation suggests that the basic program introduced under the label 'MES' has had a favorable impact on the adults in these schools, in terms of their observed behavior, their views of the programs, and the general climate of the school. But it has not had a comparable impact on the observed behavior, perception, or achievement of the children who attended.

Interestingly, Alsop talked with Dr. Fox and his colleagues before going out to spent two hours at two schools, so he cannot plead ignorance of their conclusions. We quote from a report of the Alsop visit written by Joseph Krevisky, chairman of the Center's Field Research and Evaluation Committee, and published in *The Center Forum,* July 5th:

> All consultants stressed the very tentative nature of our findings, and the great difficulty of generalizing about the success of this program or about the broader implications that MES is a possible solution to the crucial problems of education of Negro and Puerto Rican children.
>   . . . In general, these cautions made very little dent on Mr. Alsop, who disagreed with almost all the comments made and was irritated by some of them. He said at that point it was futile to discuss such points any more as *nobody would change his mind.*

There is also the little matter of money. Alsop disposes of desegregation as impractical, but does not explain how practical it will be to get the nation to "invest until it hurts cruelly." MES costs $1,263 per child, $700 more than in regular primary schools in the New York system. It also requires 30 percent more schoolrooms and roughly twice the staff members of regular elementary schools in the city. And since MES has so far obtained only modest test score increments at best, these costs are gross underestimates for achieving Alsop's goal of average performance at grade level. The newspaperman is advocating a national educational program which, if possible at all, would cost well in excess of ten billion dollars annually. We salute Alsop's resolute refusal to choose between guns and butter, but the question remains: will even the richest country on earth simultaneously support the Vietnam war and a national MES program?

The MES requirement of 30 percent more schoolrooms raises yet another difficulty. So far in New York, only schools with underutilized facilities have taken part. But nationally the program would require many new schools; and Alsop would have them built deep within the ghetto. This would institutionalize racial segregation and seal Negro children in the ghetto for generations. Instead, new school construction must take the form of large complexes, such as campus parks, which draw upon wide attendance areas, guarantee quality education, and maximize desegregation.

WHY INTERRACIAL SCHOOLING?

But to dwell on costs and construction would be to allow ourselves to be deflected from the fundamental souces of our disagreement with Alsop. Let us suppose that his facts are right, that we do have evidence that by spending $1,263 per child we could raise the reading scores of ghetto children to the level of those of suburban children. This would indeed signify equality of educational opportunity, and it would be a distinct improvement over what we now have. But would this fulfill the primary aims of a public school system in a multiracial society? Reduced to its simplest terms, our belief is that interracial contact is an essential component of quality education, that schools which are isolated by virtue of race, social class, or religion deprive their students of adequate preparation for a diverse society and world.

We don't want to fall into the trap of seeming to assert that integrated education is by definition good education; obviously, the mere presence of whites and Negroes in the same classroom is no guarantee of anything. But when we compare the findings of the Coleman and Civil Rights Commission reports with those of such compensatory programs as the More Effective Schools, we must conclude that the evidence suggests that minority group students perform better in integrated than in isolated settings.

Are the reasons for this so hard to discern? To quote again from the Krevisky report of Alsop's visit to the MES schools:

> The teachers stressed that neither MES nor other programs have yet succeeded in overcoming the sense of hopelessness in the community, and the powerful barriers to incentives posed by discrimination in housing and jobs. . . .

Unless we are willing to change the fundamental realities of ghetto life in

America, aren't we deceiving ourselves to think that any amount of money can buy quality segregated education?

Let there be no misunderstanding. We believe MES and other dedicated remedial programs are necessary efforts at this desperate juncture in American race relations. But they constitute neither a national model nor a permanent solution. At best, they buy time until racial desegregation becomes a widespread fact of American public schools. Full desegregation must be the goal, and all efforts, including MES, must point toward it. Indeed, MES was originally conceived in this spirit, as the May 1964 program description made clear on its first page. And Alsop encountered on his hurried visit the same position from MES teachers:

> ... the teachers, mostly experienced and mostly Negro, sharply disagreed with Alsop's line. They refused adamantly to accept the solution of quality segregated education and questioned him insistently on what he was doing to educate white people to accept Negroes trying to break out of the 'ghetto'. They sharply challenged a statement he made that education was the only key to integration — by elevating the abilities of the Negro people, and leading to their acceptance by the white community. (*The Center Forum*, July 5.)

We agree with Mr. Alsop that "it is always wicked to hold out false hopes and offer fake panaceas to those in desperate need of hope and help." But even the best funded and most dedicated "compensatory" ghetto program is just such a "false hope" and "fake panacea" if it is advanced as a "complete victory."

Ghetto Education
Joseph Alsop Replies to His Critics *

Joseph Alsop

Although some time has passed since the publication of "Fake Panaceas for Ghetto Education" (Sept. 23), this very strange document demands a reply, however belated. For the sake of those *New Republic* readers who may have missed the angry outburst by Messrs. Thomas Schwartz, Thomas Pettigrew and Marshall Smith, "Fake Panaceas" was an attack on an earlier article of mine. In this earlier article, I did no more than suggest that pursuit of the vital goal of school desegregation must not be permitted to interfere with a parallel effort — the urgently, even desperately needed effort to educate the millions of Negro children now in ghetto schools or soon to go to ghetto schools, who have little hope of experiencing integrated education either now or in the foreseeable future. I shall pass over everything that was personal to me, all of it grossly inaccurate, in this Schwartz-Pettigrew-Smith attack; for all this is of no special consequence. What is profoundly consequential is quite another point. To put it bluntly, Professor Pettigrew, the real author of the Civil Rights Commission's report on "Racial Isolation in the Public Schools," is either unwilling to look the harsh facts of ghetto education in the face, or has never troubled to gather these basic facts concerning the problem he discusses so glibly. If the real author of such an important government report does not know or refuses to consider the basic facts, we are in a pretty bad way.

The thrust of the Pettigrew argument is that emphasis on ghetto school improvement — emphasis, in fact, on truly educating the millions of children now in ghetto schools or destined to go to ghetto schools, where they are not now being truly educated — will provide "the self-fulfilling rationale for socially segregated schools for years to come." Hence the first basic facts to consider are those bearing on the question: how many Negro children actually have the faintest chance of escaping from segregated ghetto schools "for years to come"? Even the most eminent academics' desire to avoid "self-fulfilling rationales" must after all be subordinated to the needs of the children themselves — and their prime need is *decent education.*

Let us begin this part of the inquiry in 18 American cities — most of them among our largest cities. All of these 18 cities have total school populations that

*Joseph Alsop, "Ghetto Education," *The New Republic,* November 18, 1967, Vol. 157, No. 21, pp. 18-23.

include at least 40 percent of Negro children. These cities are printed in italics in the table on the next page, which gives the Negro percentage of school populations of 48 major cities, as estimated by the office of the US Commissioner of Education. Concerning the figures in the table, it must be noted, first of all, that in each case they cover the whole public school population, from kindergarten through twelfth grade. In all cities, the percentage of Negro children in the primary and elementary schools is substantially higher than the percentage in the high schools. Thus, Cleveland, with a school population 49 percent Negro, has a Negro majority in the primary and elementary schools; and much the same upper-lower relationships may also be assumed for all the other cities in the 40-50 percent bracket. These few bits and pieces of data should be enough to indicate the total falsity of the Schwartz-Pettigrew-Smith assertion that "neither Washington nor New York are prototypes of American cities." New York is, indeed, not a prototype because its Negro percentage of the school population is no more than 28.4, hardly higher than Boston, which has 26 percent. (But in New York, the ghetto schools also include unusually large numbers of Puerto Ricans, who are not counted in the attached table but are another major element in the ghetto school problem.) Washington *is* a prototype, alas, in the literal sense of the word; for Washington is merely the most advanced case of an urban demographic trend which will surely produce many other super-ghetto center-cities unless drastic steps are taken to solve the ghetto school problem. Where St. Louis and Baltimore are today, for instance, Washington was only a few years ago; and the same observation applies, in varying degree, to just about every other city in the table with 40 percent and more of Negro children in its schools.

The table on the following pages requires two comments. In the first place, the given percentages of nonwhite school populations do not include Puerto Ricans. Thus they grossly understate the true dimensions of the ghetto school problem in several major cities. Per contra, *they do include children of Asian origin. Hence they overstate the problem in one or two cities, like San Francisco and Los Angeles, which have large populations of Chinese- and Japanese-Americans.*

Second, the figures themselves are almost certainly on the low side. In Washington, for instance, the Negro percentage of the school population is given as 88. Last year, however, the true percentage was 90.3, close to 93 percent in the primary and elementary schools and 85.6 percent in the high schools.

Here, then, are the 18 cities with the most acute current problem. In these 18 cities, there are now close to a million Negro children in the elementary schools alone. Officially, a school is defined as segregated if it is 50 percent Negro or above. Even if the entire school populations of all these cities could be automatically homogenized, so that each school would contain the exact citywide percentage of Negro pupils in the whole school system, every one of these cities would still have segregated or borderline-segregated primary and elementary schools; and in many of them, all the schools, including high schools, would still be segregated under the official definition. As a practical matter, of course, this kind of total homogenization of the entire school population is absolutely out of the question in any city of considerable size. It can be done — and often should be done — in small cities, and even in big cities where the Negro percentage of the school population is not too unwieldy. It has been done, for instance, in White Plains, N.Y., where the predominantly Negro center-city school was closed, and the center-city children are now being bused out to the four white, middle-class schools in White Plains' outer ring. But in White Plains, this involved no insurmountable physical problem, whereas in cities like Chicago and Detroit, mere physical problems put anything like the White Plains solution utterly beyond reach. In such cities, the great majority of ghetto children are inevitably going to be educated *in ghetto schools* for a very long time to come; and this is why the prospects of *improved education in the ghettos* now constitute a subject of such urgent interest and importance.

By "physical problems" I mean, for instance, the hopeless difficulty of busing scores and even hundreds of thousands of children back and forth, often for very long distances, over the length and breadth of such a city as Chicago. As the sinister example of Boston has all too plainly shown, meanwhile, no sane man who gives a tinker's damn for Negro education can dare to forget about political problems. In Boston, after all, there are only 26 percent of Negro children in the entire school population, and not much more than 30 percent in the primary and elementary school population. I do not admire Louise Day Hicks any more than Professor Pettigrew does. Thank God she was defeated, though by a disturbingly narrow margin. But the voters she appealed to are a fact of life, however sordid and regrettable this fact may be. In Boston, moreover the real problem was rather small in dimension, and should have been manageable by persons of reasonable goodwill. Thus it is obvious that situations even more threatening than Boston's can all too easily arise elsewhere. Unless, once again, swift and drastic steps to solve the ghetto school problem begin to be taken in the ghettos themselves.

In summary, school desegregation is literally impossible, even by forcible homogenization, in 18 cities which now have a Negro elementary school population of nearly a million, with scores of thousands more in high school. In 17 more cities — those with 20 percent of Negro schoolchildren or above — serious school desegregation is probably politically impossible; for a new Louise Day Hicks can all too easily emerge from limbo, in every one of these cities, if the right steps to solve the ghetto school problem in the ghettos are not taken in the first instance. And in only 12 cities on the Commissioner of Education's list — those with school populations under 20 percent Negro — is anything like truly and fully integrated schooling an imaginably feasible aim. Even where it is imaginably feasible, any realist must further note that the road to school

Nonwhite Public School Population in 48 Major Cities, 1965-66 School Year

City	Nonwhite K-12 Population as Percent of Total K-12 Population	Percent of Total Negro Elementary Students in Schools 90-100 Percent Negro	Percent of Total Negro Elementary Students in Majority Negro Schools	Percent of Total White Elementary Students in Schools 90-100 Percent White
New York	28.4	20.7	55.5	56.8
Chicago	52.0	89.2	96.9	88.8
Los Angeles	21.0[1]	39.5[3]	87.5[3]	94.7[3]
Philadelphia	55.1	72.0	90.2	57.7
Detroit	55.5	72.3	91.5	65.0
Baltimore	61.0	84.2	92.3	67.0
Houston	34.0	93.0	97.6	97.3
Cleveland	49.0	82.3[4]	94.6[4]	80.2[4]
Washington	88.0	90.4	99.3	34.3
St. Louis	60.0	90.9	93.7	66.0
Milwaukee	21.2	72.4	86.8	86.3
San Francisco	43.0	21.1	72.3	65.1
Boston	26.0	35.4	79.5	76.5
Dallas	24.0[2]	82.6	90.3	90.1
New Orleans	63.0	95.9	96.7	83.8
Pittsburgh, Pa.	36.7	49.5	82.8	62.3
San Antonio	13.0	65.9	77.2	89.4
San Diego	13.0	13.9	73.3	88.7
Seattle	15.2	9.9[5]	60.4[5]	89.8[5]
Buffalo	32.1	77.0	88.7	81.1
Cincinnati	40.0	49.4	88.0	63.3
Memphis	52.0	95.1	98.8	93.6
Denver	13.0	29.4	75.2	95.5

City				
Atlanta	*52.0*	*97.4*	*98.8*	*95.4*
Minneapolis	6.0	..	39.2	84.9
Indianapolis	32.1	70.5	84.2	80.7
Kansas City, Mo.	*40.9[1]*	*69.1*	*85.5*	*65.2*
Columbus, Ohio	26.0	34.3	80.8	77.0
Phoenix	12.0	NA	NA	NA
Newark	*53.8*	*51.3*	*90.3*	*37.1*
Louisville	*41.9*	*69.5*	*84.5*	*61.3*
Portland, Ore.	8.6	46.5	59.2	92.0
Oakland	*50.6*	*48.7*	*83.2*	*50.2*
Fort Worth	22.0	NA	NA	NA
Long Beach	*76.6[1]*	*NA*	*NA*	*NA*
Birmingham	*57.7*	*NA*	*NA*	*NA*
Oklahoma City	16.8	90.5	96.8	96.1
Rochester, N.Y.	20.1	43.6	74.6	65.5
Toledo	25.9[1]	NA	NA	NA
St. Paul	6.0	34.4[3]	64.2[3]	93.9[3]
Norfolk	36.0	NA	NA	NA
Omaha[1]	17.8	47.7	81.1	89.0
Miami	*45.7*	*91.4*	*94.4*	*95.3*
Akron	25.0	40.9[3]	68.1[3]	26.6[3]
Jersey City	39.6	NA	NA	NA
Dayton	36.0	NA	NA	NA
Tulsa	15.2	90.7	98.7	98.9
Wichita	14.3	63.5	89.1	94.8

[1] City and school district are not coterminus.
[2] Does not include kindergarten.
[3] 1963-64 data.
[4] 1962-63 data.
[5] 1964-65 data.

integration can be all too rocky, although the task should theoretically be as easy as in White Plains.

Such, then, is the first set of basic demographic, practical and political facts that Messrs. Schwartz, Pettigrew and Smith have either refused to face, or have failed to take the trouble to discover. If fear of "self-fulfilling rationales" is going to prevent radical ghetto school improvement in a large majority of the cities on the list, something like a million and a half Negro children will then be permanently condemned to grossly inadequate schooling — and thereby in turn condemned to permanent inability to compete in modern society. This seems a heartless and antisocial decision to take.

There are also some additional facts to consider, which are of very great interest. Let us begin with busing, which was recommended as the sovereign remedy for urban school segregation in the Civil Rights Commission report, to which Professor Pettigrew contributed so importantly. In my previous article I called that report "scandalous" because it offered busing as its prime remedy, yet was datelined Washington, D.C., where the public schools are almost entirely Negro. The report would not have been scandalous, to be sure, if it had included a recommendation for a constitutional amendment, permitting forcible imposition by the federal government of some sort of general homogenization of the school populations of the District of Columbia and its white middle-class suburbs — plus the same sort of thing, of course, in other cities nearly as deeply afflicted by the white suburban emigration. If this degree of honesty and fact-facing had been practiced, the Civil Rights Commission report would not have been scandalous; it would merely have been silly. The report would have been silly, in the first place, because it would then have asked the center-city and suburban parents to tolerate their children wasting anywhere up to three hours a day on buses, in order to achieve homogenization. And the report would have been silly in the second place, and above all, because there is not the remotest chance of carrying the necessary constitutional amendment, in the highly improbable event that it is ever offered. I strongly favor busing wherever it can be of any use; yet it is abundantly clear that busing is useless as a *general remedy*. It can produce modestly useful fringe results within center-cities, although even in the center-cities, the results are bound to be more and more marginal in proportion to increases in the percentages of Negro children in the school populations.

On busing from the center-cities to the suburbs, Messrs. Schwartz, Pettigrew and Smith reassuringly declared that "efforts . . . in Rochester demonstrate" that "effective consolidation" of center-city and suburban schools "by no means necessitates a single metropolitan school district." Note those words, "effective consolidation." As usual, Schwartz, Pettigrew and Smith either neglected to inform themselves about the proud case of Rochester, or else they were once again guilty of citing nonsense-evidence. In Rochester, to be sure, some hundreds of children are being bused within the center-city, and others are being bused to the suburbs. But those being bused to the suburbs number only 220, out of a total Negro grade school population in Rochester that is close to 10,000. The children being bused have been carefully chosen for good past performance and high future potential. Even so, the majority of Rochester's suburbs are now resisting a plan to bus out a few beggarly hundreds of additional children. If this kind of "initial effort" demonstrates anything at all, it demonstrates the precise point made in my earlier article. And in Hartford, Boston and all other cases known to me of center-city-suburban busing, it is again the same story of a few hundreds, usually specially selected, out of the many thousands of children who constitute the true problem. In short, center-city-suburban busing is no more than a very minor virtuous gesture. I must add that I am not against virtuous gestures of this sort, however minor; indeed, I favor them, because even the smallest addition to our future totals of effectively educated Negroes will also be an addition to the number of Negroes equipped to compete successfully and to achieve conspicuously. But the crucial difference between remedies and gestures is another key fact that Schwartz, Pettigrew and Smith have failed to face or have not bothered to figure out.

Finally, at the very heart of all the key facts the Schwartz-Pettigrew-Smith team have either failed to face or do not know about, there is the major role of *unprepared* school desegregation in transforming more and more of the great center-cities into proto-ghettos surrounded by rings of prosperous white middle-class suburbs. In my previous article, I cited the case of the nation's capital, which has 250,000 remaining white inhabitants, with only 13,500 children in the public schools, as against nearly 500,000 Negro inhabitants, with over 134,000 children in the schools. Obviously a white population of 250,000 with only 13,500 children in the public school system (including teachers' colleges) is a demographic monstrosity in normal circumstances. Obviously, this is the situation in Washington simply because virtually all white families with children in need of schooling have automatically moved to the suburbs, except for those few in neighborhoods where the schools are still predominantly white, plus another, even smaller group who can afford to send their children to private or parochial schools. In the same article, I also cited the really tragic case of PS 7 and PS 8 in Brooklyn — one segregated, one white — the pairing of which was sponsored by the PTA of the white school. The result, as I wrote, was that school quality declined very gravely, because no adequate measures had been taken to maintain both schools' educational effectiveness in the face of a heavy postpairing admixture of extremely deprived children. In consequence, the very same white parents who had sponsored pairing either moved to the suburbs or put their children into private schools, leaving two segregated public schools where there had been only one before. This case is particularly significant because the white flight from the paired schools took place *before* any very striking change in the neighborhood the white children came from.

A large allowance for the influence of change in the neighborhood must be made, in contrast, in the cases of the schools in "transitional areas," also in New York City. In order to try to maintain a reasonable racial balance in these schools, New York has been spending some millions of dollars each year on extras intended to improve school quality. The extras have been valuable, but the improvements have been insufficient to hold the schools' white population, which has declined by one-half in three short years. The school principals themselves attribute this emigration only 50 percent to the change in their neighborhoods, and admit that the other 50 percent is attributable to continuing white dissatisfaction with the schools. Yet sufficient improvement can indeed be made to hold and even to increase the white population in a predominantly Negro school, as is proved by the case of PS 307, also in Brooklyn. Here the school principal, Dr. Irving Carlin, had to speak on the Brooklyn church-circuit to get his first 30 or so white pupils, when PS 307 was reopened as one of New York's More Effective Schools. In addition, he was able to offer the special inducement of pre-kindergarten, which is only provided in New York by schools in the MES program. But that was more than three years ago. Today, PS 307 has over 200 white children going to school — being bused in, too — in a near-complete ghetto neighborhood. Seventy of last year's kindergarten whites have stayed on into the first grade; these first-grade white children's parents show every sign of intending to keep them in PS 307 until their primary schooling is finished — always supposing school quality is maintained; and the school now *has a waiting list of another 100 white children* who cannot be accepted because there are no places for them. This is no trifling business, either, for with 200 white pupils at present, PS 307 is already above 20 percent white, solely by *reverse integration,* solely resulting from the attractive power of outstanding school quality.

Evidently, however, facts like these are either too unsettling for Messrs. Schwartz, Pettigrew and Smith to digest, or they are too troublesome for them to ascertain. In their article they passed over, in resounding silence, the uncomfortably difficult problems of Washington's strange demographic pattern and the story of PS 7 and PS 8. Probably they had not bothered to learn about the results of the New York program for schools in "transitional areas," and they had certainly failed to inquire into the achievement of PS 307. Without offering any sort of detailed proof, they contented themselves with grandly remarking that "only about one in 25 white suburbanites gives" racial problems in the schools as his reason for moving to the suburbs. If you can believe that this is indicative or meaningful, in the face of Washington's demographic pattern, for instance, you are capable of believing six impossible things before breakfast, in the manner of the White Queen in *Alice.* The plain fact of the matter is that unless radical measures to maintain school quality are taken in advance, white middle-class families will almost always begin to exercise the option to move away, either to the suburbs or to another center-city neighborhood, whenever the percentage of deprived children in a given school rises above a certain level – generally about one-quarter of the total. It is not so much a matter of race, either, as it is a matter of the effect on school quality of the addition of large numbers of children who are educationally retarded; for the white middle-class emigration has also occurred in numerous cases where the educationally retarded children were Mexican-Americans, Puerto Rican-Americans and Appalachian poor whites. In contrast, moreover, there is more than a glimmer of hope that extreme (and costly) attention to school quality can quite successfully maintain a reasonable racial balance. Here, see the case of PS 307.

Add it all up. For anyone who is willing to find out the facts and to face up to them, several conclusions are unavoidable. First, no amount of court-ordering, no further dubious report-writing by the Pettigrews of the academic community, nor any other influence that one can think of, will save millions of Negro children from receiving mainly segregated schooling, either now or for a long time to come. Second, providing those millions of Negro children with a decent education, and thereby fitting them to compete in our increasingly technological society, is therefore one of the most desperately urgent problems confronting this country, which *must be solved, no matter what the cost.* Third, however, for all the reasons cited, the problem *cannot be solved* by exclusive, too often vain pursuit of school desegregation; in fact, the only available *overall* solution is radical improvement of the ghetto schools, in parallel, of course, with efforts to obtain desegregation wherever this is practically feasible. To these all too amply buttressed conclusions, one may also add another, extremely tentative conclusion. It just may be that radical ghetto school improvement, on a very big scale, will not only help to secure the school integration that Professor Pettigrew and I both fervently believe in as the ideal result; in addition, this kind of school improvement in the center-cities may even tend to reverse the terrible demographic trend that is threatening to turn so many of our larger cities into super-ghettos surrounded by endless rings of rancidly complacent, fatly affluent white suburbs.

That leaves the question whether sufficiently radical improvement of ghetto schools is really possible, given the cruel character of the ghetto environment. The answer is, thus far, that we cannot be quite sure about this, because all experiments with really radical ghetto school improvement are too recent to have produced final results; yet we already have very good grounds for hope. As giving grounds for real hope (but no means as a "panacea" or even as a final model) I cited the longest established effort of really radical school improvement, the More Effective Schools program in New York City, which was only started in the 1964-65 school year. There is no space here for detailed refutation of the Schwartz-Pettigrew-Smith attack on the MES program. It is enough to make a single, very simple point. Briefly, one of the cardinal requirements – perhaps *the* cardinal requirement – of the MES program is to catch the children young, in order to overcome basic ghetto handicaps like speech difficulties when the children are still malleable and receptive. This is why all MES schools have an extra pre-kindergarten year. For this very reason, too, the earlier grades, whose children really were caught young, are the only fair tests of the MES schools that are as yet available, whereas the higher grades are not fair tests because the children were not caught young enough. For reasons which are extremely mysterious, the Center for Urban Education based its most recent report on the MES schools (though not its two earlier reports) exclusively on the higher grades. The explanation privately given at the Center was that in Grade II, variations in test results between MES and other schools were too trifling to be interesting. But this, as will be seen, is flatly untrue. Before using the Center's last report as their test, one must add that Schwartz, Pettigrew and Smith could have discovered the untruth by totaling up last year's test results.

The New York Board of Education has just made available its more recent sets of test results for all the schools in the city. In order to get a fair comparison, I have eliminated three schools in partly middle-class neighborhoods (originally included in the MES program to see whether they could hold their white pupils) which have shown extra-high performance. I have used as my bases of comparison only the 18 MES schools that were formerly "special service schools" – which in New York means ghetto schools – and the more than 200 non-MES ghetto schools still in the "special service" group – not excluding "special service" schools with university or college affiliations, unusually helpful neighborhood situations, or other advantages. As the new figures were barely in hand when this went to press, I have only the reading scores; but these are exceedingly impressive if correctly interpreted.

Let us begin with Grade II. At the opening of the 1966-67 school year, when the norm was 2, the children in the special service schools showed a reading average of 1.7. And when retested in April 1966, by which time the norm was 2.7, the special service schoolchildren showed a reading average of 2.4. In other words, their reading skills were equal to those of more fortunate children with only two years and four months of schooling, instead of children with two years and seven months, as should have been the case. Serious retardation had therefore set in already. In contrast, in the schools in the MES program, the children also started the school year below norm, but they were only one month behind, with an average score on the reading tests of 1.9. On the April retest, moreover, they were performing above the norm – in fact, above the average of more fortunate children – with an average score of 2.9. Of the 18 schools, furthermore, only three were more than a point below the norm (all of them in particularly horrible neighborhoods); and a few were also really well above the norm. There are many reasons for variations from school to school, which are also dramatically present among New York's special service schools. Centralized direction of the More Effective Schools program – which the Board of Education has just struck down – is badly needed in order to get at those reasons and to secure better performance in the small minority of less successful schools. Overall, in any case, the MES children were performing above grade level, on average, when they were nearing the end of the second grade. In Grade III, again, where the children had been caught less young, but still young enough to show the effects of earlier learning and better work habits, the two groups of schools still showed nearly the same contrast. At the beginning of the school year, when the norm was 3, the reading tests of the special service schoolchildren averaged 2.5, while those of the children in the MES program averaged 2.7. And in the April 1967 retests, when the norm had reached 3.7, the special service schoolchildren averaged 3.3, while the children in the MES program averaged 3.7 — on the nose of grade level, in fact. Finally, in Grade V, there was still a marked contrast, although the Grade V children had certainly not been caught young enough to offer a fair test of MES. At the beginning of the school year, the norm was by now 5, and both special service and MES schoolchildren scored only 4. But on the April retests, when the norm had reached 5.7, the special service schoolchildren scored, on average, only 5, while the MES program children had an average score of 5.3.

This talk of test scores and grade levels may seem bewildering to the average reader, but the figures are bursting with significance, nonetheless. They mean that in the representative earlier grades, the average child in the MES program *does not show the terrible, progressive retardation which is the curse of ghetto schooling,* whereas in those same grades, the curse already begins to show very clearly in the average performance of the children in New York's other ghetto schools. Furthermore, I have talked or obtained opinions from a long series of principals of successful More Effective Schools; and they are unanimous that their second-graders will go forward, on average, at grade level or above — in other words, be educated like more fortunate children — as they move upward in their schools to the higher grades. If this proves true MES will then be a solution of the ghetto school problem — but one must wait and see.

At this juncture there is only one point, indeed, concerning which one does not need to wait and see. If millions of Negro children are highly unlikely to escape from segregated, ghetto education for years to come, something has got to be done to give those children an education, *in the ghettos if need be,* that will fit them to compete in modern American society. The present system, of allowing the heaviest kind of educational handicap to be regularly piled on top of the barriers of ugly prejudice, is simply an inbuilt design for perpetuating discrimination and injustice in our society. The system must therefore be reformed, no matter what the cost. Hence educational theorists would do better to stop belaboring the arguments so dear to Messrs. Schwartz, Pettigrew and Smith; and above all, they ought to begin to study and explore every imaginable method of securing radical improvement of *the schools where the children are.* To do less than this, is callously to condemn to defeat and despair millions of Negro children who have no practical hope of integrated education.

In conclusion, I must repeat with emphasis that fully integrated schools in a fully integrated society must always be the American aim. The question is not what the aim ought to be. The question is, really, how to attain that aim — whether, for example, ghetto school improvement to equip Negro children for equal future competition with their white middle-class contemporaries is not an unavoidable prerequisite to eventual attainment of the total aim. There are many ways to approach this central question. Only one thing is already certain. Any approach that is *not* based on all the facts, that ignores current urban demography, that lets "the best become the enemy of the good," that is self-serving and fundamentally dishonest in its formulation of the problem, will surely meet with disastrous failure. And when you can find great encouragement in Rochester; when you can forget about or overlook the million elementary schoolchildren of Washington and 17 other major cities; when you can prate about busing as a general remedy and are driven to snide misstatement concerning the one promising in-ghetto solution that is well under way thus far, then your approach belongs in the class described above.

Private Schools for Black Children*

Christopher Jencks

The public school system of New York City is on the brink of collapse. No compromise between the teachers' union and the school board is likely to resolve the fundamental conflicts between the school staff and the advocates of black community control. Until the basic political framework of public education in New York City is altered, strikes and boycotts — or both — are likely to recur on an annual basis.

Nor is New York unique. It is simply first. All the forces which have brought New York City to its present condition are at work elsewhere, and the New York story will certainly be repeated in dozens of other major cities around the country during the next decade.

The origin of the crisis is simple. The public schools have not been able to teach most black children to read and write or to add and subtract competently. This is not the children's fault. They are the victims of social pathology far beyond their control. Nor is it the schools' fault, for schools as now organized cannot possibly offset the malignant effects of growing up in the ghetto. Nonetheless, the fact that the schools cannot teach black children basic skills has made the rest of the curriculum unworkable and it has left the children with nothing useful and creative to do for six hours a day. Ghetto schools have therefore become little more than custodial institutions for keeping the children off the street. Nobody, black or white, really knows what to do about the situation.

The traditional argument of both black and white liberals was that the problem could be solved by integrating black children into predominantly white schools, but experience has shown that many whites are reluctant to allow this, and that many blacks are not willing to move into white neighborhoods or bus their children across town even if the opportunity is available. Furthermore, studies such as the one done in New York City by David Fox have shown that most black children's academic performance improves only a little or not at all in integrated schools. Most people have therefore abandoned integration as a solution, at least in big cities.

Most educators are now concentrating on "compensatory" and "remedial"

*Christopher Jencks, "Private Schools For Black Children," *The New York Times Magazine*, November 3, 1968.

programs to bring academic competence in all-black schools up to the level of all-white schools. Unfortunately, none of these programs have proved consistently successful over any significant period. A few gifted principals seem to have created an atmosphere which enables black children to learn as much as whites in other schools, but they have done this by force of personality rather than by devising formulas which others could follow. Programs like More Effective Schools in New York City may eventually prove moderately effective, but evaluations to date have not provided grounds for great optimism.

The widespread failure of both integration and compensation has convinced some black nationalists that the answer is to replace white principals and teachers with black ones. But experience with this remedy is also discouraging. The schools in Washington, D.C., for example, have predominantly black staffs, and yet their black pupils learn no more than in other cities. So, many black militants are now arguing that the essential step is not to hire black staffs but to establish black control over the schools. There is little evidence one way or the other on this score, but the schools in America's few predominantly black towns are not especially distinguished.

The available evidence suggests that only a really extraordinary school can have much influence on a child's academic competence, be he black or white. Within the range of variation found in American public schools — and by traditional criteria this range is quite broad — the difference between a "good" school and "bad" school does not seem to matter very much. James S. Coleman's massive Equality of Educational Opportunity survey, conducted for the U.S. Office of Education, demonstrated this point in 1965. Coleman's work was much criticized on methodological grounds, but most subsequent analyses have confirmed his conclusions. Indeed, recent work at Harvard suggests that Coleman probably overstated the effect of school quality on student achievement. This means that the gap between black and white children's academic achievement is largely if not entirely attributable to factors over which school boards have no control.

There are, of course, both educators and scholars who disagree with this conclusion, and who argue that the schools play a substantial role in perpetuating inequality between the races. Such skeptics must, however, explain two facts documented by the Coleman survey and never seriously disputed since.

First, Coleman's work confirmed previous studies showing that even before they enter school black children perform far less well on standard tests than white children. The typical black 6-year-old in the urban North, for example, scores below five-sixths of all white 6-year-olds on tests of both verbal and nonverbal ability. These tests obviously measure performance on tasks which seem important to educators and psychologists, not tasks which seem important to the children being tested or most of their parents. But for precisely this reason they provide a fairly accurate indication of how well any particular cultural group is likely to do at such "white-middle-class" games as reading and long division. In the case of poor black children, the tests predict disaster.

The prediction, moreover, is all too accurate. Twelve years later, after the schools have done their best and their worst, the typical black 18-year-old in the urban North is still scoring at about the 15th percentile on most standard tests. The schools in short, have not changed his position one way or the other. This obviously means that his *absolute* handicap has grown, for he is 12 years older and both he and his classmates know far more than before, so there is more room for differentiation. Thus a first-grader who scores at the 15th percentile on a verbal test is less than a year behind his classmates; a 12th-grader who scores at the 15th percentile is more than three years behind.

The second fact which must be reckoned with is that while black children go to many different sorts of schools, good and bad, integrated and segregated, rigidly authoritarian and relatively permissive, their mean achievement level is remarkably similar from school to school. By the sixth grade, for example, the typical lower-class Northern black child is achieving a little above the fourth-grade level. There is a great deal of *individual* variation around this average, both because black lower-class families vary considerably in the amount of support they give a school child and because individual children differ in native ability. But there is very little variation from one school to another in such children's *average* level of achievement. The black lower-class average is within one grade level of the over-all black lower-class average in 9 schools out of 10. This uniformly depressing picture cannot be attributed to uniformly depressing conditions in the schools Coleman surveyed. Many of these schools were predominantly white, and some had excellent facilities, highly trained and experienced teachers, relatively small classes and high over-all levels of expenditure. These differences show no consistent relationship to the mean achievement of black elementary school pupils.

The last word has certainly not been written on this subject. Indeed, a group at Harvard is planning another whole book on it. But at the moment I think the evidence strongly indicates that differences in school achievement are largely caused by differences between cultures, between communities, between socio-economic circumstances and between families − not by differences between schools.

None of this provides any adequate excuse for the outrageous and appalling things which are often done in ghetto schools. But it does suggest that even if black schools had the same resources and the same degree of responsibility to parents that the better suburban schools now have, ghetto children would still end up much less academically competent than suburban children.

It follows that the pedagogic failure of the ghetto schools must not be blamed primarily on the stupidity or malice of school boards or school administrators. It must be blamed on the whole complex of social arrangements whose cumulative viciousness creates a Harlem or a Watts. This means that, barring a general improvement in the social and economic positions of black America, black children's school achievement is unlikely to improve much in the foreseeable future, no matter who runs the schools or how they are run.

Some will challenge this depressing conclusion on the ground that black children's achievement scores could be substantially improved if really radical changes were made in the character and organization of black schools. This may well be true, but such changes are unlikely. Nor is it clear that they would be worth the cost. Despite a great deal of popular mythology, there is little real evidence that improving black children's academic skills would help any appreciable number of them to escape poverty and powerlessness.

On the contrary, studies by Otis Dudley Duncan at the University of Michigan suggest that academic competence probably explains only 10 per cent or 15 per cent of the variations in men's earnings. Research by Stephan Michelson at the Brookings Institution likewise indicates that staying in school is not likely to be much help to a Negro who wants to break out of poverty unless he stays through college.

In these circumstances, it seems to me that we should view the present urban school crisis primarily as a political problem, and only secondarily as a pedagogic one. So long as militant blacks believe they are the victims of a conspiracy to keep their children stupid – and therefore subservient – the political problem will remain insoluble. But if we encourage and assist black parents with such suspicions to set up their own schools, we may be able to avert disaster.

These schools would not, I predict, be either more or less successful than existing public schools in teaching the three R's. But that is not the point. The point is to find a political *modus vivendi* which is tolerable to all sides. (After that, the struggle to eliminate the ghetto should probably concentrate on other institutions, especially corporate employers.) How, then, might independent, black-controlled schools help create such a *modus vivendi*?

The essential issue in the politics of American education has always been whether laymen or professionals would control the schools. Conflict between these two groups has taken a hundred forms. Profressionals always want more money for the schools, while laymen almost always want to trim the budget. Professionals almost always want personnel hired and promoted on the basis of "fair" and "objective" criteria like degrees, examination results and seniority. Laymen are inclined to favor less impersonal criteria, such as whether the individual has roots, whether they personally know and trust him, whether he gets on well with his colleagues, and so forth. Professionals almost never want anyone fired for any reason whatever, while laymen are inclined to fire all sorts of people, for both good and bad reasons. Professionals want a curriculum which reflects their own ideas about the world, and this often means a curriculum that embodies "liberal" ideas and values they picked up at some big university. Laymen frequently oppose this demand, insisting that the curriculum should reflect conservative local mores.

The development of big-city public schools over the past century has been marked by a steady decline of lay control and an increase in the power of the professional staff. Until relatively recently, this has meant that control was exercised by administrators. Now the teaching staff, represented by increasingly militant unions and professional associations, has begun to insist on its rights. This is, however, an intraprofessional dispute. It has done nothing to arrest the staff's continuing and largely successful resistance to nonprofessional "intervention" by parents, school-board members and other laymen. About the only thing such laymen can still decide in most big cities is the over-all level of expenditures.

The extent to which the professional staff gets its way seems to be related to the size of the administrative unit in which it works. Laymen usually have more power in small school districts, while the staff usually has more power in big districts. Until relatively recently, most liberals saw this as an argument for bigger districts, since they thought that the trouble with American education was its excessive deference to local interests and its lack of professionalism. In the past few years, however, liberals and radicals have suddenly joined conservatives in attacking bigness, bureaucracy and the claims of enterprise. Most people on the left are now calling for more participation, more responsiveness, more decentralization, and less "alienization."

Liberal thinking on this question is in large part a response to black nationalism. More and more Negroes believe there is a cause-effect relationship between the hegemony of what they call "white middle-class" (read professional-bureaucratic) values in their schools and the fact that their children learn so little in those schools. So they think the best way to improve their children's performance would be to break the power of the professional staff. This, they rightly infer, requires Balkanizing big-city systems into much smaller units, which will be more responsive to parental and neighborhood pressure. (There are, of course, also strictly administrative arguments for breaking up systems as large as New York City's into units the size of, say, Rochester. But that would not do much for parental control.) So black militants want to strip the central board of education and central administrative staff of authority, elect local boards, have these boards appoint local officials, and then let these locally appointed officials operate local schools in precisely the same way that any small-town or suburban school system does.

This scheme has been attacked on two grounds. First, members whose values are significantly at odds with the community's. This would make schools even more homogenized and parochial than they now are. Indeed, a local district which does not give its staff substantial autonomy is likely to have some difficulty recruiting even teachers who have grown up in the neighborhood and share the parents' values, simply because most teachers do not want parents constantly second-guessing them. Once the first flush of idealistic enthusiasm had passed, locally controlled schools in poor areas would probably have a harder time getting staffs than they do now. Like small rural districts confronted with the same problem, small impoverished urban districts would probably have to depend mainly on local people who could not get better jobs elsewhere.

These two arguments against local control of big-city schools naturally carry little weight with black militants. They have little patience with the liberal claim that the way to make black children learn more is to give them more white classmates and more middle-class teachers from Ivy League colleges. When liberals oppose decentralization on the grounds that it would legitimize segregation, the black militants answer: "So what? Integration is a myth. Who needs it?" When professional educators add that decentralization would create working conditions unacceptable to highly trained (and therefore potentially mobile) teachers, the black militants again answer: "So what? Teachers like that don't understand black children. Who wants them?"

Differences of opinion like this probably cannot be resolved by "experimentation — though more reliable information about the consequences of various school policies would certainly help. For reasons already indicated, the solution must be political.

In seeking such a solution, however, we should bear in mind that a similar crisis arose a century ago when Catholic immigrants confronted a public school system run by and for Protestants. This crisis was successfully resolved by creating two school systems, one public and one private.

It seems to me that the same approach might be equally appropriate again today. Since such an idea is likely to shock most liberals, it may be useful to recall certain neglected features of the parochial-school experiment.

The motives of the Catholic immigrants who created the parochial-school system were different in many important respects from the motives of the black nationalists who now want their own schools. Nonetheless, there were also important similarities. Just as today's black nationalist does not want his children infected by alien, white "middle-class" values, so many devout Catholic immigrants did not want their children to imbibe the alien values of white Protestant "first families." Just as today's black nationalist deplores the public schools' failure to develop pride and self-respect in black children, so, too, many Irish immigrants felt they needed their own schools to make their children feel that Catholicism and Irishness were respectable rather than shameful. And just as many black parents now want to get their children out of public schools because they feel these schools do not maintain proper discipline, so, too, many Catholics still say that their prime reason for sending their children to parochial schools is that the nuns maintain order and teach children "to behave."

Why, then, did not devout Catholics press for Balkanization of big-city school systems? Why did they not turn their neighborhood schools into bastions of the faith rather than creating their own separate system?

The answer is that there were very few neighborhoods in which literally all the residents were Catholic. Even where everyone was Catholic, not all Catholics wanted their children educated in self-consciously Catholic schools. Some Catholics, especially those of Irish ancestry, were extremely suspicious of the

Anglo-Protestant majority, were strongly attached to the church, and eager to enroll their children in church schools. But others, of whom Italian immigrants were fairly typical, felt as suspicious of the Irish who dominated the church here as of the Anglo-Saxons who dominated the rest of America. Such Catholics were often anticlerical, and they wanted to send their children to schools which would stick to the three R's and skip ideology.

Thus, even in the most Catholic neighborhoods, there was a large minority which thought priests, nuns and theology had no place in the local schools. This minority allied itself with the Protestant majority in other parts of the same state. These statewide majorities then kept strict limits on local control, so as to prevent devout Catholics from imposing their view of education on local Protestant (or lax Catholic) minorities. In particular, most state constitutions contain some kind of prohibition against the introduction of church personnel and teaching into the local public schools. When they do not, it is only because the Federal First Amendment was thought sufficient to prevent the possibility.

This points to a difficulty with neighborhood control which black militants have yet to face. Blacks are not a majority in many of the areas where they live, at least if these areas are defined as large enough to support a full school system. Nor are black Americans of one mind about Balkanization and its likely consequences. Some black parents still believe in integration. They think the only way to get the social and material advantages they want is to stop being what they have always been, however difficult and painful that may be, and become culturally indistinguishable from the white majority. They therefore want their children to attend integrated schools, to study the same curriculum as white children, and to have teachers from good colleges (most of whom will be white for the foreseeable future). What these families want is thus very similar to what the present professional staffs of big-city school systems want.

Other black parents feel that they can never become indistinguishable from whites, that attempts to acquire white culture only make black children feel miserable and incompetent, and that if such children are to succeed they will have to develop their own style. Such parents want their children to attend schools which try to develop distinctive black virtues and black pride, and which maintain the discipline which is so sorely lacking in the public schools. This cannot, I fear, be reconciled with what the present professional staff wants (or knows how to do).

For convenience, I will label these two sorts of black parents "integrationists" and "nationalists" — though the flavor of the distinction is perhaps better captured in the militants' rhetorical distinction between "Negroes" and "blacks."

Balkanizing big-city school systems would clearly be a victory for the nationalists at the expense of the integrationists. Schools in predominantly black neighborhoods would almost certainly end up with fewer white students and teachers. Local control would also make it easier for white neighborhoods to resist open enrollment, busing and other devices for helping black integrationists send their children to predominantly white schools. The curriculum might or might not be substantially revised once black neighborhood boards held power, but whatever revisions were made would certainly please the nationalists more than the integrationists.

Yet for this very reason state legislatures are unlikely to let black separatists exercise complete control over "their" schools. Just as legislatures earlier protected the rights of Protestant and anticlerical Catholic minorities in devout Catholic communities, so they will almost certainly protect the rights of white and black-integrationist minorities in predominantly black neighborhoods.

If, for example, the local Ocean Hill-Brownsville board wins control over the schools in that part of New York City, the New York State Legislature will almost surely go along with union demands for tight limits on the local board's right to discriminate against whites in hiring teachers and principals. (No such discrimination appears to have taken place in Ocean Hill-Brownsville's hiring of teachers, but the local board does seem to have had a strong and entirely understandable prejudice in favor of black principals.) State certification requirements are also likely to be strictly enforced, so as to restrict black local boards to hiring teachers who have enough respect for white culture and white standards of competence to have got through four or five years of college. New restrictions are also likely to be put on the curriculum, perhaps in the form of a law against teaching "racial hatred," so as to keep LeRoi Jones, etc., out of black schools. Such action would be defended on the same grounds as the rules barring religious teaching in public schools.

Restrictions of this kind are both reasonable and necessary in public institutions which must serve every child in a community, regardless of his race or his parents' outlook on life. They are, however, likely to mean that black nationalists end up feeling that, even though they have a majority on the local board, they do not really control their schools. Once again, whitey will have cheated them of their rightful pride. Local control is, therefore, likely to enrage the professional educators, work against the hopes and ambitions of the integration-minded black and white parents, and yet end up leaving black nationalists as angry as ever. An alternative strategy is badly needed.

The best alternative I can see is to follow the Catholic precedent and allow nationalists to create their own private schools, outside the regular public system, and to encourage this by making such schools eligible for substantial tax support.

The big-city school systems could then remain largely in the hands of their professional staffs. (A major change in the distribution of power between teachers and administrators would still be required, and some decentralization of big cities would also be advisable on bureaucratic grounds, but these are negotiable issues.) The public system would continue to serve white and black integrationists. Separatists who found this system unacceptable would have the option of sending their children to other schools at relatively low cost.

The beginnings of such a parallel system can already be seen in some big cities. Black middle-class parents are already far more likely than their white counterparts to enroll their children in private schools. A number of private "community schools" have also sprung up in the ghettos during the past few years. The Muslims run several schools. These schools have found many black parents are willing to make considerable financial sacrifices in order to send their children to a school they think superior to the public one. What these ventures lack, however, is substantial political and financial support. Without this they are likely to remain isolated and relatively unusual.

Some will ask why an independent black school system should need or deserve white support when the parochial schools get no such support. The most relevant answer is that, without the unity and legitimacy conferred by religion, the black community cannot go it alone. It is, perhaps, an unfortunate historical accident that black America lacks its own church, but it does — and even the Muslims have not been able to remedy the situation. Yet black America still needs its own schools, free to serve exigencies of black nationalism. Given the inevitable hostility of both professional educators and laymen who believe in integration, black nationalists are unlikely to be able to create such schools within the public sector.

Is there any justification for funding black private schools without funding other private schools on the same basis? My answer is "No."

Indeed, it seems to me that the only way a black private school system could hope to get tax subsidies would be to ally itself with a parochial school system in demanding Federal and state support for all private schools. Many traditional liberals feel this would violate the constitutional separation of church and state. The Supreme Court has never ruled on this question, however; until it does, it seems reasonable to assume that there is no constitutional objection to Federal or state subsidies for private schools — so long as these subsidies are earmarked to achieve specific public purposes, and so long as the schools are accountable for achieving these purposes.

An analogy may clarify this point. Back in the 19th century, the Supreme Court ruled that the Government could legally contract with Catholic hospitals to care for public charity patients, and today only the most strict separatist would argue that the Federal Government cannot contract with a Catholic university or a Catholic hospital to carry out scientific research. Why, then, should it not contract with a Catholic school to teach physics to 16-year-olds or reading to impoverished 6-year-olds?

Private schools should, of course, be required to show that they had actually done what they promised to do, rather than devoting public funds to the construction of chapels or the production of antiwhite propaganda. But accountability of this kind is essential with all tax subsidies, whether to private schools, private corporations or local government.

Even if a coalition between the church and the black community were put together, is it realistic to suppose that white Protestant America would actually support black schools? My guess is that it would, so long as the financial burden remains within reason. Remember, I am *not* proposing that white legislators should help create a private system for blacks which would be more expensive than the one now attended by whites. I am only proposing that black children who attend private schools should be eligible for at least part of the tax subsidy which is now available if they choose to seek an education in the public system. Far from increasing the overall tax bill, then, a scheme of this kind would actually lower it. In particular, it would help slow the rise in local property taxes, by providing black parents with state and Federal incentives to withdraw their children from locally supported schools, thus cutting local costs. Many local white taxpayers would probably greet such a development with considerable enthusiasm. It would also reduce some white parents' anxiety about the public system's being "overrun" by black children. (It would not actually diminish integration-minded blacks' interest in desegregation, but if it reduced over-all black enrollment it might make desegregation seem a little less threatening and more practical.) In addition, the creation of an independent black school system might strike many whites as a relatively easy and painless way to buy political peace and sweep the whole racial problem under the rug. I doubt if it would succeed in doing this, but it might at least help shift the focus of racial conflict away from the schools and into other more critical arenas.

At this point, somebody always says, "Well, what about private schools established by white supremacists to escape integration?" The answer to that question is already clear. The Supreme Court has held subsidies for such schools unconstitutional, and neither legislatures nor Congress should provide them.

Indeed, I would go further and argue that the state should not subsidize any school which is not open to every child who wants to enroll — regardless of race, religion or ability. Not many non-Catholics want to attend parochial schools, but some already do and others will. Their admission should certainly be a precondition for public subsidies. Similarly, black schools should be required to admit white applicants in order to get tax support. No rush of applicants need be anticipated.

One final objection to the establishment of independent black schools should be mentioned. Many whites fear that such a system would preach black nationalism and racial hatred, and that this would make racial reconciliation even more difficult than it now seems.

This is a reasonable fear. The same objections were raised against the Catholic schools for more than a hundred years. Yet despite all sorts of horror stories about anti-Semitism and other forms of prejudice in Catholic schools, a 1964 survey by Andrew Greeley and Peter Rossi of the University of Chicago demonstrated fairly conclusively that Catholics who attended parochial schools were no more intolerant, narrow-minded or socially irresponsible than Catholics who attended public schools. Indeed, the survey suggested that, all other things being equal, parochial schools had a more liberalizing effect on Catholics than did public schools.

And similarly, the Greeley-Rossi survey suggests that the black schools would not have to be especially affluent to do an acceptable job. While the parochial schools spent far less per pupil than the public schools, used less extensively trained teachers, had much larger classes, were housed in older buildings, had smaller libraries and relied on a curriculum even more medieval than did the public schools, their alumni did at least as well in worldly terms as public-school Catholics.

All other things being equal, parochial-school Catholics ended up with slightly more education and slightly better jobs than public-school Catholics. The only really significant difference Greeley and Rossi found between the two groups was that parochial school products were more meticulous and better informed about their religious obligations. This suggests that fears for the future of black children in black-controlled schools may also be somewhat exaggerated.

The development of an independent black school system would not solve the problems of black children. I doubt, for example, that many black private schools could teach their children to read appreciably better than white-controlled public schools now do. But such schools would be an important instrument in the hands of black leaders who want to develop a sense of community solidarity and pride in the ghetto, just as the parochial schools have worked for similarly placed Catholics.

Equally important, perhaps, the existence of independent black schools would diffuse the present attack on professional control over the public system. This seems the only politically realistic course in a society where professional control, employee rights and bureaucratic procedures are as entrenched as they are in America. The black community is not strong enough to destroy the public-school bureaucracy and staff. Even if it did, it now has nothing to put in its place. What the black community could do, however, would be to develop an alternative — and demand tax support for it.

Some radicals who expect black insurgency to destroy the whole professional hierarchy in America and create a new style of participatory democracy will regard this kind of solution as a cop-out. Some conservatives whose primary concern is that the lower orders not get out of hand will regard it as an undesirable concession to anarchy. But for those who value a pluralistic society, the fact that such a solution would, for the first time, give large numbers of non-Catholics a choice about where they send their children to school, ought, I think, to outweigh all other objections.

Additional Reading

Bouma, Donald H. and James Hoffman. *The Dynamics of School Integration: Problems and Approaches in a Northern City.* Grand Rapids, Mich.: William B. Eerdmans Publishing Co., 1968.

Damerell, Reginald G. *Triumph in a White Suburb.* New York: William Morrow, 1968.

Fantini, Mario and Gerald Weinstein. *Making Urban Schools Work.* New York: Holt, Rinehart and Winston, 1968.

Gittell, Marilyn. *Participants and Participation: A Study of School Policy in New York City.* New York: Center for Urban Education, 1967.

Havighurst, Robert J. *Education in Metropolitan Areas.* Boston: Allyn and Bacon, 1966.

Mack, Raymond W. (ed). *Our Children's Burden: Studies of Desegregation in Nine American Communities.* New York: Vintage Books, 1968.

Racial Isolation in the Public Schools. A Report of the United States Commission on Civil Rights, 1967. Washington, D.C.: Superintendent of Documents, U.S. Government Printing Office.

Report of the National Advisory Commission on Civil Disorders. New York: Bantam Books, 1968.

Rogers, David. *110 Livingston Street: Politics and Bureaucracy in the New York City School System.* New York: Random House, 1968.

Smiley, Marjorie B. and Harry L. Miller. *Policy Issues in Urban Education.* New York: The Free Press, 1968.

Conclusion

In one sense the following selection is inappropriate for this volume since it does not deal specifically with urban education or the urban crisis. And yet the overarching question which Friedenberg raises is an absolutely crucial one. What is the relationship between the public schools and what John Kenneth Galbraith in his book, The New Industrial State, has christened "the technostructure"?[1] For even if public schools surmount all of the specific problems of school organization, community involvement, and curriculum design, the proper relationship between public schools in a democratic society and the socio-economic power structure will remain to be worked out.

[1] John Kenneth Galbraith, The New Industrial State. New York: Signet Books, 1968.

Public Schools for Private Enterprise *

Edgar Z. Friedenberg

"To educate" has become the most transitive of verbs. It is something that is always done to somebody else, usually by adults to children. Long before *The Nation* was first published, the word had lost much of its original meaning of "to educe or draw out" the pupils' personal gifts and potentialities. This may possibly be what Aristotle did — rather irresponsibly — for Alexander of Macedon, later to be called the Great. It is seldom what American public schools do for the students who are obliged by law and circumstances to attend them.

Self-education, in the older, eductive sense, is really no longer permitted. Our society has become too anxious for credentials to allow it; the student may read and listen on his own time, or flee the attendance-taker and the draft board by going on the road; but such self-cultivation has become eccentric and socially dysfunctional even when not strictly illegal. Students who try to practice it risk bogging down in revolt and preciosity, and losing the self-esteem they started with. Education, today, means schooling. Some readers, perhaps, may find it pedantic even to suggest that it might mean anything else.

Education, or schooling, has been a recurrent concern of Americans — as it must be, perhaps, to all immigrants, who can have no natural feel for their new and alien surroundings. Those who would build a New Jerusalem must arrange for instruction in Hebrew; yet, it takes a while to feel at ease in Zion. Our preoccupation with education has, however, been suspiciously protracted and obsessive. This is not our usual style; our customary habit is to leap from problem to problem like a clumsy and overconfident moose, declaring each in turn to have been solved by our exceptional technical gifts and ignoring the wreckage we have strewn behind us. But we ruminate about our schools; which is to say that we have never quite been able to stomach them.

People only become obsessed with difficulties they are dealing with dishonestly, and whose actual basis they dare not quite face. Our fretfulness about education masks, I believe, an unwillingness either to accept or renounce certain of the most important social functions of our schools. Centrally, these have to do with status and success, and the conditions youngsters must meet in order to have a chance to achieve them. Among those conditions, of course, is that status and success must be the rewards they want and seek; and the schools must intensify their urge to do so, on the terms society makes available.

*Edgar Z. Friedenberg, "Public Schools for Private Enterprise," *The Nation*, September 20, 1965. Vol. 201, No. 8, pp. 171-175.

Community leaders are likely to find themselves in conflict when they face what those terms have become. In fitting American youth for its destiny in the free world of tomorrow, our schools may be virtually compelling them to become a bunch of ratfinks. So, in effect, Jules Henry in *Culture Against Man* and Paul Goodman in *Compulsory Mis-Education* maintain. Though this is not the whole story, they are right, I think. We are inclined to regard our interest in education and our huge expenditure on it as evidence of enlightened commitment to social progress and to the spread of economic opportunity. When we still complain, as we continually do, it is because we believe our schools are not functioning properly; standards are too low, or the dropout rate is too high, or discipline is too lenient, or college entrance is overstressed and competition is too keen. Educational evils are attributed to *defective* schools. In fact, they are as likely to be the work of *effective* schools that are being directed toward evil ends by the society that supports and controls them.

There is a sense in which great emphasis on formal education is a sign of stress and social conflict, quite apart from questions about whether the schools are working right. I do not refer here to the overworked and nostalgic idea that primitive people have more *elan vital* and fun, because they lead more natural lives. This is probably sentimental and is in any case irrelevant to my point. Great educational zeal is a trouble sign in other ways than as a token of possibly excessive artificiality.

Schools, as separate, formal, social institutions, do not appear in a society simply because it is growing more complex and specialized. In fact, the more complex and specialized a particular social role is the more likely it is that it will have to be mostly learned on the job. But, as Margaret Mead pointed out more than twenty years ago,[1] schools are a definite indication that a society is divisible into a dominant and a subordinate group, and that the dominant group want to teach the subordinate group something they could not be trusted to learn if left to themselves. Schools are expensive; and when the church, or the state, or the taxpayers set them up and arrange for the young and ignorant to attend them, it is either because they anticipate that they will have to draw on their pupils in the future for the skills and attitudes necessary to maintain and expand their enterprises, or because they have set society up and are running it in such a way that the young can make no contribution to it and become a nuisance if allowed at large (their confinement seems less arbitrary if the place in which they are kept is called a school). These reasons are neither exhaustive nor mutually exclusive; but in our society they are, I believe, paramount.

There need not, of course, necessarily be a conflict of interest between those who run the schools and those who are obliged to attend them. But if public instruction must be heavily institutionalized and strongly supported by legal sanctions there probably is such a conflict. People do tend to learn what

[1] "Our Educational Needs in Primitive Perspective": *American Journal of Sociology*, p. 48, May 6, 1943.

fits their pattern of life and their conception of their own interests without other people making a special effort to teach them; though they may want and need assistance in making the necessary arrangements. On the other hand, those social forces that mold the educational establishment also set the terms for later success and even survival as adults; and in this sense, of course, children need to become what schooling makes them. Whether education is conducive therefore, to economic opportunity or economic exploitation is a highly subjective judgment. Supporters of the school system insist, quite sincerely, that education develops talent and potential by suiting the pupils' skills and character to the opportunities society provides and helping them to make themselves useful. This, indeed, has been the historic function of public schooling in America. Only Paul Goodman, I believe, has spoken of this process as a kind of subsidy by which the personnel problems of private enterprise are solved at public expense. The schools train youth to be the kind of employees corporate bureaucracies need, and do the dirty job of weeding out the unfit by establishing dossiers on them to warn prospective employers away, or guiding them into humble jobs for which their deficiencies of character or competence, from the corporate point of view, are not disabling.

Corporations, in any case, pay a large proportion of the taxes that support education; so this is no less biased a way of viewing the function of the schools than eulogizing them as the fountainhead of economic opportunity would be. Every society is a kind of organism, and its schools serve as a kind of digestive system, breaking pupils down into goodies that can be transported to and utilized by remote organ-systems. Our school system is excessively faithful to the analogy in its tendency to degrade youngsters it cannot assimilate or finds toxic, and to treat them like excrement. And today, American youth no longer has an alternative to being ingested by the schools. Throughout our history, the average number of years of schooling completed has risen steadily from one generation to the next, as has, of course, the proportion of youth of any age still in school. Our currect attention to the "dropout problem" is not the result of any increase in the dropout rate — the rate is still falling, as it always has been — but to our increased difficulty in utilizing adolescents out of school and, I suspect, to the increased political potential of the Negroes who drop out at a rate disproportionate to their enrollment.

We now expect all adolescents to complete high school, and most of those who do have declared at some point in their high school career that they expect to attend college, while communities, faced with a higher unemployment rate among youth than among any other age group, strain their resources to give young people some sort of respectable civilian social role in institutions they hopefully call colleges.

This process is supposed to be progress: more and more young people, both relatively and absolutely, are being granted greater and greater educational opportunity. Perhaps; but only if we assume that what is taught in school is necessarily more valuable than what might have been learned outside it, if society had troubled to provide alternatives, so that youngsters might be free to stay out and make their own way, and had legitimate opportunities to get jobs and live according to their natures. This too is an American tradition, celebrated most triumphantly, perhaps, by Huck Finn in his closing statement. Only recently have we refused absolutely to permit adolescents – as would now say – to program their own activities.

So, instead of citing our approach to total school attendance as evidence that youth is being served better and better, I should prefer to accept it for what it certainly is: one more instance of the centralization of American life, with corresponding elimination of the "path less traveled by" that might have "made all the difference." For some youngsters this constitutes reduced educational opportunity; and for all it constitutes more limited – that is, less diverse – educational opportunity. Expansion of the scope and authority of formal education in this country is a pivotal part of the process by which human diversity is stultified or extinguished; not just because of the simple fact that all must now attend school for ten years or longer, but because of what school is usually like. With school consolidation, the increased dominance of standards and curricula set through state departments of education, the consequent practice of state adoptions leading to the growth of a mass textbook industry, and the emergence of an ideologically uniform educational establishment represented by the NEA, there is not as much variation in that as there used to be, either. If Dr. Conant's recent proposal for an "Interstate Commission for Planning a National Educational Policy"[2] is accepted there will soon be still less.

In compensation for the more limited range of his educational opportunity, the increased term of compulsory school attendance is supposed to provide the student who completes high school – and, preferably, college – greater economic opportunity. This is the argument advanced by those who most vigorously combat the "dropout problem." I have never heard a participant at any of the numerous conferences on this topic that I have attended argue that what was learned in school would have improved the quality of the dropout's life except insofar as it made him more employable and raised his income; nor have I heard it suggested that such an argument, even if valid, would have moved many dropouts to reconsider. The case for protracted school attendance usually rests on its economic merits. But the economic argument is largely circular. It is certainly true that people with diplomas get further and have less trouble than people without them. So do people with passports, and for the same reason; there is general agreement to require them. Employers who refuse to hire anyone but high-school graduates hardly ever specify what it is that the job requires that could only have been learned in school. If they did, they could usually find out whether a youngster had it with much greater certainty by

2 James B. Conant, *Shaping Educational Policy*. New York, McGraw-Hill, 1964.

testing than by asking for his diploma. Nevertheless, the requirement is not irrelevant; they most often want the *kind* of employee who could have succeeded in high school; who is docile, reliable, not a troublemaker; who is punctual and symbol-oriented, though not actually literate or responsible.

We are back, then, to the point that the schools are an integral part of the system by which the dominant social and economic institutions of our society staff themselves and propagate their values. What is new to us is the *totality* of the process. Society no longer brooks any alternative to school attendance; the schools no longer permit their students much voice or choice about what kind of persons they shall be encouraged to become. There is, of course, variation in the curriculum: there are IQ groupings in elementary school, with offerings tailored to the school's assessment of its pupils' abilities; there are general, commercial, and academic tracks in high school, with only the last leading to college. But students are *placed* in these by a counselor, partly on the basis of test scores and previous academic record; but to a large degree on the basis of his estimate of the fitness of things and the kind of student he is dealing with. This is not, as is sometimes thought, a simple function of social-class bias, for the bias works only negatively. In their subtle and perceptive study of the counselors' role in the educational careers of the students assigned to them, Cicourel and Kitzuse[3] found that though counselors usually kept students with pronounced lower-status characteristics out of college preparatory courses to which they would have admitted most middle-class students with the same grades and aptitude scores, the counselors also excluded qualified middle-class candidates with too much hubris: who were arrogant, or highly confident, or who professed to be happy and self-satisfied and refused to provide the counselors with the "problems" they needed in order to maximize their own operation. Very able upper-status students, if they were blithe and insouciant, were put-down as "underachievers" by counselors who made dire — and self-fulfilling — prophecies that such rogues would never get into a good college. "He thinks he's handsome," one counselor snapped in appraising such a student. "He's nice looking, but not handsome."

Considering, then, that there is no longer an alternative to school attendance, the schools' assumption of the right to prescribe the student's personal tastes and style of life is wholly insupportable. I have discussed elsewhere[4] the means, both subtle and brutal, by which students were kept in line in certain exemplary high schools whose climate of values I was studying. More recently, some schools have become so egregiously presumptuous that their actions have been reported by a press not notably zealous in defending the civil rights of adolescents. Thus, on December 16, 1964, *The New York Times* carried a story from Hartford, Conn., that Edward T. Kores, Jr., has been

---

[3]Abraham Cicourel and John Kitzuse, *The Educational Decision-Makers*. Indianapolis, Bobbs-Merrill, 1963.

ordered to change his hairstyle or face prosecution as a truant. The school
superintendent had suspended him on November 13 "for wearing his black hair
in bangs Beatle fashion" though

> . . . trimmed in the back and on the side. Edward, with the backing
> of his father, Edward Kores, Sr., a carpenter, refused to change his
> haircut. His father denounced the subsequent suspension as an invasion
> of personal rights. . . Westbrook's Board of Education voted unanimously
> last Thursday to uphold the suspension. Yesterday Mr. and Mrs. Kores
> came here and met with [State Education Commissioner] Dr. Sanders
> after trying unsuccessfully to file a complaint with the State
> Commissioner on Civil Rights.
>
> Dr. Sanders heard their case, then pointed out that a state law
> required all children to attend school until the age of 16, which Edward
> will not reach until February. Today, a spokesman for the Commission-
> er said he has written the Westbrook School Superintendent asking him
> to seek the cooperation of Westbrook's Town Counsel in enforcing the
> law against the family.

As I read this account in *The Times* I recalled – too vaguely, unfortunately,
to be able to look it up and check out the details – a local case which had
recently been reported in *The Sacramento Bee*. This, too, involved a boy who
had been suspended for having a Beatle haircut, and who had appealed his
suspension. *But the courts had sustained him,* on the grounds that he was a
member of a musical group that got paid for its services, and his haircut was
therefore a necessary item of professional equipment and not, like Kores', just
personal.

Many school personnel are exceptionally wellsuited to the role of Delilah
the Philistine, and I would not deny them their dramatic triumph in it; though
one might have hoped they would choose to appear in a more significant vehicle.
One should not, however, underestimate the significance of the role they *have*
chosen. It is no small thing to serve as the instrument by which the entire youth
of a great nation is subdued in spirit and taught that it has no rights except those
it can wheedle and no inherent dignity that anyone is obligated to respect. This,
too, is an indispensable part of the program by which youth are fitted into a
mass society, which protects itself from faction and bitterness by discounting
the claims of distinction in advance, before they can become a threat or arouse
envy and resentment. Young Kores' experience sums up, in microcosm, the
entire social transition by which the word "character" changed its meaning from
something we were proud to develop to something we are ridiculed for being.
This must all have been a very important lesson to him.

In principle, however, it has its ironic side, which becomes more apparent
when the lesson is carried to extremes. A few months ago I had occasion to visit
a Juvenile Hall, or detention prison, in a nearby county. This was not a punitive

4"The Modern High School: A Profile": *Commentary,* November, 1963.

institution. Some of the kids who were locked up in it were being held for trial. But most of them had not been charged with any offense; they were "dependent minors" or "potential delinquents" or, in some cases, simply abandoned and homeless. These had not been confined by any formal legal process; and no process existed by which they could demand release. They would have hearings, in the course of time, at which the juvenile authorities would dispose of their cases administratively; but some would be kept there, though accused of no misconduct, till they were 21 if there seemed to be no place else to put them. They lived in cells that smelled like cells; but the place was humanely run, and some effort was made to give it a normal, institutional atmosphere. There was an enclosed garden, though the youngsters were not permitted in it except under guard; and there was a wing with schoolrooms. In the corridor to this, as usual, was a framed facsimile of the Constitution, open at the Bill of Rights.

"What would you do," I asked, "if one of them read that?"

"Then," the Director replied, "we'd be in trouble."

It seemed discourteous to say so, but I had the distinct impression that we already were; and had been for some time.

Additional Reading

Carmichael, Stokely and Charles V. Hamilton. *Black Power.* New York: Vintage Books, 1967.

Clark, Burton R. *Educating the Expert Society.* San Francisco: Chandler Publishing Co., 1962.

Dentler, Robert A.; Bernard Mackler; and Mary Ellen Warshauer (eds.) *The Urban R's.* New York: Praeger, 1967.

Ellul, Jacques. *The Technological Society.* New York: Vintage Books, 1967.

Erikson, Erik H. *Identity, Youth and Crisis.* New York: W.W. Norton, 1968.

Fantini, Mario D. and Weinstein, Gerald. *The Disadvantaged: Challenge to Education.* New York: Harper & Row, 1968.

Galbraith, John Kenneth. *The New Industrial State.* New York: Signet Books, 1968.

Hickerson, Nathaniel. *Education for Alienation.* Englewood Cliffs, N.J.: Prentice-Hall, 1966.

Kvaraceus, William C.; John S. Gibson; Thomas J. Curtin; *Poverty, Education and Race Relations: Studies and Proposals.* Boston: Allyn and Bacon, 1967.

Levenson, William B. *The Spiral Pendulum: The Urban School in Transition.* Chicago: Rand McNally & Co., 1968.

Mack, Raymond W. *Transforming America: Patterns of Social Change.* New York: Random House, 1967.

Nordstrom, Carl; Edgar Z. Friedenberg; Hilary A. Gold. *Society's Children: A Study of Resentment.* New York: Random House, 1967.

Rudman, Herbert C. and Richard L. Featherstone. *Urban Schooling.* New York: Harcourt, Brace and World, 1968.

Contributors

Philip Allsworth, assistant professor of Education at Richmond College in New York City, was formerly associate editor of the quarterly journal, *Urban Education.*

Joseph Alsop is a Washington columnist who writes on foreign and domestic problems.

McGeorge Bundy, former advisor to Presidents Kennedy and Johnson, is president of the Ford Foundation. He headed Mayor Lindsay's Advisory Panel on Decentralization of New York City schools.

Kenneth Clark, professor of psychology at City College of the City University of New York, is the author of *Prejudice and Your Child* and *Dark Ghetto: Dilemmas of Social Power.*

Robert Conot, a graduate of Stanford University, has been a newspaper reporter, an editor, and a tv writer. He is the author of *Ministers of Vengeance* and *Rivers of Blood, Years of Darkness.*

J. L. Dillard is director of Urban Language Study at the Center for Applied Linguistics in Washington.

Edgar Z. Friedenberg, professor of sociology and education at the State University of New York at Buffalo, is the author of *The Vanishing Adolescent, Coming of Age in America,* and *The Dignity of Youth and Other Atavisms.*

Estelle Fuchs, an anthropologist, is associate professor of education at Hunter College. In addition to *Teachers Talk* she is the author of *Pickets at the Gates.*

Herbert J. Gans is senior research sociologist at the Center for Urban Education and adjunct professor of sociology and education at Teachers College, Columbia University. He is author of *The Urban Villagers* and *The Levittowners.*

Alfred A. Giardino, an attorney, was president of the New York City Board of Education and was a member of Mayor Lindsay's Advisory Panel on Decentralization of New York City Schools.

Paul Goodman, poet, playwright, therapist, and social critic, is a fellow of The Institute for Policy Studies in Washington, D. C. His books include *Growing Up Absurd, The Community of Scholars,* and *Compulsory Mis-Education.*

Jean D. Grambs is associate professor of education at the College of Education, University of Maryland, and the author of *Schools, Scholars, and Society.*

Mary Frances Greene, a graduate of the University of Chicago, began teaching elementary school in New York City in 1961. She co-authored with Orletta Ruan *The School-Children, Growing Up in the Slums.*

Robert J. Havighurst, professor of education at the University of Chicago, is the author of *Education in Metropolitan Areas, Society and Education,* and *The Public Schools of Chicago.*

Nat Hentoff's writing has appeared in *The New Yorker* and *The Village Voice.* He is the author of *The New Equality* in addition to *Our Children Are Dying.*

Charles S. Isaacs teaches eighth grade math at J.H.S. 271 in the Ocean Hill-Brownsville School District, New York City.

Christopher Jencks is executive director of The Center for Educational Policy Research at Harvard, on leave from The Institute for Policy Studies in Washington. With David Riesman he wrote *The Academic Revolution.*

Jonathan Kozol, author of *The Fume of Poppies* in addition to *Death at an Early Age,* is a consultant in curriculum development to the federal government. His articles have appeared in *The Atlantic, The New Republic, Esquire, The New York Review of Books,* and *Harvard Educational Review.*

Charlotte Leon Mayerson edited *Two Blocks Apart,* the stories of Juan Gonzales and Peter Quinn from taped interviews of two seventeen year-old boys living in New York City.

G. Alexander Moore, Jr. is assistant professor of anthropology at Emory University in Atlanta, Ga. Dr. Moore completed *Realities of the Urban Classroom* in conjunction with his work as a member of Project TRUE at Hunter College.

Thomas Pettigrew is an associate professor of social psychology at Harvard University and author of *A Profile of the Negro American.* He served as chief science consultant to the U. S. Commission on Civil Rights for its report, *Racial Isolation in the Public Schools.*

Orletta Ryan, a graduate of Mundelein College, teaches in the elementary schools of East Harlem. She co-authored with Mary Frances Greene *The School-Children, Growing Up in the Slums.*

Thomas Schwartz, formerly a high school English teacher, is a doctoral candidate at Harvard Graduate School of Education.

Patricia Cayo Sexton, professor of the sociology of education at New York University, is the author of *Education and Income* and *Spanish Harlem.*

Marshall Smith is an instructor at Harvard's Graduate School of Education. He was formerly the director of research for the Harvard faculty seminar on *The Coleman Report.*

Walter Williams, assistant chief of the research and plans division of the Office of Research, Plans, Programs and Evaluation which plans programs for The Office of Economic Opportunity, has written on monetary theory, consumer and other social behavior and income maintenance.

Roger R. Woock, who teaches at Hunter College, has been a consultant to The Office of Economic Opportunity and the National Teacher Corps. He is on the editorial board of the quarterly journal, *Urban Education.* He is co-editor of *Man Against Poverty: World War III* and the co-author of a forthcoming text on urban education.

Index